UNLEASHING THE
IMPROVEMENT
MINDSET

A better strategy for adopting a culture of
continuous improvement for next level performance

DARCY MELLSOP

This is ten percent luck
Twenty percent skill
Fifteen percent concentrated power of will
Five percent pleasure
Fifty percent pain
And a hundred percent reason to remember the name

It's not about the salary
It's about reality and making some noise
Making a story

Fort Minor, *Remember the Name*

Be the change that you wish to see in the world.

Mahatma Gandhi

First published in 2024 by Darcy Mellsop

A catalogue entry for this book is available from the National Library of New Zealand.

ISBN: 9781923007826

Book production and text design by Publish Central
Cover design by Julia Kuris

Contents

Introduction   1

Loop 1 Map   7

Loop 2 Map   11

Part I: Introduction to Continuous Improvement   15

Chapter 1   Understanding the What and Why   17

Part II: Loop 1   51

Loop 1 Map   53

Chapter 2   Build the Right Team Dynamic   55

Chapter 3   Understand Your Current Level of Performance   75

Chapter 4   Improvement Initiative Plan, Roles and
             Baseline Data   103

Chapter 5   Determining Why We Experience the Current
             Level of Performance   131

Chapter 6   Developing Better Solutions   145

Chapter 7   Embedding Proven Solutions   175

Part III: Loop 2   195

Loop 2 Map   197

Chapter 8   Understand Your Current Level of Performance   201

Chapter 9   The Customer   207

Chapter 10   Determining Why We Experience the
              Current Level of Performance   229

Chapter 11   Developing Better Solutions   241

Chapter 12   Embedding Proven Solutions   283

References   297

Appendices   299

Appendix 1   Facilitation   299

Appendix 2   Visual Boards   308

Appendix 3   Improvement Initiative Plan Template   313

Appendix 4   Pilot Plan Template   315

Appendix 5   Embed Stage Planning Template   317

Appendix 6   Team Dynamic Example   318

Appendix 7   Sample Size Calculations   319

Appendix 8   Gemba Questions for Leaders   322

Appendix 9   Key Terms of a Benefit Realisation Framework   324

Appendix 10   Control Charts   326

Appendix 11   Pareto Charts   330

Appendix 12   Box Plots and Histograms   332

Appendix 13   Everything on One Page, the Cheat Sheet   335

Appendix 14   Homework   336

About the author   337

Introduction

The purpose of this book is to support leaders and guide teams through better practices that will impactfully embed a continuous improvement culture in organisations producing tangible results. This book focuses on how to best adopt a continuous improvement culture, highlighting vital elements that include:

- starting with energy
- ensuring leaders and teams stay resilient and focused
- quickly experiencing tangible improvements in performance.

Establishing a continuous improvement culture is not easy, but there's no need to make it harder than it needs to be by making common mistakes, such as the excessively slow progress of improvements, scoping work that's too complex and overwhelming for the team's capability or providing underwhelming improvements.

We need to start somewhere, we need to start simply, and we need to start by generating results. Nothing establishes good practices like good results coming from those practices. So, rather than a methodical collection of tools in the supposed order of their usefulness, this book is more of a map of the right things to do to support the adoption of continuous improvement thinking (and the benefits that come from that) at a cultural level in the organisation.

There are two distinct sections to this book. The first section is about engaging and maintaining your team's interest in continuous improvement. The focus of this – what I've termed

Loop 1 – is to start by igniting and nurturing the appetite for continuous improvement and reinforcing it with good results as we loop through the stages of continuous improvement, over and again, which is why I've used the term *loop*. The approach of the first loop is to specifically unleash your team's capability to make improvements without over burdening them with methodology. Too commonly teams are overburdened with complex problems that they don't have the capability to solve when an organisation initially adopts a continuous improvement methodology. Our approach for our first loop will resolve that.

In the second section we explore the second loop – a deeper understanding and application of continuous improvement skills, further enhancing the team's capability. Continuous improvement, like anything, can become entrenched in the culture and honed by the team for greater gains. As the team gains expertise and capability, it excels in finding and removing more complex and deep-seated obstacles to good performance.

Beginning with simplicity allows the team to achieve significant results without being hindered by a rigid and over-engineered methodology. The focus is on building the team's capability and, most importantly, fostering an emotional connection with continuous improvement in Loop 1. In Loop 2, the emphasis shifts to strengthening capabilities and improvement skills to tackle more complex problems in sophisticated processes.

Recognising that each organisation is unique, the approach to continuous improvement outlined in this book is designed so that it can be adapted to fit your organisation. The method provides a path for improvement while allowing enough flexibility for customisation by your team, for your team's specific needs.

WHY THE TWO-LOOP APPROACH?

The two-loop approach stems from a common challenge teams face when navigating methodologies. Often, teams encounter obstacles during transitions between stages. For example, many teams spend too much time capturing customer insights – because they haven't set up that stage purposefully enough to know exactly what they need – enabling them to swiftly transition to the next stage. Teams frequently become stuck when moving from customer and process performance insights to then determining root causes, and then transitioning to developing solutions, and then again to piloting solutions.

Using the loop approach, the first loop, being your team's first foray into solving a performance-related problem, focuses on the crucial steps that enable an organisation to start to build and then unleash their continuous improvement capability. The second loop follows the same approach but delves more intricately into addressing the complexities of subsequent improvement initiatives. This approach ensures a strategic start in the first loop rather than starting too big and overwhelming the team – especially at the key points of transition from one stage to the next for teams new to continuous improvement.

PROBLEMS AND PURPOSE

In this book, you'll see the word **problem** used purposefully over **opportunity** or **challenge** because problems need to be solved more than opportunities taken and challenges faced. There's a sense of urgency and energy that comes with the word problem – and that is a good thing.

Too often for teams, the word problem is cloaked with negative connotations – and accompanying negative behaviours, including the hiding of problems. A problem is simply that – just a problem to be solved. Problems are useful because they indicate exactly where a solution can be applied for better performance. Our concern should not be the prevalence of problems but our failure to recognise or be aware of the problems that need to be solved.

You're also going to see the word **purpose** a lot. Everything we do needs to be purposeful. We need to understand the purpose of what we're about to do so our efforts are aligned to affect strategy. Before we start anything, whether it be a large piece of work or just the next step in an improvement initiative, we should always be clear on the purpose to ensure our initiatives are lean, without waste, and effective.

Purpose serves as a crucial lens to evaluate the value and impact of any activity. All analyses of a process, system or parts thereof should include analysing the purpose of that element. In essence, purpose becomes the perfect go-to tool for assessing the value of any undertaking and how it contributes to the wider process and system.

GETTING THE MOST FROM THIS BOOK

This book has been written to serve a singular purpose, its success will be measured by how well it helps you and your team in adopting a continuous improvement mindset. Given this core objective, I had to rethink the conventional way of structuring a book to ensure it best serves its purpose by delivering you the right information in the right order and written in the best way to maximise comprehension.

So here are the points of difference I built into this book:

1. A one-page cheat sheet covering the key steps in this entire book is included for quick reference in Appendix 13, and most importantly, a map of how all the elements tie together and in what order, and in relation to the four key steps of an improvement initiative. This will help any team know what they are about to do, as the next step, and how that next step purposefully relates to the step after.

2. The methodology is presented in two loops. The first loop (being the first time your team undertakes an improvement initiative) focuses on the core things your team needs to know to navigate it successfully – stripping out everything that likely doesn't offer your team value in getting the first wins with continuous improvement. The second loop delves deeper into the details needed for subsequent loops, allowing your team to enhance their capabilities gradually. This two-loop approach ensures swift progress without overwhelming your team with tools that may not be immediately necessary.

3. The book stays focused on the purpose, which is to offer the essentials of adopting a continuous improvement methodology, thereby ensuring compatibility with all other major continuous improvement methodologies.

4. And the key essential is the team dynamic, so I've addressed that coming from a number of different angles to ensure that one angle (at least) resonates with you, and to reinforce key messages that I know will be extraordinarily helpful to you. I need there to be times where you think 'You've already said that' – and that's perfect, as it means I've landed something vital that will be significantly helpful to you.

5. The appendix includes tools that you might already be familiar with and allows a more in-depth exploration of them without unnecessarily expanding the core content of the book.

6. I've blended analogies, some are personal and some in a business context, and they have been purposefully written in the context that will help you most likely remember and translate them easily for use in your work environment.

7. In a similar vein, my aim has been to craft passages primarily to stimulate the right thought rather than ensuring effortless clarity. Admittedly, some of these passages may come across as cumbersome to read (some are), but their deliberate construction will likely stimulate exactly the right thought that will serve you – which is where the value is.

8. I use the word 'leader' a lot. Let's be clear – that's you. The fact that you are reading this book means that you'll likely be leading and supporting others to adopt or contribute to a continuous improvement mindset that makes life easier for the wider team and customers. You'll have people come to you with questions and needing support. You're a leader. So, when I'm referring to a leader's perspective (and that's the core of this book), that's for you.

9. I've purposefully used some terms interchangeably, because different words (though meaning the same thing) will resonate with readers to differing extents. But by 'covering

the bases' with the use of different terms as I repeat the message in different contexts and stages in the book, it almost ensures that it is easier for you to understand, and reinforces your understanding of the point being made. I've worked to make sure that the context is the same for those words used interchangeably.

10. And finally, I only include what has been proven to work, and I explain why it did.

Above all, I've drawn from my extensive experience to share insights that are likely to be effective in your environment, too. I've not held anything back for 'later' because I believe that every improvement we make, if only initially in a single organisation, will emanate outwards to benefit society. My purpose for this book is to provide the best possible insights to adopt a continuous improvement mindset that will manifest in improvements that benefit us all.

Finally, as a tip, please read ahead from whatever stage you might be in with your team. This way, it will be clear to you and your team how the outcome of the current stage will be utilised in the next stage, providing clarity of purpose for the stage you are currently in. This will significantly reduce the chances of your team having to rework any steps. For example, read ahead and be clear on root cause analysis before undertaking data capture, and be clear on what happens post pilot before you start pilot planning.

If you need a break from this book and want to watch something entertaining that is continuous improvement based, see the homework I suggest for you and your team in Appendix 14.

Loop 1 Map

The first loop covers the fundamental aspects that any team would be able to affect in their first attempt without it being becoming overwhelming or hindering progress. The purpose of the first loop is to ensure that your team is engaged and is actively contributing to building a mindset and culture of improvement.

Even though there will be a significant learning curve and capability building within the team during Loop 1, it should still be a swift process, taking only days or weeks at most to achieve positive results.

The first step of Loop 1

1. Build the team dynamic:
   a. building cooperation with building and using facilitation skills
   b. building a collective understanding of a process and understanding who does what in that process.

Understand the current level of performance

2. Build a map of the process:
   a. capture problems and pain points we currently experience and know can be fixed
   b. understand any inter-relationships that exist between the problems and pain points.
3. Choosing what can be improved:
   a. decide on what is to be improved (initially) using decision-making tools

      b. choose who owns the improvement initiative and who is involved in the improvement team.

4. Problem statements are developed:
    a. Develop Improvement Initiative Plans.
5. Capture baseline data.

Determine why we have the current level of performance

6. Root cause analysis (analysis of baseline data):
    a. setting up stand-up meetings for updates.

Develop and pilot solutions

7. Who develops the solutions?
8. Good solution development.
9. Planning for and piloting solutions:
    a. determining the solution we will pilot
    b. how long the pilot will be
    c. measures for the pilot
    d. decision to go live or not.

Embed proven solutions

10. Implementing and embedding a proven solution so it becomes the new norm.
11. Benefit realisation.
12. Celebrate success (for an enduring appetite for continuous improvement).

In the first loop, our aim is to identify the easiest way to produce a tangible improvement while following the fundamentals of continuous improvement. This involves addressing the initial and relatively uncomplicated problems (low-hanging fruit) that we choose to improve. The goal is to see rapid results – crucial for the continual engagement of the team.

The primary focus of the first loop (highlighted as the path the team travels in Figure 1) is quick and tangible improvements that generate an appetite for continuously tackling problems and generating benefits. We want to avoid getting bogged down by strictly following a rigid methodology or applying tools that don't add value, offer insight, or that impede progress.

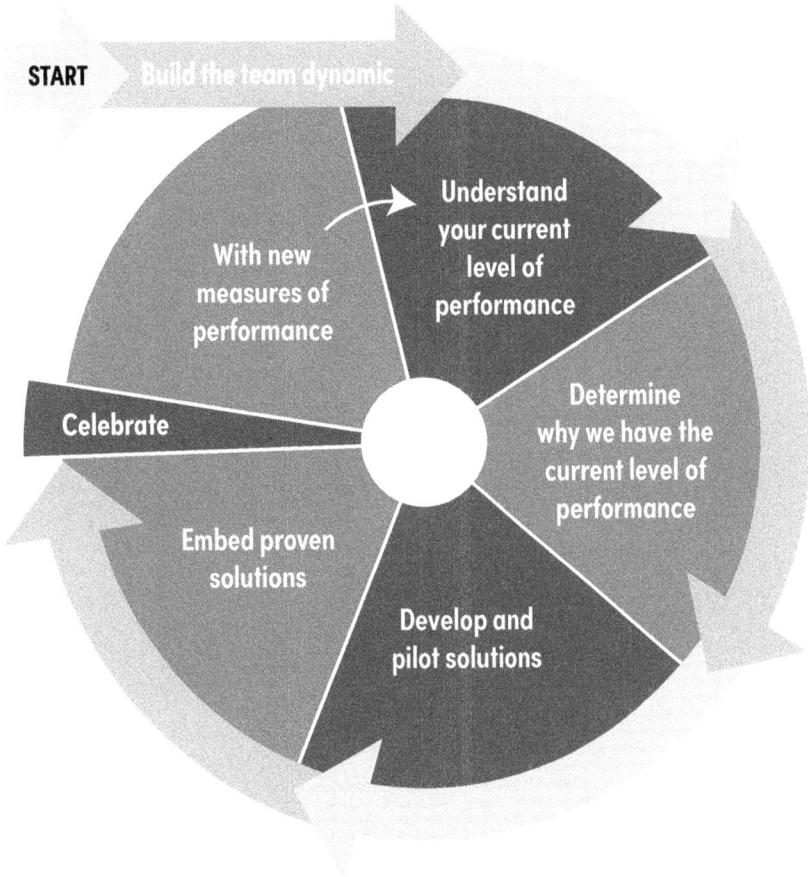

START Build the team dynamic

Understand your current level of performance

With new measures of performance

Celebrate

Determine why we have the current level of performance

Embed proven solutions

Develop and pilot solutions

Figure 1: Loop 1

Loop 2 Map

Any method of continuous improvement also has to be continuously improved. That means our ability to hone a culture that keeps our organisation dynamic and customer-centric will continue to evolve. When your organisation is looking at adopting continuous improvement, the initial focus should be on *just starting* – not having it perfect but performing well enough to do the right things and be able to start with some good principles. Where the first loop purposefully provided speed of early success to ensure an appetite to embed a continuous improvement mindset in your culture, the purpose of Loop 2 and subsequent loops is to permeate, customise and entrench the refined data-based problem-solving thinking throughout the organisation.

Understand the current level of performance

1. Build the value chain:
   a. determine the good measures of performance for the steps of the value chain.
2. Focus and notice – what's going on in the organisation. Having insights and performance data on the things to improve:
   a. knowing from customers what to do and what not to do – a better understanding of customer insights
   b. capturing further improvement ideas from the team, from their experiences and validated with data.

Determine why we have the current level of performance

3. Facilitating Gemba – leaders being closer to the work.

4. Analysing the system around a process.
5. Better data analysis.

Develop and pilot solutions

6. Process improvement (with Lean, and other tools and concepts).
7. Good measures and the use of visual boards:
   a. do we have the right performance metrics? Refine the metrics we have: are they lead or lag measures? Are they driving the right behaviours?
   b. the third link – measuring three steps deep.
8. Better piloting.

Embed proven solutions

9. Post-implementation review (applying continuous improvement to improve your team's methodology).
10. Constant review of performance:
    a. dashboards
    b. sustaining the momentum of improvement, into the next loop.

As the team progresses through further improvement initiatives, they will develop the confidence, gain the experience and enhance their capability to tackle and solve more complex performance problems. This advanced stage will require a wider range of tools and is illustrated in Figure 2 by the widening paths through the loop representing the capability build of the team through different experiences gained through various improvement initiatives.

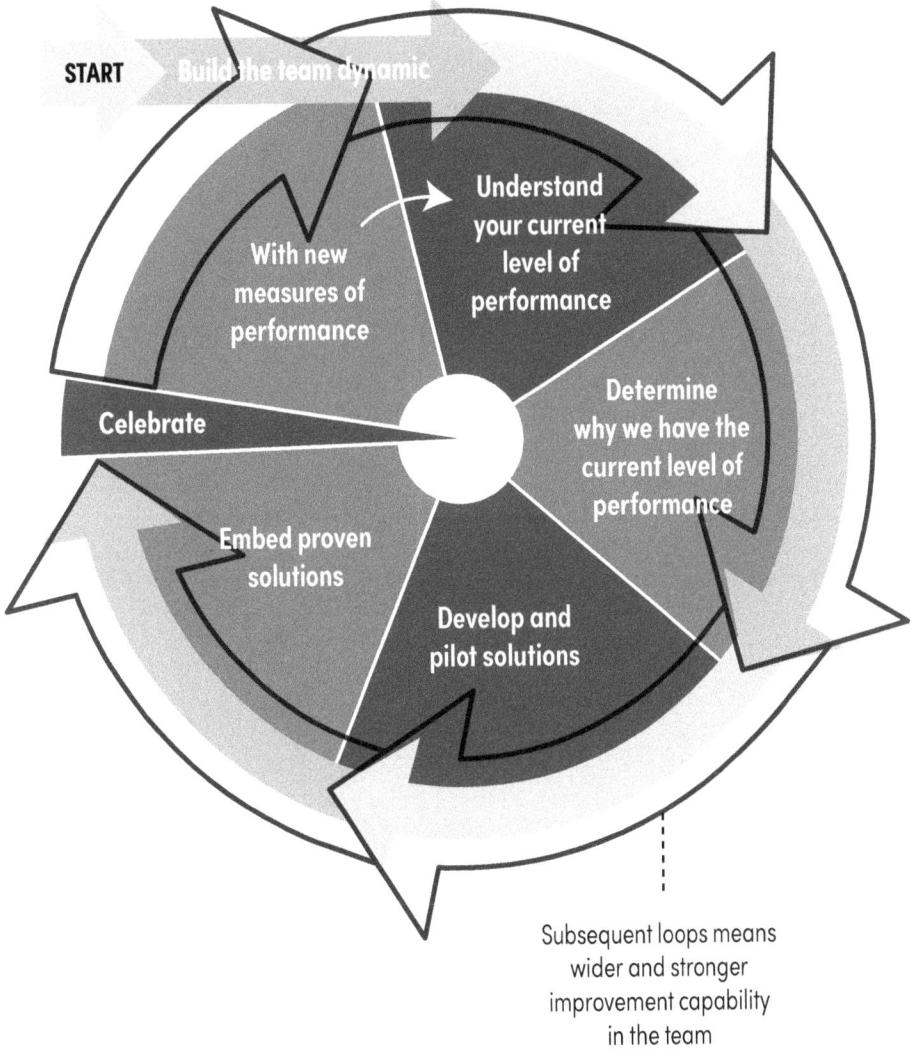

START Build the team dynamic

Understand your current level of performance

With new measures of performance

Celebrate

Determine why we have the current level of performance

Embed proven solutions

Develop and pilot solutions

Subsequent loops means wider and stronger improvement capability in the team

Figure 2: Loop 2

PART I
INTRODUCTION
TO CONTINUOUS
IMPROVEMENT

CHAPTER 1

Understanding the What and Why

In this section, we'll explore why, as leaders, it is compelling to invest in building a continuous improvement culture in your organisation. We'll examine the advantages and the challenges associated with this approach, including:

- the compelling *why* – the benefits of continuous improvement
- defining what continuous improvement is and is not
- crucial team dynamics and cultural elements
- key principles for teams and leaders
- leadership in continuous improvement culture and the leaders' role in that culture
- challenges to adopting continuous improvement
- how to start/starting the right way.

If performance isn't where it should be, it's not because of the lack of high-performing people but, more likely, the void of a high-performance environment. As a leader, steadfastly focus on building an environment that fosters performance.

WHY CONTINUOUS IMPROVEMENT?

Continuous improvement is about making life easier for ourselves and our customers. It is about looking at processes, the purpose of those processes, and making a series of continual and informed improvements so the outcomes are purposeful and provided as effectively and efficiently as possible.

So much of the work we do is wasted. We need to work conscientiously to remove that waste and enable the team to build their capability to perform better, where performance means achieving results rather than exerting effort.

Having a team perform at a mediocre level takes the same energy as a team performing with excellence.

Imagine a team in a leaky boat, spending all their energy bailing out the water coming in through the leaks. This is similar to working tirelessly to address the constant stream of problems stemming from a flawed process.

Alternatively, the team could invest the same amount of energy by first repairing the leaks in the boat. Once they've sealed the leaks, they can then focus on bailing out the remaining water just once.

There are some key messages in this short analogy:

- If we persist in channelling all our energy into bailing out water from the leaks, we'll only sustain mediocre performance. However, once the leaks are fixed, and the water is cleared from the boat, the team will have the time and energy to engage in something new, productive and strategic.

- Teams can only look to fix leaks when they know they exist and can locate them. Often, teams can be a victim of being so engrossed in alleviating symptoms of issues (in this case, the bailing out of the water) that they can't see or even realise there's a cause that can be acted on for the problems exhausting them.

- Achieving improvement requires the courage to invest in medium to long-term performance enhancements. When the team stops bailing water to fix the leaks, the water level in the boat will most likely rise, giving the appearance of poor performance. This phase takes courage to redirect energy from bailing water to fixing the leaks in the boat. It is only from this point onward that performance starts to improve markedly. This challenge is exacerbated by the prevalent and often toxic culture in companies, where there is a preference for executing a flawed process correctly rather than attempting to improve it and risking making mistakes in the process.

- It often takes less energy to fix problems at the root than it does to constantly alleviate the symptoms of the problem. Additionally, fixing the root cause of a problem (the leaks) then frees up capacity for strategy; there's no (smooth) sailing happening while you are bailing.

Too many organisations inadvertently reinforce their prevailing culture of performance apathy by measuring adherence to a poor process rather than rewarding courage, and even rewarding mistakes, endeavouring to improve performance.

Continuous improvement is important for all teams because *we make poor use of our talents* (Robinson 2020). When we fail to tap into our team's full capability, we miss out on valuable opportunities. Often, the fear of making mistakes holds us back from unlocking the team's full potential in the pursuit of improvement. Staying anchored to our adherence to conventional wisdom, while seemingly safer, continues to suffocate our taking of opportunities. It really is a case of choosing between continuous improvement or continued mediocrity.

Shutting Off Autopilot

Adopting continuous improvement is a great way to shut off the autopilot mode that can often exist in organisations. Autopilot occurs when people do their work without taking the opportunity to consciously step back and determine how they can improve performance by improving their work. Without that deliberate approach to improvement that comes through the continuous improvement culture, we are effectively running on autopilot, reproducing existing levels of performance as programmed. A team running on autopilot generally means that your opportunities to improve performance is effectively switched off.

Adopting a continuous improvement approach deactivates autopilot. The team start to wear two hats in their work, not only executing their tasks but also donning a **second hat** focused on improving their work. They consciously seek ways to improve the performance of their work. Of course, there are some factors that need to come into play for this to happen.

Doing the Right Things Right

Continuous improvement is about ensuring we know and are doing the *right* things. This means knowing our purpose, that what we are doing is relevant for the customer (because we have asked the customer) and we have insights through data that shows us that we are doing the right things.

Doing the *right things right* means knowing the specific behaviours of our team to meet the specific outcomes that our customers need and continually honing those behaviours. Helping us to do the right things right are:

- performance measures that support, reinforce and drive the right behaviours
- continually improving our team's capability to improve how we do the right things – more effectively and efficiently
- freeing up our team's capacity to continue to evolve and, importantly, have visibility of whether we are continuing to do the right things for our customers.

In this book, we will focus on how leaders and teams can determine what the right things to do are and how to do those right things right.

Continuous Improvement Can Help Strategy

Harmonised processes that run smoothly, swiftly and with few errors, are important because poorly performing processes choke the life out of strategy, suck up a lot of team capability and capacity, take too long, and generate too many mistakes and a need for lots of rework. This results in your team spending time fixing those elements before they do anything else.

Process improvement is about changing how we think and perform by improving our processes for better outcomes – either in terms of efficiency or experience – for both the team and the customer. Any strategic initiative should be a priority. But affecting strategy is hard and procrastinating with those urgent, familiar and time-sapping tasks is too much of an easy choice for our teams.

Teams tend to only work on normal day-to-day work, with work on strategy often barely getting a look-in. It's a classic case of actions perceived to be urgent being worked on before those that are important or purposeful. Again, think of the bailing water out of the boat analogy. For teams, it can be easy to think of bailing water as being important work and taking priority – even over an organisation's strategy to find and fix the leaks, which the team simply feel that they don't have time to do. That's the kicker; unless a change is made, bailing out water stays as the day-to-day work at the expense of working on strategy.

Harmonising processes frees up a team's time and allows you to use that new capacity for strategic initiatives to continue to improve your organisation. How your team reinvest their time and capacity is something that you can choose.

The huge benefit of continuous improvement is that the team's capability improves. Instead of relying on a team of, let's say, six, with its associated productivity, the improvements can effectively empower your team to operate with the impact and efficiency equivalent to a team of 15 or 18. So when we talk about building continuous improvement capability in the team, always couple that, in your mind, with building the team's capability to perform better, faster and easier – and be better aligned to the customer's needs – that is the purpose of continuous improvement at its core.

As we'll discuss in the first loop, begin by picking a process – ideally, have the team involved to choose a process to improve, which will mean they are already invested in improving that process. Harmonise the chosen process and be deliberate about how the freed-up time is re-invested. Reinvestment could involve improving another process, influencing your organisation's strategy, reducing customer wait time through improved processing time, providing team members with a well-deserved holiday, or progressing towards a four-day work week, among other initiatives. The key is to ensure that the newfound free time and capacity don't go to waste.

That point is crucial. Make sure that you work with your team to determine, even at this early stage, how they will use the freed-up capacity through improvements and how the freed-up capacity will benefit the team. Determining this with your team is a great way to have them connect with the reason why you are looking to make improvements.

> Harmonious and purposeful processes free up huge
> swathes of your team's capacity. As a leader, you
> can use freed-up capacity to enable your strategy.
> Harmonised processes unleash your team's capability
> to grow the organisation.

The Compelling Proof for Continuous Improvement

The unleashing of continuous improvement onto processes – led by the teams – in the work has been transformative and profound. We've experienced substantial improvements across various industries for improvement initiatives typically lasting no more than one month/160 hours, with most initiatives being vastly less than that as improvement initiatives should be short and fast-moving. Here are some results, which the benefits will replicate for the teams, year after year:

Streamlined application processes:

- A queue of 120 days improved so that 80% of the applications are processed in an hour, saving 10.1 hours of capacity per application (and the 120 days), with the value of time saved being $1.29m per annum.
- Reduced report writing from 142 minutes to 52 minutes per report, reclaiming 3,900 hours per year, value of time saved being $182k per annum.
- Improved application completeness (all the information is there) and accuracy (all the information is right) from 6% to 90%, and days to process from six to three days, saving 64 minutes per application, value of time saved being $126k per annum, and internally promoted a member from the team due to the freed-up capacity.

Enhanced customer focus and support:

- Improved the ability of the customer contact team to answer all three key customer questions at the first time of asking (by the customer) from 0% to 100%, in turn reducing average call length from 96 seconds to 26 seconds and saving 2,760 hours annually across the organisation, being the customer contact team and those in the wider organisation who needed to reply to the follow-ups.
- Customer waiting time of an application reduced from 16 working days to five working days – 11 days faster for the customer, significantly reducing follow up calls to the contact centre.
- Improvements in providing better visibility of charges to the customer, reducing customer queries by 79%.
- Application rework rates with customers reduced from 61.2% to 14.3%, in turn reducing overall rework questions to customers from 4,100 to 555 questions asked, saving 1,030 hours of team capacity per annum.

Faster customer queues:

- Reduced queuing time at an airport's international and domestic terminals of at least 48% – meaning all queues were almost effectively moving twice as fast, during peak times, with zero reduction to passenger safety or changes to passenger safety processes and protocols.

Optimised invoicing and cash flow:

- Reduced the reworking of invoices from 74% to 24% and, combined with improving the automation of invoices through optical character recognition software from 0% to 61%, experienced an improved process for processing of invoices from 4.6 days to one, saving 2,292 hours of team capacity per annum, with the added benefit of late payments of the invoices dropped from 32% to 10%, improving the organisation's reputation.

Waste reduction:

- Process improved for better notification of visits to a customer (from two weeks prior to two days prior) saving 12.5 km of driving per day, equating also to a saving 23 minutes per representative per day, saving 63.4 kg per week of CO_2 emissions and reducing forgotten appointments from 19% to 0%.
- Removed wasted capacity in a process amounting to 15,347 hours per year across a team, freeing up that capacity, value of which was $400k per annum.

Revenue recovered:

- Reducing days to handle and determine applications from 39.5 days to 19.3 days, reducing the queue of applications from 200 to 0, enabling the future recovery of revenue and reduction of penalties of not meeting timeframes amounting to over $600k per annum (and the opportunity for the team to move to a four-day working week).

WHAT DOES CONTINUOUS IMPROVEMENT LOOK LIKE?

Energising a team culture through continuous improvement enables an entire team to contribute to the responsibility of organisational improvement rather than resting on only a few people – using the team's cumulative intelligence and cognitive ability. Get the team involved by enabling them to be involved.

Improved process performance often includes better visibility of process performance for the team and leaders. A team and its leadership with a full understanding of actual performance helps result in customer-centric thinking, improved and consistent customer experience, the ability to swiftly improve the customer experience, and more organisational capacity for customer growth strategy implementation.

Continuous improvement helps:

- reverse current and unhealthy business protocols
- enable an organisation to perform better while consuming fewer resources, having less environmental impact and needing less team capacity to perform the same tasks
- enable better customer retention and relationships with new customers.

When continuous improvement is entrenched in the organisation's culture, these are the things you'll see happen:

- Teams make informed decisions with the support of performance and customer experience data.
- Teams understand the difference between improvements that tackle *root causes* versus improvements of *symptoms*. And almost without exception, they choose to adopt *root cause* improvements.
- Everyone in the team knows that contributing to organisational excellence is part of their role, and continuous improvement practices are adopted throughout the organisation.
- Clear measures are established that drive the right behaviours in the team to underpin excellent customer experience and your organisation's strategy.

- Layers of misinformation between any levels of the organisation are removed, and there is clear visibility of performance, especially for leaders, related to the purpose of all work in the organisation.
- The organisation is continually performing better in established measures – at least relative to economic conditions – and there is a clear understanding of the contributing factors to the improved performance.
- Pilots and tests of new solutions and innovations occur continually and with increasing regularity.
- There are fewer and fewer longstanding frustrations and problems in your organisation, with problems being raised and resolved more quickly and permanently rather than being experienced in subsequent quarters or years.

Defining Continuous Improvement

Every organisation wants to improve. Continuous improvement is a conscious approach to improving organisational performance by seeing and taking all the opportunities to improve.

Continuous improvement offers a methodical way to measure, analyse, improve and report on performance. But more than that, it is also a conscious focus on making that improvement happen quickly and continuously. In that way, continuous improvement is a mindset, and the widespread adoption of this mindset leads to a culture of consistently improving, again and again, the work that is done in the organisation. And because it is a mindset, continuous improvement applies to all sectors and industries, regardless of services or products.

Adopting a continuous improvement culture means having an engaged team ready to gain every advantage, eliminating today's problems and preventing their recurrence in the future.

Continuous improvement is about ensuring we are not carrying today's problems into tomorrow, it's about making life easier for your team and your customers.

The adoption of continuous improvement needs to be driven by the culture. If organisational performance is not where it should be, it is likely not because of the lack of high-performing people but rather the void of a high-performance environment. As a leader, steadfastly focusing on building a high-performance environment fosters excellence.

As your team adopt a continuous improvement mindset, along with others in the organisation, this will shape the culture, especially when everyone in your team actively embraces and adopts the concepts. You'll likely first notice the change when you hear them organically using certain phrases related to the core principles of continuous improvement.

Continuous Improvement and Organisational Transformation

The need for transformation often occurs when what we do has lost relevance, especially in how we serve our customers, and we need to make a significant change because we have not kept up with the changing needs of our customers. A substantial gap has grown over time between what our customers want and what we offer or provide. At that point, an organisation needs to transform.

That's not to say that transformation is bad or unnecessary – if we need to make big changes, perhaps because of the state of health of something we have inherited, these changes must be made.

Facilitating a transformation now might be crucial for the seismic shift that an organisation urgently needs to realign itself with its customers' needs and demands – or the more efficient delivery of meeting those customer needs and demands. But it does mean that the fact that transformation is crucial is unfortunate as the changes in the customer have been ignored or the organisation has been tone-deaf to. What is troubling is how an organisation lets itself fall into a state where it needs to transform instead of making the changes when needed.

A further issue with transformation can be the reliance on restructuring and redundancies to pull the organisation 'back into shape'. However, a key principle of continuous improvement, without expending energy on blame, is to determine: How do we improve from this current level of performance?

**'The best time to plant a tree was twenty years ago.
The second-best time is now.'
Chinese Proverb**

It becomes our responsibility not to replicate that mistake, ensuring that a substantial aspect of any transformation extends beyond our systems and processes and granting our teams the freedom to implement smart, customer-centric improvements.

A vital role of continuous improvement is to monitor our customers' changing appetites and demands, and make frequent, dynamic and timely changes to keep what our organisation offers aligned with the customer – largely negating the need for transformational change.

Whether or not we've recently joined the organisation, as leaders, we own the current state of performance and the responsibility of creating a culture that doesn't let an organisation stagnate into irrelevance again at the expense of the customer and our teams.

Continuous Improvement After Transformation

The **customer echo**, encompassing all events and thoughts after interactions between the organisation and the customer, offers crucial insights for the organisation to enhance its customer-centricity.

The role of continuous improvement is to ensure that the customer echo is understood, captured and acted upon to ensure the effectiveness and efficiency of the organisation, so an organisation can swiftly show the necessary agility to meet the changing and dynamic needs of the customer and eliminate the need for transformations, as illustrated in Figure 3.

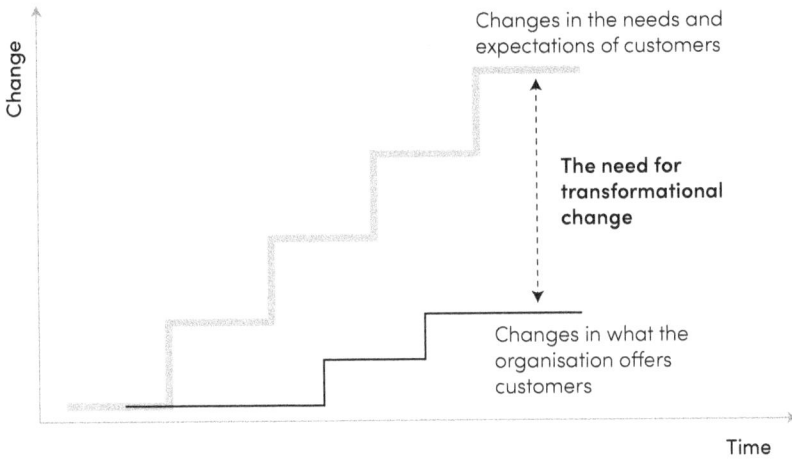

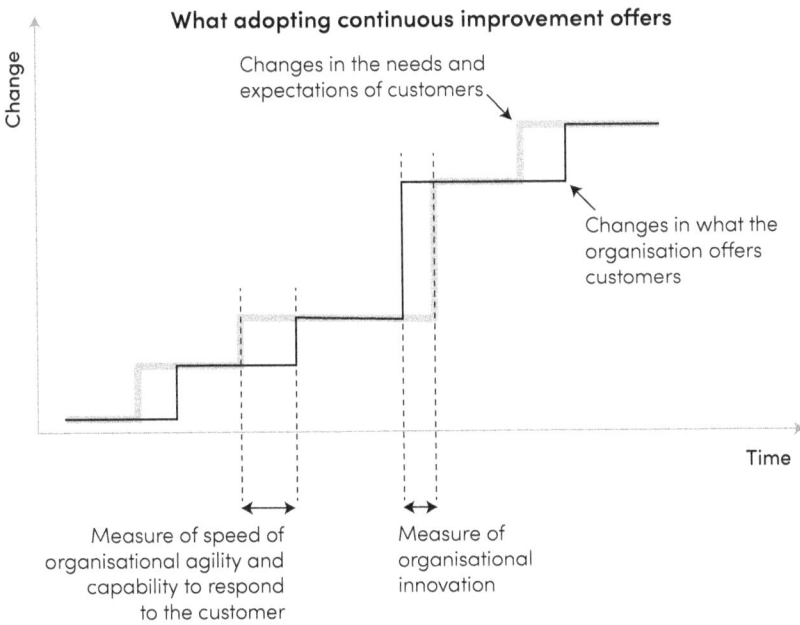

Changes in the needs and
expectations of customers

**The need for
transformational
change**

Changes in what the
organisation offers
customers

What adopting continuous improvement offers

Changes in the needs and
expectations of customers

Changes in what the
organisation offers
customers

Measure of speed of
organisational agility and
capability to respond
to the customer

Measure of
organisational
innovation

Figure 3

Adopting a continuous improvement approach after any transformation is important, as it offers longevity to the revitalised
relationship with agility to shift with the customers' ever-changing
needs. Embedding continuous improvement in your culture means

that the team are less likely to experience an organisational transformation again.

In this respect, an organisation's agility is how quickly the teams can adapt to meet their customers' needs effectively without significant defects, errors, rework, or other quality or service delivery issues.

A measure of innovation would be any time a new product that exceeds the customers' expectations and needs is released. In this scenario, the organisation represented by the black line would rise above and surpass the customers' expectations and needs, symbolised by the grey line. This not only grants a competitive advantage to the organisation but also reshapes the broader industry by redefining customers' expectations.

Significant improvement, akin to what might be achieved through a transformation, comes from a plethora of continuous, small incremental improvements. Embracing continuous improvement can stave off the need for transformation as the organisation continually and swiftly adapts to, rather than diverges from, the needs of customers and the customer echo.

'The paradox of true continuous improvement is that, at times, the improvements can be so small that they appear to be non-consequential and may not be able to be quantified. It may not have a Return on Investment (ROI), or that operational dynamic may not even be visible to the average onlooker. However, these small incremental improvements will, over time, create processes and operations that are highly efficient and effective.' (Martichenko n.d.)

Continuous Improvement is Not Cost-cutting

To lose weight, we don't amputate body parts; instead, we change our nutrition. Similarly, we know that driving costs down and improving performance are not the same thing. They stem from two very different mindsets. Yes, there can be a relationship; improving your processes and systems will have a positive side-effect of reducing costs, but a focus entirely on cutting costs will not have a positive effect on improving your system.

Continuous improvement is not cost-cutting. Good continuous improvement provides holistic and wide-reaching improvement. Rather than focus on where you can save, broaden your focus to identify areas where you can improve. A focus on cost-cutting resembles an amputation, whereas continuous improvement is a holistic nutritional and exercise program, improving your appeal to customers.

CRUCIAL TEAM DYNAMICS AND CULTURAL ELEMENTS IN ADOPTING CONTINUOUS IMPROVEMENT

The purpose of this section is to support your organisation's culture and improve the dynamics between the teams to underpin an effective foundation for a culture of continuous improvement.

Not all of the team that will be exposed to the improvement of the dynamics in your organisation and will go on to be part of an improvement team specifically focusing on an improvement initiative, but their value is in their impact of understanding, adopting and helping to embed the right culture that supports a continuous improvement mindset to flourish throughout the organisation.

Mindset Over Toolset

A well-established continuous improvement culture manifests in two ways: innovating new and enhancing current processes by doing clever new stuff and stopping ineffective practices.

For continuous improvement to become established in a culture, it has to be understood and adopted as a mindset rather than a toolset. Cultures are comprised of mindsets, not toolsets. So, any discussion about which improvement methodology is better, based on its toolset, is relatively pointless.

The extent to which a team has adopted continuous improvement is reflected by their mindset rather than their use of a toolset.

Adopting the perspective that continuous improvement is a mindset rather than solely reliant on tools empowers your team.

Once ingrained as a mindset, the skills for continuous improvement can seamlessly transition across various aspects of both work and personal life.

> **A continuous improvement mindset should be adopted in an organisation for a number of reasons; however, the crucial reason is it enables the team's ability to take every opportunity to improve organisational performance.**

Adopting continuous improvement is primarily about enabling your team to think the right way rather than using what is perceived to be the right tools.

The organisation's commitment to continuous improvement and building the teams' capability means a lot of intensive coaching. How do we know when a team has authentically adopted a continuous improvement approach? What are the clues to the maturity of continuous improvement in your team?

The extent to which a team has adopted continuous improvement is reflected by their mindset. If your team is using a toolset without the right mindset, you will likely see them rigidly apply the toolset and the method, using the terminology and lexicon that is congruent with that methodology and doing so with a sense of reluctance. They may think of (and verbalise) continuous improvement as an additional burden to their workload, hindering their 'real work'. As a result, improvement initiatives often drag on.

If your team has adopted continuous improvement as a mindset, you can expect them to:

- apply it to everything they do – even to their personal lives
- not be wedded to any particular methodology and use the best tool from any methodology that is the most purposeful to their needs
- display a cooperative dynamic with each other including the sharing of information and data with the sole purpose of transparency and working together to solve problems

- develop their own tools (or make adjustments to the tools they have been trained in) and develop their own terminology
- consider continuous improvement as a vital part of their role.

Expertly understanding a methodology and toolset is undoubtedly important and fundamental, but it is the mindset that transcends the expertise in the use of a toolset and shows that a team has wholly adopted continuous improvement.

A continuous improvement mindset is extraordinarily good value for money mainly because, in essence, it is free. A continuous improvement mindset applied to one process or system to improve it can be replicated repeatedly to continually improve elements of that organisation.

Continuous improvement can only work to contribute to your organisation if you, as a leader, fundamentally believe that your team have the ability to improve how your organisation performs, and you want to see that ability realised as tangible improvement.

Tools are important for continuous improvement; they are the product of proven and honed practices. However, it's important to note that tools can be misused, where a good tool isn't being used the right way, in the right situation. All tools are good, but they can be used in an imperfect situation (the purpose of the tool being used is misaligned with how the tool is being used) or could be a complete waste (where the tool is being used without benefit). The key to utilising the right tools is in the experience of using them, possibly coupled with good guidance, which I'll provide some tips on later.

The catalyst for continuous improvement is the team having the right mindset rather than the organisation choosing 'the right' toolset. This might sound a bit blunt and over-simplified, but the difference, in my experience, between an organisation that has adopted a toolset and an organisation that has adopted a continuous improvement mindset is this: A team with a continuous improvement mindset will apply that mindset to everything they do. When this happens, it shows a comprehensive understanding of continuous improvement, an appreciation of the value and impact of continuous improvement, and an appetite and commitment to apply continuous improvement.

Facilitating a team to adopt a continuous improvement mindset – and the resulting realisation of its benefits – is contingent on several factors, with a crucial factor being the flexibility to adapt a methodology. Allowing teams this autonomy ensures that the principles of continuous improvement are not just tools but evolve into their prevailing approach and their mindset.

And that's the premise of this book, and especially Loop 1 – exploring what's proven to be the effective strategies to enable and support the growth of the continuous improvement mindset among teams.

Building Capability in the Team

To build the mindset, the team needs to build their capability for continuous improvement. Similar to how playing tennis improves your tennis skills, practising continuous improvement strengthens your capability and application of those skills.

For your team to consistently strive for improvement as part of their work every day, they must possess the necessary skills. As we encounter problems daily, like poor customer experiences, rework, faults and the like, the imperative to address and resolve these problems also needs to be a daily commitment. This ongoing effort is an investment aimed at saving time, improving the customer experience and your organisation's reputation, and freeing up the capacity of your team to do better things by fixing problems permanently rather than constantly alleviating the symptoms of the problems.

One common reason teams fail to make improvements daily is the lack of capability. This deficit extends to continuous improvement capability in the team, the environment and, in turn, the culture.

As an organisational culture doesn't take a day off, then continuous improvement, if ingrained in your culture, won't take a day off either. It has to be something that is done every day. This underscores why continuous improvement is a mindset rather than a toolset.

Moreover, this mindset should consistently refine the organisation's toolset and methodology using continuous improvement to enhance the very process of continuous improvement itself. 'Indeed, continuous improvement is a process and needs to be managed in the same way as we manage other important processes.' (Martichenko n.d.)

One of the best ways to help the team improve daily is to empower them to own and adapt the improvement process over steadfastly and perhaps robotically following a chosen methodology. This could involve actions like improving the **Improvement Initiative Plan** or the **Pilot Plan**, where new sections can be added to better serve the organisation (see examples of these plans in Appendix 3 and 4), or it might mean developing and improving a case study overview (covered on page 190) to highlight the key elements and benefits of a completed improvement initiative.

Have the Team Develop Their Own Rules

The key to enabling the team to adopt continuous improvement is unleashing their freedom to challenge the rules and behaviours they have inherited so they can evolve and perform better. This means the team can develop their own set of rules that they *know* work for them and that they will live by with full commitment. These rules could be about their team dynamic – how they will work together, what tools are used when, or their use of plans – or the Improvement Initiative or Pilot plans, the fields in the plans, and renaming the tools to better suit the environment.

Where teams often become unstuck and disengaged with continuous improvement methodologies is when they meticulously follow each step without adequate support. Navigating through each methodology step can be challenging, especially without guidance to know which tools within each step properly contribute to the improvement initiative. Without such guidance, teams may invest time and effort in using tools ineffectively, which can strain their feelings towards the methodology, leading to apathy and indifference.

Over time, the continuous improvement adoption initiative flails and then fails in the team's mind because (they feel) the methodology wasn't good. It's important that teams receive support in the application of a continuous improvement methodology to ensure that the tools they use serve a clear purpose and offer value in improving the process. Teams should have the flexibility and support to customise and adapt these tools to align with the nature and context of the organisation.

The Challenge of Challenging Conventional Wisdom

We all know the utterance (often used as an excuse): 'But that's how it's always been done'. Though that phrase likely serves as an indicator of a process that needs to be improved – and that hasn't been improved for a very long time – the problem with this phrase is that, too often, it's the sole catalyst for an organisation's process improvement. It's a significant problem that teams only look to improve processes when that phrase is expressed, and even then, often, the attempt to make a positive change is too meek or justification of the current process is wrongly accepted.

Any action that becomes a habit without thoughtful consideration may negatively impact your performance, particularly if these habits make your organisation less dynamic than your customers. When you first start wearing a watch, you consciously decide which wrist to use with a specific purpose. However, as days pass, this decision becomes less deliberate, and putting the watch on the same wrist becomes a habit – something you do without thinking. The danger lies in the fact that you're choosing a wrist out of habit, not because it's the best choice for the day's activities. Over time, this habit can become a subconscious action, transforming into an uncontested conventional wisdom. This phenomenon is what I refer to as process calcification or process muscle memory.

Imagine you clench a fist, and it stays clenched for ten minutes. Trying to unclench that fist if you need to is like trying to meet new customer demands without having regularly changed processes before. Without frequent improvements, our ability to be dynamic diminishes.

Nothing inhibits innovation and improvement in performance as significantly as the continual adherence to conventional wisdom.

There's a common misconception that changing your processes too often will cause confusion. However, in my experience, changing your processes too infrequently, without purpose, and without those changes being led by the right people causes confusion and leaves an organisation vulnerable and lagging behind the needs of the customer.

Too many changes are only a problem when the changes are done to the team rather than led by the team that needs the change. If the right people make each purposeful, customer-focused change, there is no issue about making too many changes – but we'll get into that later.

Conventional wisdom is more about convention than it is wisdom. Constantly looking to make improvements in our processes needs to be part of our work, not something we become conscious of through happenstance when we hear someone utter the phrase, 'But that's how it's always been done'.

As a final point, saying that you did continuous improvement once is like saying that you breathed once. Continuous improvement, like breathing, is something that you need to do, well, continuously.

KEY PRINCIPLES FOR TEAMS AND LEADERS

Regardless of the chosen methodology – be it Lean, Six Sigma, Systems Thinking, Theory of Constraints, or design-oriented approaches such as Human-Centred Design, Co-Design, and Service Design – certain key principles underscore success. Ensuring these principles are used across various methodologies is crucial for a comprehensive approach to continuous improvement:

- use data to make informed decisions
- focus on root causes
- have the right mindset/don't play the blame game
- have good performance metrics and measures that drive the right behaviours
- have the right people develop the right solutions
- start smart rather than starting big
- continuous improvement is part of everyone's role
- know your customer intimately
- the customer is central to the solution development
- better is good, always take better – don't wait for perfect
- cooperation first, IT last – focus on building cross team cooperation and collaboration to improve processes first, and then with honed processes, automate processes and make system changes.

Principle-based Mantras

When adopted, these principles can become catchcries within your organisation. The principle of using data to make informed decisions could become your team expressing this to each other as: 'Show me the data!'

Based on the above principles, here are some other terms that teams have used to fuel the fires and keep these good principles alive:

- Let's move from what we think and what we feel to what we know (**data of performance**).
- How do we know that we are working on the **root cause** here and not another symptom?
- Let's actually get to the contact centre and listen to some customers (**know the customer**).
- Have we scaled and scoped this work properly to be able to get the crucial parts done fast? (**Start smart.**)

The Inter-relationship Between the Principles

There is a strong inter-relationship between all the principles. The principles mentioned above are intricately interconnected, with each one reinforcing and being bolstered by the adoption of others. No single principle operates in isolation; instead, they collectively enhance the team's approach to continuous improvement.

Examples of the inter-relationships between the principles include:

- When you focus on the root cause, the benefits are greater.
- You can articulate benefits when you have a good baseline. A good baseline of performance data means that you can tell if you have a good improvement, as you can see a change in performance.
- You can better see changes in performance when you measure variation rather than averages.
- Root causes are easier to work out if you measure variations rather than averages, as you'll know which events to specifically look at and look for common occurrences.
- Good measures drive the right behaviours.
- Knowing the root causes means that we know the right behaviours to support, monitor and measure, and how frequently.
- Knowing the root causes means that we determine better lead measures for performance and can improve the chances of better outcomes for our customers.
- Knowing the customer means that we know better measures.
- Knowing better measures means we can hone the elements of our behaviours that count.
- Better measures mean that we make better-informed decisions.

THE LEADERSHIP ROLE IN A CONTINUOUS IMPROVEMENT CULTURE

If we hope for change, then any change that happens does so because of chance or dumb luck. There is only a place for hope when you have no control over influencing any change or result whatsoever.

If we are in a position of control, as leaders, we have an opportunity to influence performance, and any energy we spend hoping for better is wasted energy.

Too often, continuous improvement is thought of as something that is hard to understand and complex to do. It isn't. Continuous improvement is simple. It can only live in simplicity. What it does demand is courage and commitment to gain knowledge and to make improvements fuelled by that knowledge. Hope is the hollowest of all tools to affect change. An antidote for hope is courage.

Continuous improvement takes courage because an early step is to understand your organisation's performance and *why* you experience the level of performance you do, especially related to your customers.

It is the finding out the *why* that takes courage – as you'll discover a lot of ugly practices that exist.

It takes courage to discover the previously hidden issues, problems and practices in your systems and processes. They can be labelled as opportunities but only if we know they exist.

As a leader, delving into the limiters and inhibitors of your organisation's performance will likely reveal some unhealthy practices and behaviours, often to game the system to meet targets. It will take a lot of courage to look and see exactly what is happening within your organisation and know exactly how you are performing, especially from a customer's perspective.

Courage is the single most valuable element that is needed to support continuous improvement in an organisational culture.

If you are prepared to look at and understand the reasons for your organisation's performance, you'll find bad news. That's good.

In fact, it's fantastic, and unquestionably, it's better than not finding it or ignoring the possibility it doesn't exist.

An example of this is the **hidden factory** – the processes and events that produce defects, waste or cheat measures of performance that are usually only known by those operating within the hidden factory. Some hidden factory processes are deceitful, but more often, they are just habitual, and there's a lack of awareness of their consequence and appetite to improve. It takes courage – on everybody's part – to share the actualities of the hidden factory practices.

It's better to know what needs to be improved than to remain ignorant. That's what adopting a continuous improvement culture helps expose, and that's why it takes a lot of courage, fortitude and resolve. Facing reality is gruelling but incredibly rewarding. You might or might not have a leadership title in your organisation, but trust me, if you're prepared to properly understand the performance of a process to understand the bad and ugly stuff going on, you are a leader.

Continuous improvement can never be thought of so thinly as just a methodology if the rewards for adopting it are to be experienced. Crucially, continuous improvement needs an organisational culture that supports courage – as just one of a number of important traits.

As a final point, having the courage to solve problems and selecting which problems to solve, like the holes in the boat scenario I've talked about before, is essential. Leaving the leaks open is another reason why continuous improvement (and the principles that underpin it) takes courage – to fix only some of the problems you and your team know exist while leaving the others is crucial to getting good stuff done, as having to make those decisions (especially on what problems gets fixed now and which are left for later) takes courage.

Let me ask you this. Would you, as a leader, accept a performance improvement of 127% over the next year if that meant you'd be down by 32% at the end of the first quarter of that year? Courage is needed to stick to the plan, especially when you are 32%

down at the end of that first quarter, as you can't know that your team will be 127% up by the end of the year.

Cultivating a Problem-solving Culture

One of the best things a leader can do to foster a continuous improvement culture is to facilitate the sharing of ideas in their team, so the team thinks smarter and acts faster. Let's focus on how we can facilitate that.

It starts with leadership being seen to embrace problems. There's a key issue with the saying: 'Don't bring me problems, bring me solutions'. The issue is this: the organisation has to have a healthy culture towards problems because if it doesn't, people won't even raise problems with leaders because that also means bringing them solutions – it's a double-edged sword. The way an organisation treats a problem, and certainly the prevailing culture of how a person who brings a problem to a leader's attention is treated is crucial.

Leaders will always find out about problems, but a healthy culture will ensure leaders find out about problems early – or better yet, that leaders are involved in the early discovery of the problem, as opposed to something far more significant later.

How an organisation treats the team members who raise problems is vital. You have the option to foster a culture where you become aware of issues that have impacted thousands of customers after the fact or identify problems that have affected a few customers early on, preventing broader repercussions if immediate action is taken.

We need the right culture that is not punitive and short-sighted when it comes to problems. All organisations have problems, and any organisation that thinks they don't, has a really big problem.

CHALLENGES IN ADOPTING CONTINUOUS IMPROVEMENT

A mindset of continuous improvement cannot exist in a culture where teams believe that only hard work equates to good work.

Continuous improvement is about making life easier for your customers and your teams.

How Are we Going to Find Time?

Often, teams know of and feel the frustrations of the problems typical of their environment, either directly or through their customers. The cruel irony is that the teams that have the most to gain through the improvements tend to be the most under pressure and have less capacity to look at making improvements.

They ask: How are we going to find time to start to improve?

We typically become so invested and focused on the continual problem-solving of inherent issues in our processes that the thought of making improvements to the process itself is perceived as something extra. Improvement is something *instead of* rather than extra.

Usually, there are already pockets of time available, but teams, for example, often spend that time airing grievances during meetings. Leaders need to steer this energy away from complaining and towards active problem-solving, and how to do that is a key focus of this book.

We need to transition to a mindset that fixing problems is seen as not only non-disruptive, but an integral part of their work – an improvement focus is not additional to their work but is a crucial element of it. In their roles, the team should both do their work *and* improve how they do their work. For that to happen, they need a methodology, the capability to use it, and the permission and support to unleash that capability.

As a leader, don't let improvement initiatives only occur when your team feel that they have the time available to make improvements – as that likely won't be any time soon. Rather, dedicate some of their capacity to making improvements, so they have the time to get started now.

I often share this with teams: It's too rare that we have the feeling that we did something really special in any given day. We won't likely remember this time next year the work that we are processing, but we will remember the significant changes we made to improve the way our work is done for ourselves and our customer.

The Executive Challenge

What can seem obviously compelling at a team leader or senior manager level can be just one of a noise of options at the executive level – and this graft through options means that the argument for an organisation to adopt continuous improvement struggles to get the oxygen (like everything else) at the executive level.

The biggest problem continuous improvement practitioners, or those that are trying to build a continuous improvement culture in an organisation, face is convincing and getting the executives on board by answering this question from the executive's perspective: Why is this important?

A primary factor contributing to this challenge is the short-term demands placed on the executive team to consider short-term impacts on shareholders, who themselves might have short-term thinking. Continuous improvement is not a short-term approach.

Simply, there is never a single short-term fix to realise long-term results. Ever.

The key issue lies in the framing of continuous improvement, as it often falls short of addressing the fundamental question: Why would we adopt continuous improvement? And it's a fair question.

Continuous improvement is an investment. It takes time to fully realise the benefits of the investment in the team's capability and the capacity dedicated to improvement initiatives. Often, things go slower before they become faster; we have to slow down to be able to speed up.

As with any investment, there is a bit of pain early on before the benefits are harvested later. It rests on the team to provide compelling reasons why it is good for the executives to support the organisation to adopt continuous improvement.

Convincing executives about the importance of progress and gaining their buy-in to a continuous improvement culture requires more than just conversation. Like anyone else, they need to be shown what continuous improvement looks like in action and the effects of it. Conducting site visits to observe teams that have successfully adopted and benefited from continuous improvement work well.

Continuous improvement might face resistance because executives have to relinquish control over certain processes, including decision-making authority within those processes. This shift is crucial as those directly involved in the work are best positioned to make timely decisions for performance improvement.

Executives might be hesitant for various emotional reasons. As performance improvement becomes a decentralised task, decisions for changes are embedded within the work rather than being another hierarchical layer, which enables a dynamic organisation. Empowering those who identify problems to make decisions about them allows for better and more timely decisions. What hinders executives' ability to make real-time decisions is that they often receive lag data of performance that has already occurred.

If you, as an executive, want to actively contribute to improvement decisions, staying engaged in the actual work where these decisions should be made is crucial. While well-designed dashboards with meaningful measures can provide insights into performance, being present in the work fosters interpersonal relationships and trust. This presence allows you to receive early warnings about problems and gain a deeper understanding of intricacies, facilitating swift and significant improvements when addressed promptly.

DEFINING CONTINUOUS IMPROVEMENT FOR YOUR ORGANISATION

The information in this book has proven effective for various organisations. While some elements may work better for some than others, consider these elements as ideas to be tested at this stage. Some will prove successful and should be persisted with, while others may not yield the desired results. What we know is the approach which has proven to be most likely to work is what has become the core of Loop 1.

By thoroughly testing these ideas and making informed decisions about what does and does not work for your team, you will define your method and approach to continuous improvement. And that's the crucial outcome you want: your team to build and continually develop their improvement method. Embrace ideas from others (you'll find that the continuous improvement community generally loves to share) and define your ethos.

Everything I'm about to share with you is either right, wrong or somewhere in between. The effectiveness of each element depends on the context and will either work – or not – to a varying degree for the situation you and your team are in. What works and what doesn't is a crucial part of defining what continuous improvement is in your organisation.

How and Where to Start – the Right Way

An organisation adopting continuous improvement will usually take one of two common approaches:

1. They will look to map and catalogue all their processes and have a full set of processes ready for improvement with the added benefit of having visual representation and standardisation of those processes. I refer to this as a *horizontal* approach to continuous improvement, where work is completed in layers – the first layer being the mapping and capture of processes.

2. They will adopt continuous improvement one process at a time – mapping and analysing then improving and embedding the better process before moving on to the next process. I refer to this as a *vertical* approach to continuous improvement.

In my experience, adopting a vertical approach – the combined mapping and improving a process – yields significantly better and faster results. This method accelerates wins and allows incremental refinement of your continuous improvement approach.

Conversely, a horizontal approach, focusing on mapping processes first, does not substantively improve processes – simply because improvement is not the initial aim of that first layer of work. Further, hiring consultants (or simply those outside of the work) for the reasons of capacity and speed to map processes in this approach can impede team capability development and the lack of substantive wins or immediate benefits can hinder the establishment of an energised 'thirst to improve' mindset within the organisational culture.

Think of it this way: if you had a lot of invoices to mail out (just bear with me for a moment, I know my example sounds old-school), so many that it would take a week to do, you could take the approach to fold all the invoices first, then put them in all the envelopes, then apply the postage to the envelopes, and then post them. This would be the horizontal approach of batching and performing all the similar tasks before moving on to the next task. There are some inherent risks and disadvantages in this approach. There is the risk that after folding all of the invoices, we find that the invoices don't fit in the envelopes with the way that they've been folded (another reason why we run pilots, which we'll cover later), and because this process is batched, it's only when all the envelopes are completed that we would post any, meaning that no one receives (and can pay) their invoice until *all* the invoices have been prepared and sent.

The vertical approach is more beneficial. We fold an invoice, then we put it in the envelope, which means if there's a problem with this step in the process, we immediately see what the problem is. After processing one invoice completely, we can implement any lessons learnt and refine our approach in the preparation of the next invoice, which is what continuous improvement is. A further benefit of this approach is that by the end of each day, we can post the completed invoices, which will be significant if this process is related to cash flow – with a good portion of our customers getting their invoices sooner than they would have.

Embracing a vertical approach leads to early benefits, including improved processes, immediate building of team capabilities and showcasing the dividends of continuous improvement. This is ideal, as it paves the way for your team to take the lead in embedding a culture of continuous improvement. This approach is congruent with the 'start smart' and 'start where the love is' principles, allowing teams to strategically improve processes simultaneously – it does not need to be completely linear. You might have five teams and:

1. Have some people from each of the teams work together on a process (one process improved).

2. Then have those members lead further improvements in their own teams on another process (five processes being improved simultaneously).

3. Then each of the teams continues to line up and work through processes to be improved, which could be two or three processes in each team (between 5–15 processes improved simultaneously).

Either way, whether this is the best approach for your team or not to use their capabilities, the key is that *there is a plan* to leverage the strengthening capabilities of your team and grow the continuous improvement capability and culture across the wider team.

The Formalisation of a Process

Formalising a process through mapping provides value by aligning the entire team involved in the process. Mapping often reveals variations in how team members handle specific process steps, highlighting areas for improvement and fostering consistency. An example of a variation in a process step is where we find that some of the team members are following up with a customer to capture the customer's experience after the sale, while other team members didn't know that there was something that needed to be done.

There's an irrational fear that mapping or articulating a process causes restrictive uniformity and reduces any needed flexibility in the process. This is a mislaid fear. A process is a snapshot benchmark reflecting what we know is the best way to perform the process at that point in time – though this 'best way' could still be heavily flawed. It is with a continuous improvement mindset that we constantly study that process and its performance, in parts or as a whole, to improve it. And when we know what is better, we improve that part of the process to then perform better. Keeping the integrity of a mapped process should never restrict the improvement of a process. A mapped process is the baseline for improvement and is not intended to be a static standard to inhibit betterment. Good performance measures ensure that the process remains dynamic through informed improvements.

Start Where the Love Is

If you run a large team or organisation, you'll most likely want the entire team to adopt continuous improvement. With a larger team (even 100-plus is a large team), there are also likely subcultures with varying views on its value and adoption. Irrespective of whether or not they are informed, they will exist. These differing views, a number of which will be negative, will only hinder and dilute the adoption of continuous improvement.

Rather than trying to enforce it organisation-wide in one go, start where the love is – where the energy is – to get started right now, and let those who want to adopt continuous improvement do it first. Start with the team that has the largest appetite and the greatest energy.

Importantly, communicate to all teams that your organisation is moving towards adopting continuous improvement, emphasising that its core purpose is to make life better and easier for your organisation and the customers. The (effectively) self-selected team should be challenged to both adopt continuous improvement and contribute to the organisation-wide appetite to adopt it by being open and sharing their experiences and results with the rest of the organisation.

The feedback and interest from teams may be:

1. They get what adopting continuous improvement could mean for them, and they are energised to start now.

2. They get what adopting continuous improvement could mean for them but show limited appetite to start now.

3. They misunderstand continuous improvement (perhaps thinking it's about getting better vending machines in the café for improved employee satisfaction) and don't want to be involved in continuous improvement. They think it's essentially a waste of time and say they're 'already too busy with their work'.

Unfortunately, the teams in the last scenario probably need continuous improvement the most. However, the strategic approach remains to start where the love is – start with the teams in the first scenario. While the first scenario is the ideal starting point, the second scenario is still a good place to start the implementation process.

PART II
LOOP 1

Loop 1 Map

The first step of Loop 1

1. Build the team dynamic:
   a. building cooperation with building and using facilitation skills
   b. building a collective understanding of a process and understanding who does what in that process.

Understand the current level of performance

2. Build a map of the process:
   a. capture problems and pain points we currently experience and know can be fixed
   b. understand any inter-relationships that exist between the problems and pain points.
3. Choosing what can be improved:
   a. decide on what is to be improved (initially) using decision-making tools
   b. choose who owns the improvement initiative and who is involved in the improvement team.
4. Problem statements are developed:
   a. Develop Improvement Initiative Plans.
5. Capture baseline data.

Determine why we have the current level of performance

6. Root cause analysis (analysis of baseline data):
   a. setting up stand-up meetings for updates.

Develop and pilot solutions

7. Who develops the solutions?
8. Good solution development.
9. Planning for and piloting solutions:
    a. determining the solution we will pilot
    b. how long the pilot will be
    c. measures for the pilot
    d. decision to go live or not.

Embed proven solutions

10. Implementing and embedding a proven solution so it becomes the new norm.
11. Benefit realisation.
12. Celebrate success (for an enduring appetite for continuous improvement).

CHAPTER 2

Build the Right Team Dynamic

Whether it's an exhausted parent getting up in the middle of the night for a crying baby, a fire officer on the frontline of a fire or a medical worker feeling exhausted, or scientists working feverously to unravel a virus to determine a vaccine or reverse the effects of climate change, none of the extremes of effort in this work is being done for fame or money. We all dig deeper because the work is purposeful.

Too often, we forget about or completely underestimate the power of purpose. As a team or as individuals, without a purpose that resonates in our core, we aren't even close to tapping into our capability.

Building the right dynamic is about connecting the team with purpose and unleashing the energy to improve.

The purpose of this section is to highlight what needs to be fundamental and supported in the culture of our teams to provide the right foundation for continuous improvement to be adopted. This culture change focuses on the key elements of cooperation and collaboration – gracefully and authentically. This will provide strong benefits in their improvements as, usually, a large proportion of improvements in any organisation will mean the support and participation of other teams, which is why cooperation and collaboration are so crucial to the efficacy and impact of improvements.

In this section, we will focus on the core elements (which just happen to start with the letter c) of cooperation, collaboration, coordination and cohesiveness:

- **Cooperation** – working together for a commonly understood purpose.
- **Collaboration** – working together to solve problems.
- **Coordination** – knowing how to best work together for the realisation of the team's collective purpose.
- **Cohesiveness** – strength of the kinship between the team members to work together.

THE METHODOLOGY

Loop 1 offers a very specific approach to adopting continuous improvement in organisations and focuses on establishing the mindset of continuous improvement in the organisation. This is done by:

- building the right dynamic in teams for a continuous improvement mindset to flourish
- starting smart by using that mindset and initially inexperienced capability of the team by taking care of easier problems, with a low risk of stumbling by working on something too big
- starting earlier by not looking for the *perfect problem* to solve first
- starting smart and experiencing success to create an increased appetite in the team to continue to grow and take on gnarlier problems (which flows into Loop 2).

By taking this approach, we take the first crucial step towards entrenching a culture that ensures its longevity and facilitates continually improving performance.

The core of Loop 1 is building the appetite for continuous improvement to be part of your culture. The team start work on those problems they have the capability, confidence and desire to fix, which might not be the biggest issues facing the organisation. As they gain experience with the methodology and confidence from previous wins, they can progressively address more complex issues in Loop 2.

This continuous improvement methodology generally moves through four key stages:

1. **Understand** the current level of performance (sometimes referred to as the *current state*).
2. **Determine** why we have that current level of performance – the root causes.
3. **Develop and test** solutions that address those root causes to improve performance and prove that the solutions work through piloting and testing.
4. Implement and **embed the pilot-proven** solutions with better reporting to highlight the ongoing benefits.

In my experience, all good continuous improvement methodologies move through something very similar to these four key stages. If your organisation or team is looking to adopt any continuous improvement methodology or otherwise – like Lean Six Sigma, Systems thinking, Total Quality Management, Agile, or Human Centred Design – this book will support that. The primary focus of this book is to provide a practical guide on how to adopt continuous improvement methodologies, addressing crucial aspects related to team dynamics and organisational culture.

Often, methodologies focus on starting with understanding the current level of performance. However, they regularly overlook a crucial element that we need to build first – the right team dynamic.

The first stage of the first loop takes us through building the right team dynamic – think of it as crucial pre-conditioning for the team.

THE TEAM'S DYNAMIC

The team's dynamic means and represents their ability to work together to support each other in meeting the purpose of the team.

We're all part of the same team, and sometimes, our teams need to be reminded of this. One of the best outcomes of a continuous improvement initiative is getting the team to work together to fulfil purpose.

Both the speed and impact of improvements come from cross-team collaboration and cooperation. Unfortunately, too often, teams focus on the task that they think they should be performing rather than on the tasks that contribute to the purpose of the organisation.

One of the few ways a team can have a good understanding of how any task contributes to the purpose of the organisation is to comprehend the end-to-end process that their work resides within. Understanding the placement of their tasks within that process is crucial, offering insights into the relationship between their tasks and those of others in their team in the fulfilment of the purpose. This helps with team engagement as each team member develops a crucial understanding of their work, the work of others and the inter-relationship of that work.

Building and focusing on team engagement before they start will speed up any continuous improvement initiatives and set things off on the right foot from the start, creating a foundation for how the team can best work together throughout the improvement initiative.

Coordination, cooperation, cohesiveness and collaboration among the team are undervalued elements in the adoption of continuous improvement in any organisation. The cohesion of a team will outlast the initiative that they're in as it'll be fundamental for an ongoing continuous improvement mindset. So, for this reason, any initiative needs to start not in the work but in forming the team ready to perform the work.

Ironically, despite the abundant connectivity options offered by today's technology, our actual connection with each other has diminished – we are less connected with each other in how it matters. What used to be a vibrant exchange of ideas has been reduced to one-dimensional messages and emails. This lack of rich communication results in real waste and inefficiency, which is exacerbated by our teams needing very little in the way of permission or thought prior to sending out an email. Everyone is free to send emails to many people that can suck up large amounts of time to read, and not be important or purposeful for the recipients. Whether sent to hundreds or just a few, the repeated impact is significant.

Poor connectivity means instead of experiencing cooperation to work together to make improvements that benefit the team, we are far more likely to experience benefits for the individual at the expense of the team or for one team at the expense of other teams – such as a new edict that saves one team five minutes but costs another team 20 minutes to perform.

Harmonise Teams Before Processes

Teams who look to adopt continuous improvement must start with building and supporting healthy team dynamics throughout the whole team – obviously including leaders who have a specific role to play in setting and supporting the dynamic.

Only with healthy team dynamics can we have honest conversations about the performance being experienced and, more crucially, *why* we are experiencing the levels of performance that we are. This is where the gold is: Understanding why we are experiencing the performance we currently have means knowing all the contributing factors we have, which together manifest as the performance we experience. If we are looking to change our performance, then it's these components that we must change, adapt, remove or add to.

We need to have open and candid conversations about the components that we must change, adapt, remove or add, and the team dynamic is crucial for the authenticity and openness of these conversations.

Commonly, the reasons for the level of performance we are currently experiencing are not just one step removed – usually, there are a number of interrelated but linear factors that need to be worked through to get to the root cause. I'll introduce (or reintroduce) you to tools later that can help unravel the symptoms to find the root cause.

These tools and concepts help minimise the likelihood of teams thinking, often incorrectly, that there is just one factor in the reason for the level of performance being experienced. In cases where teams are in really bad shape and exhibit that thinking, they can mistakenly blame the customer, saying, 'If the customer only...' That's a sure sign that the team are oblivious or in denial about the reasons for their current level of performance.

STARTING WITH COOPERATION

Cooperation is essential, if not critical, for continuous improvement and anything good happening in your organisation, like an engaged team working to meet the needs of the customer and keep the organisation relevant. With cooperation, attitudes in the team prevail, such as: *We share a common goal. We are passionate about that goal. I want to help you contribute to that goal and I can feel that you want to help me.*

Team dynamics and the cooperation and coordination that exist among the team are crucial for team performance. For example, imagine a sporting team where there isn't cooperation and coordination throughout the team. If the team manager or coach has a plan and the team is not following that plan, then the team might still win despite not following the coach's plan – and those few wins will come down to luck and won't be consistent as they are not a high functioning and performing team. They will not win often. If the team is split in half, and half wants to follow one plan – one set of tactics – and the other half wants to follow another, then that team is even less likely to win, if at all. It is crucial that any team works together cooperatively and in a coordinated fashion – this is the single most important determinant of successfully adopting continuous improvement.

The single most important determinant of a team's success in adopting a continuous improvement mindset is cooperation being a core team dynamic.

For the organisation to present a unified and holistic view in service to the customer, cooperation must permeate through its teams. This involves asking, 'How can we work together to best help the customer?'

To reduce the chances of a potentially good solution being incorrectly dismissed through poor team cohesion – where some of the team don't understand the process thoroughly enough to see the benefits of a solution others in the team are proposing – we need to have the team authentically cooperate with each other. Cooperation is important because it removes the intentional (and unintentional) sabotaging of applying continuous improvement to improve performance when people think: *Why on earth are we doing that? It will never work.*

Cooperation, irrespective of how it supports your continuous improvement initiative, will support all future interactions among your team. A team that cooperates is simply a better team than one that does not.

To determine what does and does not work, experimentation is necessary. After all, we'll only know if it works when we try it. Everyone has to be committed to trying it properly with the hope that it will work. Good, healthy and authentic cooperation among the team not only means effective trials of new improvements but also provides the willing environment to trial ideas from the wider team.

The team needs to be cognisant that anything that works well is a win for the team. And for that to occur, cooperation is crucial.

Cooperation in a team generates approachability, which in turn supports cross-team collaboration for performance. For two teams to collaborate with each other to improve performance in a way that they individually can't, there needs to be a willingness to collaborate, and that comes from a good attitude – one primarily of cooperation.

The Cooperative Quotient

People measure their intelligence quotient (IQ) and emotional quotient (EQ) – but as teams, we need to understand our ability to work together and how we can measure and improve on that ability, a **cooperative quotient**.

Every team can be measured by their cooperative quotient, and a high-performing team has a strong/high *cooperative quotient*, as they understand among themselves how they best work together, and they abide by that understanding. An example of a high cooperative quotient among a team is when there is no fear of asking each other questions to help understand or asking for help. It is a worthwhile session to have your team develop its own definitions and standards for what aids the cooperative quotient of the team.

> **Tip:** Your response to news of poor performance sets the tone for your team. Display grace, fortitude and resilience. Avoid unhealthy phrases like 'Don't bring me problems, bring me solutions'. Teams reacting negatively to this statement can display behaviours like hiding or altering results, justifying, minimising, rationalising, or making excuses – a culture of denial. Encourage openness and problem-solving instead.

Your Team Needs to Think Differently

For a continuous improvement mindset to flourish, we often need to think differently. There is a critical difference between thinking *why can't we?* and thinking *why we can't*, and just that slim difference in that energy of thinking substantially changes the outcome.

When teams are thinking *why can't we?* they are in an innovative mindset and are expressing a state of mind to try and discover a way to do something. But when someone is in a *why we can't* mindset, all they're trying to do is shut down the possibility – the irony is both those mindsets are applicable at that point in time, leading to two similar expressions but with very different outcomes. The difference is where the 'we' is in our statements and, thereby, our mindset.

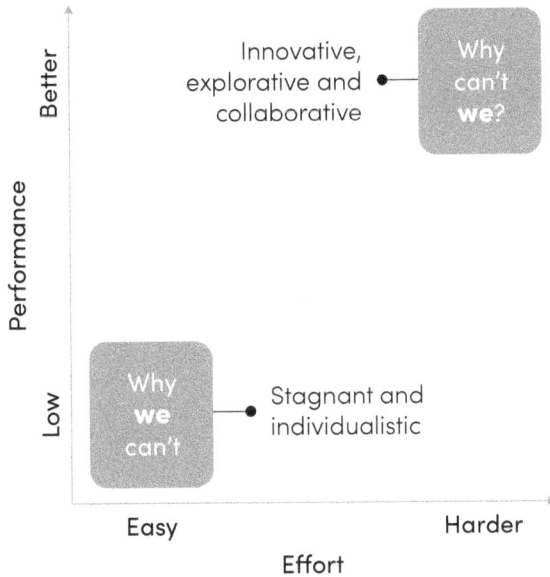

You can't find the path of least resistance in a process by taking the path of least resistance in your thinking. The *why we can't* mindset is the path of least resistance as it is so easy to shut down or dismiss a thought, an idea, a suggestion to be teased out, a problem to be solved or a solution to be piloted. A *why we can't* mindset dismisses, easily, all those options and opportunities at the outset. That's easy. And lazy.

The *why we can't* mindset shuts down innovative thought and does not progress the possibility; alternatively, the *why can't we?* mindset is energy towards enabling that possibility, unravelling and uncovering, and solving that possibility. It is a challenge to conventional wisdom. These two mindsets can occur simultaneously; when someone has a *why we can't* mindset, they can't think in a *why can't we?* mindset, so the team or the individual needs to deliberately decide which mindset they take.

It is crucial for the team to foster the right thinking. As a leader, it is essential for you to listen carefully to what the team says. Additionally, listen to what you're thinking and make sure it's *why can't we?* and not *why we can't*.

Setting the Team Dynamic

The ultimate goal in establishing a good team dynamic involves establishing some key traits and characteristics – the dynamics that the team will share – to enable a cooperative team dynamic. If we were to refer to these traits as mantras or sayings, they would be something like:

- The fastest way to do something is to do it properly.
- Don't fix breakages with craftsmanship (don't do bad stuff or irrelevant stuff well) – use craftsmanship to fix the reason why things break.
- Don't volunteer an improvement to be done unless you are prepared and willing to be part of the team that affects the improvement (don't suggest work for others to do – but suggest work you'd want to lead yourself).
- The way in which you perform one thing will become the mindset that permeates everything you do (how you do one thing is how you do everything).
- We all have two jobs – to do our work and to improve the work that we do.
- We can either bail water out of a leaky boat or focus on plugging the holes.
- When we talk to each other, it is always on the spectrum between the extremes of authenticity and gamesmanship – we've chosen to be authentic.
- We'll always display our willingness to work together and support each other to fulfil the purpose of the team. We're all on the same team.

There's an example of a team dynamic in Appendix 6 that can be replicated by your team. By collectively following the standards they set for their team dynamic, the behaviours in the above list will manifest.

ACTIONS TO START BUILDING COOPERATION

At this stage, the team's opinions may lack full insight. To clarify, the distinction between opinions and solid knowledge lies in having the data of performance. While we'll work on obtaining it, our immediate priority is practicality. The team's primary goal is to sustain effective collaboration. Together, they can explore areas already identified for improvement without delving into intricate details at this early stage.

Energy and Emotion in the Culture of an Organisation

When teams possess high energy and courage, they excel at problem-solving. They actively seek out challenges, not worried about finding problems or the consequence of finding problems, because they are supported by leadership, and they have the capability, resilience and capacity to solve the problems that they find.

Additionally, we experience teams collaborating and supporting one another in resolving problems. The collective effort of teams collaborating to solve problems also cultivates a culture of cross-team collaboration and innovation within the organisation. This dual focus of problem-solving and seizing opportunities drives continuous improvement and enhances performance.

Our aim as leaders is to nurture a blend of emotions that contribute to the right elements in our culture and drive optimal performance. We also value the tools that high-energy teams employ, especially those that streamline processes and save time, ultimately freeing up capacity.

Start With Who Does What

Too often, teams make decisions to reshape processes and systems without a thorough enough understanding of the work. Achieving healthy gains in performance can only be experienced through good improvements in the work, which in turn come from insightful and intricate knowledge of the work. This means everybody who is involved in, responsible and accountable for the work and looks to tangibly improve performance needs to have an intimate understanding of what's actually going on first, across an entire process, then build and unleash the capability of those in the team to improve performance.

To support the growth of cooperation between the team and to get them talking to understand the intricacies of their teammates' roles, and also as a catalyst to develop the desire and energy to improve the work that the team does, start with a session where the team can ask each other questions. This is literally an opportunity for them to ask everything they have ever wanted to ask for the purpose of a better understanding of how their work inter-relates with others.

For example, one team member might ask another: 'When this [explained event] happens, do you follow up with the customer? Because I assumed it was you rather than me, and if you haven't, that means no one has been following up with the customer about this [event].'

Capture the words of the questions visually and write them on sticky notes. This helps the team become comfortable with visual representation, and the questions themselves will help later with the idea generation of improvements that the team could undertake.

The purpose of the question-and-answer session is to enable good cooperation and a better understanding of what each member does and their role within some of the organisation's processes so the team can start to understand and work to improve the process collaboratively.

This is literally an opportunity for them to ask everything they have ever wanted to ask about the work of others for the purpose of a better understanding of how their work inter-relates with others, but, for whatever reason, haven't – proving the value of this exercise.

Like all sessions run with the team, nothing should come as a surprise. Let the team know in advance – at least a couple of days, if not a week – that they will have an opportunity to ask each other questions about the work performed so they can prepare. Tell them it would be a good idea for them to note and capture questions in their work over the week prior to the session and bring these questions along.

The team has to feel safe to ask questions that will support them to cooperate better with other members of the team. We know that some ideas have been lost and not captured, and some people don't have a voice in meetings, and this is why the building of a healthy and cooperative team dynamic is important. Of course, many of the questions that will be asked should have been asked before, but the very nature that they have been asked in the session means there wasn't a foundation to ask them before.

Another reason they may not have asked these questions before is that they felt vulnerable. It's important that you build an environment where the team feel comfortable asking questions of each other about the work that they do. I usually start the session by making sure that the team understands that it is better to know the answer to these questions than to not ask them, so any question asked is a good question because it needed to be asked.

Often, when the team ask each other questions about the work they do, it is not unusual that they start to jump to solutions at this stage for the problems that they hear. As the facilitator, it's important that you preface the session by saying the problems will be revisited later and that the focus of this session is just to ask each other the questions we want to ask. Using a **parking lot** is a good way to park conversations that are important, but not important to have right now during the session. Capture and park peripheral conversations so you don't lose that thought, but in capturing the thought, you can swiftly return to the purpose of the session. Your parking lot might simply be a designated space where you put a sticky note that reflects/captures the discussion point that you won't discuss now but do want to capture for a later session.

Like most Q&A sessions, they can be a bit slow to start, but momentum can build quickly when the team think of questions after hearing others. If you are facilitating the session, you could have some questions you ask first, or if some of the team is comfortable sharing the questions they have prepared, and if they set the right tone, let them start. How would you know? Catch up with some of the team and ask them what questions they have beforehand.

Most questions are along the lines of: *What do we do when a particular event happens?* Other common questions include:

- Jeremy, do you deliver to our customers once or twice during the day?
- How often does Vanessa get to talk to the customers, and what sorts of things are talked about when she does?
- What do you do when you can't find an empty container to pack the customer's order?
- When we ask for customer feedback and they rate us on the scale, at what point, or ranking, do we call them back to understand why we got that ranking and who sees that feedback?
- What happens when we can't supply what a customer has asked for?

These are all valuable questions. It's both important and highly beneficial for those in the organisation to know the answers to these questions. By engaging in this type of questioning, not only do team members gain a better understanding of each other's roles and processes in the organisation, but most importantly, it cultivates an awareness of how individual actions impact others and how they can start to do things in a way that supports the work, and certainly alleviates the rework of others. This session can ignite the awareness and understanding they need to have ownership of their work and support and cooperate with others to work through problems and improve the customer experience together.

Tips for Running This Session

In facilitating a session like this, set it up so the team is comfortable. They might be too embarrassed to ask questions as they feel that others might assume that they should already know the answers – especially if it's considered that not knowing means they have been underperforming in their work up to now. There are three things we need to keep in mind:

1. It's now more crucial than ever that we fill that gap in their knowledge because if we don't, that underperformance will continue.
2. If they didn't know what we assumed they should, that's not their failing; it's ours as leaders.
3. We will reduce the chances of this happening again with new members joining the team through better team coordination dynamics of stand-up meetings, visual boards, and a more cooperative and courageous (*why can't we?*) culture.

So, more than anything, make sure that this session is run like an amnesty. Egos need to be put to the side, and we authentically need to understand everything that is real about why we currently have the level of performance that we do. Like so many aspects of adopting a continuous improvement culture, this, too, will take a lot of courage, understanding and empathy.

Any signs or displays of dismay, annoyance, blaming, or the like will adversely impact this session. A facilitator will likely need to continually remind the team of the purpose of this session and stay on top of any behaviours that will erode the necessary team dynamic.

> **Tip:** If your team's stuck, ask them what makes them mad, sad and glad about the work that they do and need to perform. Mad are things that frustrate the team – things they could get done but can't. Sad is those things that go wrong and are below-par performances, which are disappointing. Glad encompasses the positive aspects and successes.

Want to know more about facilitation and good skills that affect good facilitation? See Appendix 1.

Choosing Not to Play the Blame Game

Continuous improvement needs to be about how we advance from this current level of performance without dwelling on blame. Initially, our energy is directed toward understanding our current level of performance. From there, we can choose to allocate energy to blame or to progress with all our focus on improvement.

With continuous improvement, we look to understand the causes of our current performance rather than how or by whom we have inherited those causes. Consider it like this: we've discovered a rule or practice that is causing damage to our performance, so the practice or rule is a problem we need to develop a solution for. And that's precisely where we spend our energy. Rather than finding out how or who is responsible for us inheriting the rule or establishing the practice, we focus only on solving that problem to then perform better in the environment we are in and for our customers.

Certainly, the rule might have worked well before, but changes in our environment have turned it into a problem. We just need clear data and facts to confirm it's an issue. If we don't address it, this problem will keep affecting our performance, so our focus should be on making improvements.

NOT JUMPING TO RESOLVE PROBLEMS TOO EARLY

Early on in the process of adopting continuous improvement, the team will have plenty of opportunities to both discover and discuss problems that could be resolved. It is important, though, that we don't spend energy too early trying to resolve problems because we likely have a very immature understanding of those problems – what it is about those problems we need to fix and any interrelationship between those problems.

If we mistakenly spend our time and resources on fixing symptoms of problems without fixing the core problem, we will continue to experience symptoms that we will continually need to resolve. This is an ineffective and expensive approach.

There was one team I worked with who, in the first minutes of meeting them, informed me they had already developed the solutions that were needed – our work was going to be done in a flash. Of course, I didn't even understand the problems we needed to resolve at that stage, so I asked if I could view where the problems were happening and if they could advise me on the problems I would be witnessing.

The team and I then went to where the problems were – an area where people queued in the airport – and we agreed as a team to write down all the problems that we saw as we stood there for two hours. Even though each of the team members had at least 10 years of experience working in this location, while they were standing and watching the actual environment, they discovered and wrote down new problems that they hadn't seen before.

Back at base, we then wrote the list of the problems we witnessed on a whiteboard and then the list of solutions they had devised prior. We then systematically went through each of the problems to determine if any of the solutions listed would have resolved that problem.

We found that if we had implemented all the solutions, only 20% of the problems would have been resolved or alleviated. In other words, 80% of the solutions wouldn't have impacted the problems we were experiencing, which would have made the time and resources spent implementing them wasteful.

The valuable lesson learnt, and one that was reinforced for me, is challenging but crucial: refrain from jumping to solutions. Instead, thoroughly understand the problems before proposing remedies.

PASSIONATE TEAMS NEED COORDINATION

Just as building cooperation across the team is important, so too is the coordination of the team's energy once they start to determine the multitude of problems that need to be resolved.

Teams who are passionate and heavily invested in the purpose of their work, and who want to contribute significantly to the organisation, often have many ideas on how they can do that. They spend a lot of energy trying to pursue those ideas – and that's a good thing. However, the danger arises when an organisation's resources are fragmented and pulled in different directions because people are starting different initiatives, which increases strain on the organisation.

To reduce overlap and ensure efficient use of resources, it's essential to foster coordination across the teams. This involves sharing initiatives collectively, allowing the wider team to make informed decisions on where to allocate capacity and support. Through this collaborative approach, team members naturally begin to work in unison, offering mutual support on shared improvement initiatives.

Coordination is crucial for the engaged team that has many ideas seemingly streaming out of them in terms of new ways of doing things, improvements to your organisation's operations, different markets that could be targeted, new products and services, and technology improvements. Coordination means that not only are these ideas captured and not lost, but they are acted on and supported after the decisions have been made about what ideas your team will pursue now and which ideas will be pursued afterward.

Teams can't work together unless there are things they agree on. There needs to be a level of agreement, and what better basis for agreement than agreeing on the problems that need to be solved as a team. Instead of having a team of ten, each having two great ideas they are pursuing, those 20 ideas are shared, and the team can make an informed decision across them all. In the end, there might be only four or five of those 20 ideas that the team will focus on right now, but the team will be able to support each other in each of those ideas.

Yes, sometimes the energy needed for honing the team's focus is tantamount to the idiom 'like herding cats'. This is the power of having the right team dynamic, the stand-up meetings and the visual boards offered in terms of the coordination of your team's passion.

Somewhat humorously but accurately, I'd suggest that if the team are flat and have no energy then coordination is going to be less of a problem. So, having the coordination challenge, especially through an energised team, is a good problem to have, but ensure that your team are coordinated.

The best way to stay coordinated is to focus on just one thing at a time. As you read through the stages of continuous improvement, which are presented in a linear fashion (why make it hard? This isn't like the script for *Pulp Fiction*), focus only on that element and 'complete' it before moving on to the next individual step. Trust me, you'll get more done in less time and with better results that way.

THE VALUE OF STARTING SMART

Start with wins. *Start smart* to better ensure that those wins occur.

Starting smart involves choosing problems that are the right fit for the team and that they are emotively invested in fixing – the problems *they* have chosen to fix. There are numerous other criteria that could be used to decide what problems to start with, but starting smart means focusing on these principles first:

1. ensuring the problems are not too big (given the team's capability and experience in continuous improvement), and
2. confirming the team want to solve these problems.

Once you have an idea of what problems you'll look to solve, you still need to decide on which (as a subset) of those problems you'll start on first. This is where Loop 1 comes in. The steps in Loop 1 will ensure that you work on some crucial steps to aid the adoption of continuous improvement, such as ensuring that you capture a baseline of current performance for benefit realisation, which in turn will prove the wins and bring mana* to you and your teams' efforts in enacting meaningful change.

---

* Mana is a te reo Māori (language) word not directly translatable into English, but it means a blend of honour, gravitas and dignity. Someone with mana has words that are proven to carry weight, are well considered, thoughtful and are from a place of integrity and authenticity.

CHAPTER 3

Understand Your Current Level of Performance

In this section, we will lay the foundations of continuous improvement. It is very difficult to improve what you're doing before you know how you are currently performing, so we'll dive into the techniques that enable us to determine and capture how we are currently performing for a full and informed view of performance of a process.

This can be challenging at times, completing these steps may reveal that your performance is worse than you had thought, or it could show that the performance isn't so bad. Both of these are great outcomes because they give you more information to make better decisions.

The steps include:

1. Building the high-level process map to serve as a guide.
2. Capturing all the problems and where they occur in the process.
3. Capturing indicative data for each of the problems:
   i. the frequency with which the problems occur
   ii. the impact of the problems, including time resolving or reworking the problems (measured in elapsed waiting time and team working time).
4. Understanding the inter-relationships between the problems, which problems are precursors for, or cause the other problems.

5. Making an informed decision of which problems to fix first – led by the team.
6. Forming the teams to fix the problems.
7. Validating the anecdotal data so it becomes empirical for those problems to be fixed first, for baseline performance, for root cause analysis (next) and benefit realisation (later).

MAPPING A PROCESS

Process mapping, to provide a visual representation of the steps in the process and who performs which step and when, supports continuous improvement and enables the identification of opportunities for improvement by helping to reveal problems, issues and rework within a process. This provides a platform to create a better process. Other benefits are:

- the process of process mapping itself helps the wider team understand their role in the whole process
- a mapped process can be used as a training and induction tool
- mapping is an inclusive tool and excellent for encouraging participation, so take the opportunity to develop the process map with the team involved in the process.

Before you start to look at improving a process, there are some important steps to perform beforehand. The first is to map the high-level steps of the process. For example, if I were to map a high-level process of my day, it would be something like:

1. wake up
2. do my morning routine
3. eat breakfast
4. get ready for the day
5. commute
6. do some great work
7. travel back home
8. go for an evening run
9. make dinner
10. waste some time in front of a screen

11. do my evening routine
12. go to bed.

As you can see, there is a lot of detail missing. Even though there might be 1,000 individual steps in my day, and each day will likely be different (e.g. some days I'm travelling and other days I go to the gym in the morning), I've dropped that level of detail at this high-level process. The purpose of this is to capture what most likely happens rather than every exact detail of each of my differing days of the week, which is where teams commonly fall over in mapping a process over an inordinate amount of time.

With this high-level process mapped, we'll next want to capture some data on how long each process step takes to be performed, and the end-to-end processing time. We'll also look to capture if there are issues or problems that occur within a process step.

For example, I might find that getting ready for work might be a process time between 30 minutes and 60 minutes each day; when it is 30 minutes, everything has gone to plan, and alternatively, when it is closer to 60 minutes, it is likely because some issues have happened.

Now I know that I can focus on that process step and understand all those issues that are happening to cause it to be 60 minutes and work out how I can stop them from happening, so this process step can consistently be 30 minutes, and I can always arrive to work on time. Having data on the process steps, typically measuring the time required for each step or the frequency and impact of errors for which process step they occur, guides the team in determining which process steps to refine. The high-level process map then acts as a spine to hang all the problems off so we can understand contextually where each of the problems occurs in the process.

Once we've created a high-level process map, identified problems linked to specific steps and articulated some data related to those problems, we can begin pinpointing areas for process improvement. I follow a specific sequence of key steps I'll detail later, which act as lenses to examine the process and initiate improvements.

HOW TO MAP A PROCESS

The key steps for setting up to map a process are:

1. Engage a **facilitator** and **timekeeper** for the mapping session:
    - The timekeeper, who can be from the team as it is an uncomplicated role, monitors the session's progress, ensuring they announce when every allotment of predetermined time (e.g. every 15 minutes) has passed so that the facilitator and team can gauge their progress against time to keep the team moving.
    - The facilitator, ideally external to the team, helps guide the mapping process. This separation allows team members to contribute fully without one of the team having the added challenge of facilitating. Additionally, an external facilitator provides a valuable language and sanity check, ensuring clarity of anything captured. For facilitation tips, refer to the facilitating and decision-making section in Appendix 1.

2. Include those who do the work in the process:
    - Mapping activities should always involve the people who do the work. Their insights are invaluable, as they possess an unparalleled understanding of the process. Make it a collaborative team effort by inviting their active participation.

It is not just the facilitator's role, but everyone's responsibility to maintain focus when developing a process map, with the core focus at this stage that the process maps reflect about 80% of all the scenarios in the process. The process map doesn't need to be to the nth degree where every single scenario is intricately captured. The process map exists to act as a spine to capture and contextualise where the problems are. A good facilitator here is useful to keep the team at the right level of detail, and to bring the group back when they have dived too deeply – trying to map every possible scenario in a process map.

The Process Mapping Session

You can approach this session in one of two ways:

1. Capture the process map, then ask the team what the problems are and add them to the process where they occur.
2. Start by brainstorming all the problems and then arrange the problems in order of how they might occur chronologically, and then capture the process map and add the problems.

The approach I'll discuss is the first option: mapping the process, brainstorming, and then documenting the problems encountered in the process. Following that, we place these identified problems in their respective locations within the process:

1. Identify an area where the map will be captured. If you're using sticky notes to capture the process steps, aim for a glass surface – they stick best there. Whiteboards can do the trick, too, just make sure they're clean without any marker residue. Otherwise, consider using Corflute or covering walls with brown paper for better stickiness and the convenience of moving the map around. Use one colour of sticky notes to capture the process (I tend to use yellow for this) and another colour(s) for the problems identified. That way the process steps and problems are visually differentiated. While it is ideal to have the team in a room while mapping the process, if that is not feasible, tools such as Microsoft Whiteboard, Miro, Trello and other collaboration tools can be useful.
2. Use consistent symbols and establish them with the team. Simple symbols are:
   - a circle at the start or end of any process flow
   - rectangles for activities
   - diamonds for decisions where a process flow is split into two or more flows from that point.
3. Map the process in chronological order of events, from left to right. Each individual step has its own sticky note. Only those involved in the process step will detail what happens in that

step and they will finish by saying who or where they hand their work to.

4. Do not capture what is thought to be happening in the process – always map the current state being what is *actually* happening. Ensuring that you are capturing what actually happens in the process is something for the facilitator to check in on and remind the team of. If there is confusion about what is happening in the process, then it's best for the team to observe the process and then replicate it on the map.

5. Always validate the process map with a final walkthrough of all the steps with the team to make sure the process is accurately mapped. Talk through all the steps to validate it and check no steps are missing and are in the right order.

See an example of these symbols in a process map in Figure 4.

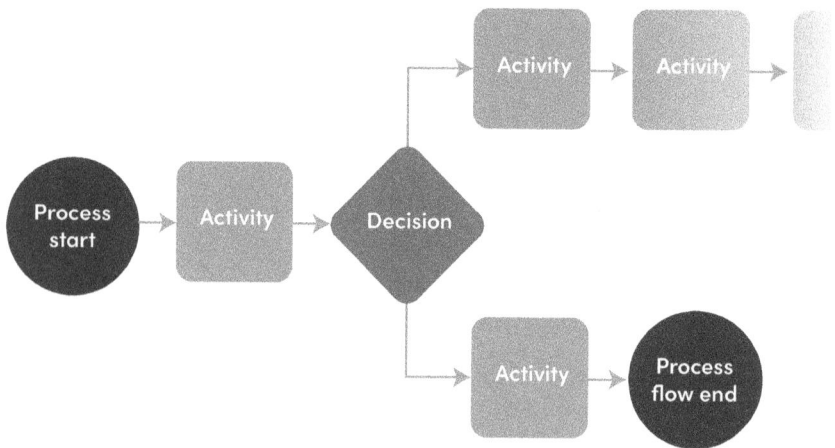

Figure 4

To determine whether a step is an activity or a decision, consider the following activity after that step. If there are at least two distinctively different activities after, then you have decision point (diamond) that splits the process into those different activities. For example, if in a process step there's an evaluation of the application, whether we process it or send it back to the customer, that's two very different next activities, so the assessment activity is a decision point (a diamond). Whereas, if in an activity, irrespective of the outcome of a decision, the next process step is the same, then you have an activity rather than a decision point. If evaluating an element of an application leads to different covering notes being added, but the application always goes to the same team as the next step, then, even though a decision is made, it constitutes an activity.

Tips for Process Mapping

- If the team are together in person, use sticky notes to capture the process rather than electronic tools at this early stage. Using sticky notes makes it easy to insert process steps accidentally missed and re-order the process if needed; they're also more engaging for a team. Because sticky notes are square or rectangular, the team will only need to draw circles or diamonds (tip: you can put a sticky note on a 45-degree angle to replicate a diamond) around those process steps that are starts, ends or decision points in the process.
- Feel free to add photos where you need to and insert them onto the process map if they help with the explanation of the process steps.
- Take photos of the process map throughout its production – especially at the end of the session – as a recorded backup of work done.
- Make sure you have the right team members in the room – only those that perform the process can talk to the process and their specific steps in the process. It's crucial we capture the process as it actually happens rather than how it is thought to happen or how it should happen.
- No process map is 100% accurate, as often there can be a huge number of variables and resulting process steps. When the process map reflects upwards of 80% of the common pathways through the process, it is likely accurate enough for its purpose at this stage to capture pain points and rework loops.

Adding Insights to the Process Map

Once a process is mapped, there are other layers of information that can be added to the process map to support the optimisation of a process. That other information can include:

- rework loops
- pain points in the process (where things go wrong and affect the team or the customer), such as:
  - ~ delays
  - ~ complaints
  - ~ failures
  - ~ waste
  - ~ alignment issues (different teams performing the same process differently)
  - ~ handover issues (ensuring that quality work moves from one team to the next)
- inter-relationships between pain points – which pain points directly cause other pain points later in the process, or pain points to be solved together
- the data we have on the process, such as how often the rework occurs at a point, how long the delay is when the rework occurs, and the time it takes between important process points – certainly from the start to the end of the process.

Let's now go through how we capture this detail.

CAPTURE THE PROBLEMS AND IMPROVEMENTS

Have the team brainstorm problems that are experienced in the process. For brainstorming tips, check out the overview in the chapter Developing Better Solutions on page 145.

This step is not about proposing solutions but exposing problems; usually a *why* statement differentiates between the two. For example, if someone suggests, 'We need to improve our ordering system', that's suggesting a solution for something that the team doesn't know the context for and a problem they aren't aware of. When we know it's a 'solution' being offered, we can ask, 'Why?'

We know that we haven't articulated the problem because we can ask, '*Why* do we need to improve our ordering system?' And the answer 'We are receiving a lot of complaints from our customers that it takes them too long to place an order' is the problem that needs to be posted at the point in the process where you receive the complaints.

The 'solution' that was proposed may not actually be the best solution or a solution at all, but with a newly formed team dynamic, it is important that the whole team understands the actual problem that is occurring before they develop a solution.

Post each problem visually under each of the steps of the process they relate to. Keep in mind that the perfect location of the problem in the process isn't as essential as simply capturing the problem – if that saves your team some heartache determining where in the process to precisely place the problem. Problems don't need to be properly categorised that way, just as long as they are captured visually for the whole team to see. There might even be a few problems that relate to the whole process itself, simply decide where you'll post those.

Make Decisions Based on Data

Make decisions based on data rather than anecdotal advice. Typically, all problems can usually be measured by two key elements: their frequency, indicating *how often* they occur, and their severity, denoting the consequences and effects on the organisation and the customer. We need to know this information because it means that we can make informed decisions on what problems we need to fix and in what order.

When we move from what we *think* or *feel* (that a problem is occurring about 200 times a week) to what *we know* (this situation has occurred between 400–550 times each week over the last eight weeks) it means we have a baseline of performance and insights for which we can develop an improvement. Having good amounts of data on current performance provides us with good insights that enable informed decisions about what next needs to be focused on for improvement.

A challenge often experienced at this stage is that teams commonly have no absolute data on how often problems occur, and when they do occur, what the consequence and effect on the organisation is. You will capture data on the problems you prioritise to fix first, but in the meantime, use what you know, even if that is anecdotal – which is often good enough to compare problems against each other to determine which are likely more impactful on performance.

Capture New Measures

Determining the essential performance measures which provide a full picture of performance often reveals gaps in existing data collection. Many measures required for holistic baseline assessment of current performance may be entirely new. When identifying these new measures, it's crucial to focus on those genuinely needed for understanding baseline performance, avoiding unnecessary data collection.

Implementing new measures may involve people capturing data during their work. Designing a process that ensures high data integrity is essential. The key is to develop a non-disruptive and manageable data capture method. Convincing individuals to adopt this new data collection requires emphasising the anticipated improvements that will make their work easier in the long run and creating a win-win situation.

CAPTURE DATA ON PROBLEMS THAT COULD BE FIXED

Usually, at this stage, most methodologies would argue (and legitimately so) that you should capture data on all the metrics and problems to be able to make an informed decision on what needs to be improved. But that comes with risks if we overlook:

1. That the team will be energised at this point to tackle problems, not capture data. Your endgame is to fuel that energy so continuous improvement becomes part of the culture. We are deliberately choosing at this stage to embed the 'continuous'

part over that quality of the 'improvement' part of continuous improvement.

2. That following this typical approach means that you will over-capture data as you'll be capturing data for all problems and elements, rather than firstly understanding the inter-relationship between the performance problems you are experiencing. Instead of working on all problems (or at least capturing full data on all problems), prioritise improving the performance in one area that will also alleviate performance problems in another. Often, some problems are symptoms of other problems, and this is a good time to find those core problems. For example, why try to improve the complaint resolution process when you can reduce the number of complaints you can resolve?

Gathering Initial Data on Problems

When identifying problems, the next step is to obtain indicative data to gauge their impact. Capture both how frequently the issue or problem is occurring and, when it does occur, the severity of the impact on your organisation and the customer. We can measure the impact of all problems by those two elements initially to understand the pain of a problem.

Of course, these indications won't be super accurate as they are estimates, but these indicators provided by those with experience of the problems will serve to give us an idea of the size of the problem and this will help when we are comparing problems to evaluate which ones the team chooses to fix first.

The key question to ask every time a problem is discovered is: how often does this problem happen, and when it happens, what is the severity of the problem?

For example, if the team identifies a problem like: 'We have to request additional information from the customer for many applications', this problem overview is incomplete. The next step is to quantify the frequency and impact both for your organisation and the customer. Use specific numbers, such as 'Occurring 35% of the time' or '30–40 times per week', instead of vague terms like 'frequently' or 'often'. Shorthand this detail on a sticky note on the process map, capturing it as: 'Request for info from customer, 35%, 1–3 weeks waiting, 1.5 hours capacity'.

As a tip, frequency is usually easy for the team to estimate and capture either as a raw number (30–40 times per week) or ratio (occurs 35% of the time), but it can be trickier to capture the impact as much of the impact might be unseen by the team. Of course, try to capture what you can, and in terms of impact, there's two key areas you might be able to establish:

1. **Waiting time** is anything that adds time to the process through a delay, or the lag time between steps in the process, like going back to the customer for more information, as it stalls the processing of the application until the customer comes back.
2. **Working time** refers to the time during which the team's capacity is dedicated to performing work. For example, when dealing with processes like sending out and receiving applications for additional information from customers, this refers to the time that the team invests in those tasks. It encompasses the duration required for sending, receiving, evaluating, and getting back up to speed with the application.

Many impacts involve both waiting time (the time it slows the process by) and working time (time of the capacity lost in the team).

Determining the Cost of Poor Quality

Once we capture the frequency and impact of the problems we experience, we go a step further and put a value on those problems, individually and collectively through a concept referred to as the **cost of poor quality (COPQ)**, which enriches the capture of our baseline performance.

Cost of poor quality is the cost of everything that we produce that is of substandard quality. Whether a product or service, it is about the cost to us when we don't meet the quality standard set by customer expectations. Anything that falls short of that is going to be rework for our organisation; when we define the cost of that rework to our organisation and multiply that cost by the frequency it occurs, we then have a better idea of the cost of poor quality. Rework, of course, isn't just the improvement of the product (for example, the cost of one defective part being replaced), but includes the cost to perform that rework.

Some softer measures of the cost of poor quality can be included if you choose (you can define it how you like to suit your organisation) and we see that with the advent of social media, with poor experiences widely shared and viewed. The consequences of that customer echo would be hard to numerate or articulate, but we can certainly capture the frequency of these events.

ENSURING A GOOD BASELINE

You must ensure that you establish a solid baseline of data for your current performance. This baseline is essential for accurately identifying the root causes of performance issues, assessing the performance of your solutions during pilot phases, by comparing performance against the established baseline, and articulating the benefits of the improvements once solutions have been fully implemented.

With good baseline data, you'll know if performance is faster, better (fewer problems) or both with:

- end-to-end process time and extent of variation of that processing time (rather than just having averages)
- times and the variations of times of the process steps, at least those process steps that your team are looking to improve
- sufficient data on the frequency of pain points (for solution development) and a focused effort to understand and capture the impact of those pain points when they do occur (for benefit realisation).

Measuring the Three Elements of Time

To create a good baseline for performance data, it's crucial to analyse the three elements of waiting time, working time and end-to-end process time. Your team's objective would be to reduce time lost in the elements of waiting time and working time through process improvements, thereby freeing up capacity and improving the performance of the end-to-end process.

Figure 5 shows some examples of where you might capture working and waiting time data within and between process steps and the end-to-end process time:

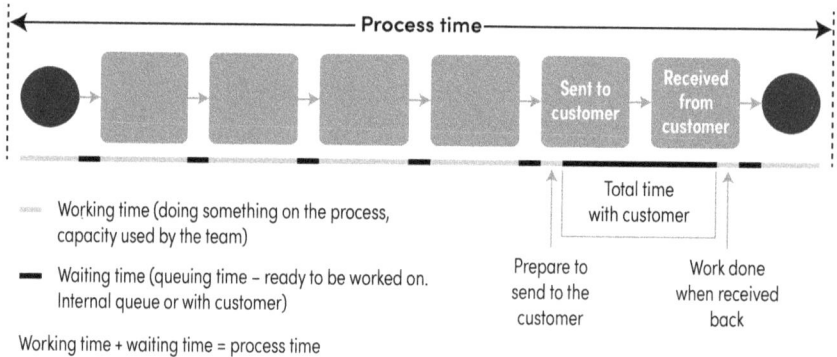

Figure 5

By scrutinising the data of all these elements in your specific process, you'll know which ones are more significant. Although the data won't provide the reasons for their occurrence, it will serve as a compass directing your team to the areas that require a closer look for becoming improvement initiatives.

UNDERSTAND THE INTER-RELATIONSHIPS BETWEEN PROBLEMS

To foster effective problem-solving, you need to also understand the inter-relationship that exists between problems. Will fixing one problem in turn solve another? If that inter-relationship exists, you would look to fix problems upstream that solve other problems downstream.

A great way of understanding the inter-relationships between problems is by mapping the problems as they occur in the process map. We have already placed where each problem occurs on the process map. Some problems are over-arching, such as resourcing issues, and they can be captured off to one side, but most problems will have a home in a specific process step.

We've named the problem and estimated the frequency and impact of the problem. For example, a problem of rework might occur 5–10% of the time and each time that occurs rework takes 50–60 minutes to sort. With all the problems layered on top of the process map, we can start to highlight the associations and inter-relationships between them. This might be as easy as using arrows to show which problem contributes to another problem. This is simply so we can understand the inter-relationships between the problems and make informed decisions about which problems we fix first.

For example, rather than focusing solely on decreasing the time required to address rework, we shift our attention to preventing the rework from happening as frequently. When we reduce the frequency of a problem occurring, we are addressing its root cause. On the other hand, if we solely decrease the severity of the problem, such as in the case of rework, we are only alleviating the symptoms.

Here's an overview of what we have done to this point:

1. Develop a process map

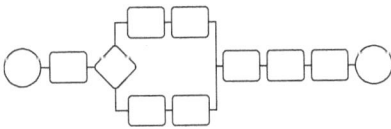

2. Add the problems which occur, where they occur

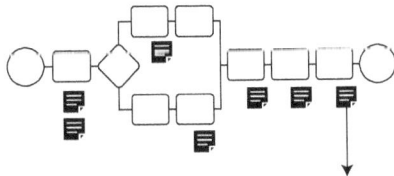

Rework of final decision. Happens about 5–10%. About 50–60 minutes to sort each time.

3. Show the inter-relationships between problems; which problems cause others

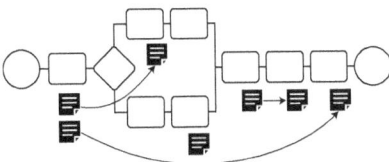

HANDLING THE PROBLEMS – TWO DIFFERENT PATHS

Generally, problems can be fixed one of two ways, either as:

- a *quick win* – where the cause of the pain point is obviously unambiguous, or

- as an *improvement initiative* that needs to be scoped to determine the root cause for the pain point and piloting a solution to prove its efficacy.

Quick Wins

A **quick win** refers to a situation where both the root cause and solution are known and can be fixed quickly and easily to benefit the team.

Usually, quick wins are identified before reaching this point. A decision is made about the action to be taken, without needing the setup of a team to go through the methodology or proceed to the next step of understanding the underlying root causes. You might have baseline data of performance at this stage, and that's great to monitor the change in performance. Let's define what quick wins are, so we can identify them at this stage if we haven't already.

One type of quick win is a behaviour adjustment. Perhaps all the sales team should be doing this one thing, but the problem is, it's only being done about 80% of the time, causing rework for others in the admin team. The quick win is the sales team agreeing that it is good action, and that they should be doing it 100% of the time. That's an example of a behavioural quick win. With behavioural quick wins, there are only two key elements that need to be done for success:

1. The teams agreeing to the behavioural change that they need to perform for the quick win, and

2. Developing a simple metric or measure that will be regularly reported back to the team to monitor performance, specifying who will be reporting back and how often.

For example, it might be captured like this (noted on the visual board about the performance updates):

> *The sales team will all hand over their sales forms to the admin team by the end of each day, noting if the customer is new or repeat. On Friday during the daily stand-up, Jess from admin will report back on the percentage of forms that were handed to the admin team correctly over the previous week.*

That's it. Captured and built into the consciousness of the team, making it something measured and reported on.

Here is another example, being of an application process:

> *With external and internal pressure to increase the number of decisions made on customer applications, the decision was previously made to streamline the process by removing the need for the team to check the customer's details on their application forms.*
>
> *Unfortunately, this meant a spike of errors occurring in the application process, where the supplied information from the customer hadn't been correctly transposed into the system, and much of these errors were not detected as they were through the manual team checks on the customer details.*
>
> *These undiscovered errors, over a period of a single month, meant that the team were overwhelmed by rework occurring from these errors – the time/cost was too large for the business to undertake.*

The re-introduction of detail checks is a quick win. These checks took up to two minutes per application, including any corrections to the customer's details. Based on success measures of five decisions a day, this amounted to 10 minutes of additional processing time a day, or 2,600 minutes per annum based on 260 working days. That's 43.33 hours per year. Comparatively, it has taken one team member on average 15 minutes to assess and correct one error – with the average error rate of 40 per week.

Sometimes you will find the solution is already there. Often the team involved in a process will be able to identify one or two things that can be sensibly and immediately changed – quick wins. For all other and more common and complex problems, we need to follow the methodology to determine the root cause as an improvement initiative with a team.

> **Tip:** A test that we need to be conscious of is making sure that a fix is better overall for the team, not better for one area at the expense of another. For example, a team producing a new form for another team to fill out that saves one team five minutes and costs another team 30 minutes is not better for the overall team.

For complex problems, here are the steps you need to go through, which we'll now cover:

1. Decisions must be made about which problems you start with.
2. In Loop 1, it is crucial to involve the team – and we'll discuss why that is important.
3. Since there will likely be too many problems for the team, we will:
   i. look at the right (smart-sized) problems to start with
   ii. prioritise the problems the team say they want to specifically fix, and
   iii. utilise a tool to help narrow down to a select few problems around which teams can be formed.

DECIDE WHAT TO IMPROVE

If I was to coin the term **Process Insanity**, I'd define it as the irrational expectation of a process that is completely out of control, meaning it delivers a lot of variation of outcomes, to perform consistently better without making any changes. This concept mirrors the idea that it is considered insanity to repeatedly do the same thing and expect different results. Similarly, it is insane to perform the same task inconsistently and expect consistent results.

Deciding what to improve is crucial for process sanity. It's unrealistic to expect improvement in a process that's entirely out of control and yields inconsistent outcomes. Expecting consistent results from an inconsistently performed task, especially across your team, is wasteful.

If you want to own your process,
you have to hone your process.

When choosing what to improve, it's important to align with the two-loop approach and look to emotionally connect your team with continuous improvement first before ramping up their capability. We'll be performing these two steps in this order:

1. Let the team improve anything that they want to improve with the methodology. This choice, often driven by a personal and emotional connection to the process they wish to enhance, is vital. It's important for the team to feel a sense of ownership and comfort, fostering their enthusiasm for continuous improvement. This is our focus for Loop 1.

2. In Loop 2, those who have been through the first loop can be assigned more challenging processes to improve as their expertise and comfort in the methodology advances.

The initial focus for the team's improvements should be on what matters to them. As they gain experience and progress into the second loop, where additional capabilities are introduced, the team can then shift their focus to improvements that matter more to external stakeholders, such as customers. This involves applying a methodology that they are more capable with.

Another Reason Why the Team Lead the Change

A quick note on my experience of culture change and how continuous improvement can be a vital part of instigating culture change.

You are likely familiar with the adage that you can lead a horse to water, but you can't make it drink. In that same vein, let's talk about how continuous improvement can help the horse want to drink before it's led to water.

Often, we can spend a lot of time planning the change we want to make in our culture – a change that means we are more agile, that we improve our performance faster, to make life easier for ourselves and our customers.

Consider this alternative approach to stimulate a culture change: provide people with the freedom to start to make the changes themselves, contributing to improved performance and making life easier for both the team and the customer. This focus is likely congruent with what you want to establish in the new culture, right?

Start by unleashing the team's capacity and capability to make the improvements that they see need to be made.

Know that you won't be able to lead all horses to the water, at least initially. And that is fine; start where the love is. Start with the teams that want to make improvements, those who want to determine the root causes for performance improvement and develop solutions to address those root causes – and pilot those solutions and adopt the visualisation of their performance.

The whole angle is don't drag the horse to water hoping it will drink – don't impose new standards and behaviours to underpin a culture you want if there's a way (and usually there is) to have the team drive themselves to that objective.

This is why, in Loop 1, we have team members who have been through the stages of mapping the process, determining the pain points and any inter-relationships that exist in the pain points and, once they have chosen which pain points to look at first, volunteer themselves to be part of the team to fix them.

We've Got 99 Problems, so a Lack of Problems Ain't One

The danger of discovering that you have a number of problems, which may have been brought to the surface through a process map littered with pain points, is the team lose too much time and energy deciding which problems to fix first. When teams are aware of numerous problems, each evoking a sense of urgency whereby teams want to simultaneously solve them all, the risk is that teams can waste vast amounts of time debating the order to solve them in and, ironically, a good number of problems could have been solved in that time spent debating.

The key to resolving all of this is good facilitation and fast decision making. Again, don't let perfection suffocate progress. Whether arguably a right decision or not, it is often better to just start than forever deliberate. Teams, especially those new to applying continuous improvement, tend to worry too deeply about doing things the right way to the right problems with the right tools, in the right order. Often, the best thing is to just start.

> **Start anywhere. The most important thing is that your team just starts.**

Start Smart Rather Than Big

Too often, teams think they will apply their new continuous improvement tools to get 'the biggest bang for their buck'. This saying sadly warns us when continuous improvement is likely to fail. It happens when teams tackle a massive problem without having the capability to solve it both quickly and effectively, causing overwhelm throughout the improvement effort. As a result, delivering meaningful benefits to customers and the organisation becomes challenging.

Starting smart also means it's best the team chooses a problem they are familiar with as they apply a methodology they are using for the first time. Once the team have a good understanding of the methodology, this is when they can look to apply the methodology to new problems in potentially unfamiliar processes. As a leader, make sure the team have something in the work that they are familiar with enough to support their task.

Any methodology can be effective, but the complexity of problems looking to be solved must be congruent with the team's capabilities. For initial improvements, begin with small, smart-sized changes and achieve success to fuel the desire for ongoing enhancements. While it may require setting aside ego, starting small – extremely small – proves beneficial and gets early runs on the board. Tackle larger problems when your team are capable to address them at the root.

An organisation's ability to change and adapt to new environments is inherently nurtured and fuelled by continually changing and adapting to new environments. Starting smart, rather than big, helps significantly with this – and constancy of improvement. Like anything – don't strive for perfection. Often, striving for perfection is procrastination in disguise and will certainly delay progress, which will erode the team's motivation and energy.

The mantra of starting smart is so important. I've witnessed organisations stagnate because of their *approach* in their pursuit of excellence. Any organisation that has truly adopted continuous improvement will experience benefits through their agility in developing and their speed of adopting every improvement as quickly as they can. Each improvement in turn becomes the platform for the next improvement.

> As crucial as inspiration is, impact only comes from implementation, not inspiration.

Start Where the Team Wants to Start

When a team leads and drives change, they cultivate their appetite for change, making it a regular part of their work rather than an exceptional occurrence. And that's our focus, as leaders, in Loop 1 – building the appetite and commitment for continuous improvement to be a crucial element of our culture, where everyone in the organisation contributes to organisational performance, rather than just a few. For this to happen, we need to start the right way.

> Don't start on big problems, start where the love is: where there is appetite to make change.

We need to ensure that we've a good foundation to ensure the energy of the team through the smart-sized improvement initiatives. To understand this, two questions I ask are:

1. Does the team know that they have problems?
2. Does the team want to solve those problems?

If both answers are yes, then I know we have a good platform to make some tangible improvements to performance that can be led by the team.

Sure, as a leader, you might not feel that that is the best starting point for the organisation – there might arguably be more critical processes or elements to be improved than what the team are suggesting, but prioritise the actions that lead to the long-term adoption of continuous improvement mindset to become entrenched in the culture, which will drive many other improvements after those in this initial loop and benefit the organisation.

Letting the team choose where to start is often a good decision, simply because having the team perform the improvement that we think they *should* do rather than what they *want* to do makes it a task rather than something they emotionally connect with. Following the methodology ensures that the team have made an informed decision about what process or element to improve first, and that the improvement will prove to be beneficial.

JUST START

The key consideration is starting in a way that best supports the cooperation and coordination across your wider team. More importantly, *just start*. Failure to start means everything counts for zero. Don't let wasted time on selecting the perfect problem to fix first suffocate progress.

'The secret of getting ahead is getting started.'
Mark Twain

THE PROCESS OF GETTING THE TEAM TO CHOOSE

Once the team has identified various pain points on the process map, estimated how often these problems occur, gauged their potential impact, and identified any interrelationships between the problems, the team will have sufficient insights to prioritise which pain points to address first.

Because we don't have the capability to work on and fix all problems simultaneously, we need to choose. It is important that the team agree on the problems to resolve first, although it may be tough reaching a unanimous decision depending on the makeup of the team having very different experiences in the process, and the differing nature of the pain points themselves. Good prioritisation of problems to be resolved happens when teams understand the purpose of the process.

Multi-voting to Decide

One of the best ways to narrow down a number of pain points to a select few can be done through multi-voting. Simply give out a set number of votes to each of the team members to vote on which of the pain points they feel the team should focus on first.

There's a bit of a rule of thumb in terms of how many votes are given out – about a third of all the possible options. If we had 20 pain points that were captured in the process, then each team member would have seven votes. Round up so you get slightly more votes than less to ensure better differentiation. You can even give away as many as half of the options as votes.

Voting can be done by giving people coloured sticky dots to put on the sticky notes – each note being a pain point and each dot being a vote for that pain point, or supplying whiteboard markers for people to allocate their votes as a mark to be tallied. If the team are using marks – make sure that they mark up their votes as bars rather than writing numbers, for ease of tallying later.

How the individuals of the team allocate their votes are completely up to them. They might:

- put all seven of their votes on one pain point

- put four votes on one pain point and one each on three other pain points
- put one vote on each of seven pain points.

The distribution of their votes is completely up to them, and it's that distribution across the team that helps really highlight the pain points they collectively feel need to be focused on first.

> **Tip:** Make sure that there is enough space around each individual pain point for people to put their votes. When you tally the votes, it's easier when it is clear which votes relate to which pain point. Also, having space allows the team to vote directly on the process map at the same time.

After the voting is completed, and it should only take a couple of minutes with everybody up at the process map voting simultaneously, then simply tally the votes so you can start to rank the pain points by appetite to be fixed. Usually, the facilitator would tally and total the votes in front of the team as there might need to be clarification if some votes are unclear. It's usual for some pain points to not get any votes, which simply reflects the team's focus is on other pain points and is great to know.

Once you have totalled the votes for each pain point, rank the problems in terms of the greatest appetite to fix. There might be 30 pain points on the process map and perhaps only 15 have votes; I would suggest you only look at the top three, four or five. You need not order past that point, especially if you have a team of, say, six people, then five problems will likely be way too many for them to solve. Again, a rule of thumb from my experience is that for six people, you'd be looking at two or three pain points, and splitting the team up, with perhaps some of the team volunteering to be part of two separate teams to fix two separate pain points.

Next, we'll look at the next stage of determining the teams to tackle the highest ranked pain points.

Want to know more about fast team decision making and how to perform it effectively? See Appendix 1.

FORM THE TEAMS TO FIX EACH PROBLEM

At this point, the team have collectively decided on the more pressing pain points that should be worked on now. The next step involves identifying team members interested in working on the selected pain points, which the team has deemed worthwhile to address immediately. This is a straightforward process – simply ask team members to volunteer for the issues they want to fix, forming natural teams. They'll likely want to fix the problems that they have personally raised and voted for. When people volunteer for a team to tackle a specific issue, simply note down their names next to the corresponding pain point on the process map.

Make sure that team members do not over commit – that's crucial for their energy levels. The problems that were not selected to be worked on now are not going anywhere, you can revisit those later when the team have capacity. It is better that they are working on as few problems as possible and get through each quickly and on to the next rather than trying to crunch through too many problems simultaneously.

Begin by allowing the team to make improvements and experience the success of those improvements. This requires improving problems within their current capabilities. Avoiding a large problem combined with strict adherence to an unfamiliar methodology provides the team with the freedom to initiate effective change. Successful change far more likely ensures they cultivate practices that integrate improvement into their team mindset. If the team has selected a large problem, they can focus on a specific aspect of that problem only, to avoid overwhelming themselves. For instance, if the issue involves rework at a process step, the team might concentrate on solving one specific reason for the rework.

Tip: Once teams have formed and selected a pain point to work on, allow them some time to decide when regular meetings will occur for collaborative work on the pain point.

As a final tip, if the teams break into smaller teams each owning a single pain point, encourage them to support each other by trusting the process. Trust that each team will follow the methodology, perform great data capture, identify the root cause and develop a fantastic solution to be piloted that can be trusted by all not directly involved.

Trust is crucial because teams may not fully understand the other team's journey as they analyse a pain point, and they might be asked to participate in piloting a solution. It's important not to reevaluate the solution during the pilot but to trust the team and give their best effort. Encourage teams to express their mutual trust to each other in the development of their respective solutions.

QUICK RECAP

Let's quickly recap and connect the linear progression from what you and your team have already accomplished to what lies ahead and why.

You've compiled a list of problems based on your team's input, giving you a broad understanding of them. You've then assigned high-level metrics to compare the problems in terms of frequency and impact, though not with pinpoint accuracy, but accurate enough to be able to compare the problems to each other.

Mapping these problems onto the process diagram reveals where they occur and helps uncover possible interrelationships – where some problems are a result of others earlier in the process.

All these steps lead you to determine, as a team, which problems to prioritise. At this point, you have a clear idea of the problems you aim to solve first. Now, as the next steps in this loop, you need to develop an approach and assemble the team to address them.

To achieve this, you'll refine your understanding of the problems by developing problem statements. These statements will each be integrated into an Improvement Initiative Plan, where you'll specify the team, scope and support needed.

We'll now focus on building the problem statement and wrapping an Improvement Initiative Plan around it, and capturing the baseline data of current performance.

CHAPTER 4

Improvement Initiative Plan, Roles and Baseline Data

Once you know what problem you are going to start on, and the team that will be involved, you can capture these details in a short document called the **Improvement Initiative Plan**. An Improvement Initiative Plan is a clear and concise overview of the work to be done, outlining the problem to be solved and identifying the key participants. A well-crafted plan provides insights into the expected benefits, and how those benefits align to the values of the organisation. Its purpose is to define the initiative's elements, ensuring clarity for all involved and minimising issues arising from assumptions.

There's a template in Appendix 3 to capture the key elements that you'll determine at the start of the improvement initiative to coordinate the work.

The core elements you'll capture are:

- an overview of the process and the problem the team are looking to fix
- what is in and out of scope as part of the improvement initiative – what will and will not be worked on and improved, and expected outcomes

- how resolving this problem will support the values or strategy of your organisation
- who will be the team involved in the improvement initiative and their roles and the capacity they will make available as part of the improvement team, including who's the leader
- who is the sponsor of the improvement initiative, and the process owner.

Like any template, adjust it to suit your team and add any fields that are purposeful. More importantly, make sure that this document doesn't go over two pages (or at least, not by much) – it should be a short and sharp though a comprehensive representation of the body of work that will be undertaken. Keep it concise for regular team checks, such as during a daily stand-up meeting, ensuring focus on the task at hand without distractions or diversions into other issues that are likely to be discovered through this improvement.

Want to know more about stand-up meetings and how to perform them effectively? See Appendix 2.

PROPERLY UNDERSTANDING AND ARTICULATING PROBLEMS

One of the core elements of continuous improvement is making sure that we develop excellent solutions that focus on positively impacting performance and alleviating or eliminating the root causes of problems. This starts with properly understanding and articulating problems. Too often, we hear problems being referred to in a way that lacks the detail we need.

For example, a problem being defined as:

- a lack of capacity
- an under-skilled team
- long customer queues.

Defining problems in this way doesn't offer us enough to work with. We need to articulate problems more thoroughly:

- Unfilled orders affecting at least 20% of all orders reducing revenue by $400,000–$500,000 per annum – is a better defined problem that we can get our teeth into and offers the opportunity to deliver a number of potential solutions, *rather than* a lack of capacity.

- A product rework rate of 31% costing on average $470 to fix each item, against an industry average rework rate of 7% – is a problem *rather than* an under-skilled team.
- A processing rate at peak times being 20–24% slower than the rate of customers joining the queue – is a problem, *rather than* long customer queues.

The reason why we need to be specific and accurate about understanding the actual problem is because we need to ensure that the solution we are developing is the most efficient and effective in addressing the problem at the root. Any solution that doesn't, though it might be relatively effective, will be inefficient and could be more expensive than a more effective solution.

The other reason why we need to better understand the problem is often it affords us a wider range of solutions. Think about the examples that I've just shared with you: If we believe the problem is *lack of capacity* then we only have a few solutions all centred on increasing capacity. Whereas, if we understand the problem better, we have a wider range of solutions we can deploy to address the problem: An unfulfillment of at least 20% of all orders.

If we look to address what we only understand as capacity issues with hiring more staff rather than improving our processes to free up capacity, hiring more staff would certainly prove to be both an expensive and an inefficient fix.

Once we embed a culture that looks for a better level of understanding of our problem, we can make a better-informed determination of how we can alleviate the problem, and as in the above example, increasing capacity should be considered among various solutions, not the sole option.

Here's a simple test to understand if we have the problem framed at the right level:

Has what's been stated as the problem also described the impact of the problem?

If the answer is no, such as lack of capacity, there's no understanding of the frequency of the problem's occurrence (meaning having data on the actual frequency) and we don't yet know enough about this problem. If the answer is yes, your team are moving towards a healthy position of being able to determine the root cause of the problem. It is the root cause of a problem that we want to design our solutions to address, and proper framing of the problems is the crucial first step for that.

A great way to capture problems is through **problem statements**, which are an important part of defining the improvement initiative.

PROBLEM STATEMENTS

The development of full, comprehensive and insightful problem statements is a significant tool for understanding your current state of performance.

Problem statements are a very important stage contributing to the success of any improvement, but because we tend to almost innately jump to solutions, we rip through this phase too quickly, which usually leads to poor results and an uncoordinated team effort.

Uniformity in the understanding of the problems that the team face is important. We know that for a basis of cooperation and coordination it is important for teams to unanimously agree on the problems that they collectively face as a team. Any disparity in their understanding of the problems that they face as a team means individual team members will likely be pulling the focus and resources of the team in different directions to resolve their interpretation of the problem.

Further, in addition to teams consistently understanding the problems, they also consistently articulate the core nature of each problem. This means not just agreeing what the problems are, but also agreeing the extent and the nature of those problems and aligning the definition of the problems. For this to occur, we need to be more articulate about the scale and nature of the problems your organisation is experiencing.

Problem statements are one of the best tools to help you with conveying the problems to your wider team in a uniform way for effective comparison and decision making. For the current performance, you need to make sure that you know what is actually going on rather than being anecdotal. Understanding the actualities of current performance helps to make informed decisions on whether to prioritise the work over other potential improvements.

Developing a Problem Statement

Start by establishing a good baseline of current state performance. In many cases baseline data may not be readily available, or is of a questionable quality, integrity or relevance. So, the improvement initiative team will almost certainly need to consider methods for how the data will be obtained that do not result in an unsustainable burden for themselves or others, such as through data collection.

Performing this work upfront is essential for realising benefits at the end. Embrace the fact that, more often than not, additional or new data will be required to ensure an accurate and comprehensive baseline of current performance. This proactive approach not only aligns with the ultimate goal of realising benefits but also streamlines the improvement process.

A problem statement is useful because it:

- provides a quick summary of the benefits of doing the work
- helps us to sell the story of what needs to be done (so others can easily understand the pain points)
- enables ongoing reporting of the key metrics of performance, especially customer-focused metrics, which should be used to monitor future performance
- ensures we capture a thorough baseline of current performance, which is what is needed to complete a problem statement.

A problem statement will likely be 2–4 paragraphs covering the answers to these questions:

- Where is the problem occurring in the organisation?
- How frequently is the problem occurring?
  - When the problem occurs, how large or severe is the problem?

~ What is the measurable impact on the organisation and your customers?

- When did the problem start or was first noticed?
  ~ Over what time period do you have data on this problem?
- What will be the measurable effects on your organisation and your customers if this problem isn't addressed over the next year?
- Which of your organisation's strategies or values will be supported by fixing the problem?

A problem statement does not:

- state an opinion about what is wrong
- describe the cause of the problem or prescribe a solution. If the root cause of the problem and thereby the solution are obvious, then there should be effort to affect this rather than an improvement initiative to develop a solution after determining the (currently unknown) root causes
- assign blame or responsibility for the problem
- combine several complicated problems into a single problem statement, which is usually an indication of the scope of work being too wide.

If a problem statement can't be completed properly because data is missing, then you need to capture data.

Test now if you can write a comprehensive problem statement.

If data for the above points is missing then we don't have a comprehensive enough view of the current state, which limits our ability to understand the benefits of our improvements and reduces the effectiveness of our solutions to address the issues that exist. In that case, capturing the missing data is needed before you can develop a solution to address the underlying root cause.

You can use a placeholder (either anecdotal data noted as such or simply an 'x') in a problem statement while you capture and validate the actual performance data. The placeholder might look something like this: the current rework rate of the initial vetting of the application forms is x%, and each time rework occurs, the capacity it absorbs of the team averages $x.x$ hours.

A comprehensive problem statement supports your teams to then determine and understand the root causes and develop informed solutions.

Here are some examples of complete problem statements properly captured.

Problem Statement Example One

For the last year, our organisation has experienced many issues in the onboarding, offboarding and **New Employee Notifications** processes. The issues include New Employee Notifications not being actioned, resulting in varying levels of quality and experience of those being onboarded, with some crucial induction experiences not happening and crucial information not being passed on to the new team member. This problem affects almost 100% of all onboarding experiences:

- We process on average 1.5 New Employee Notifications per day, taking 6.6 minutes each to complete and send out, only when all the information is available, which occurs 62% of the time, resulting in the HR team following up for missing information 38% of the time, losing on average 92 minutes of capacity (as rework) each time they need to follow up.
- Many teams receiving New Employee Notifications also experience rework through the lack of or incorrect information on the New Employee Notifications. For 24% of the notifications, at least one team is impacted by this problem, costing the HR team 37 minutes on average to get and resupply to the team the right information.
- 82% of the onboarding New Employee Notifications are not affected at all or properly, with the new team member missing out on or delayed in important training and information.

If these processes are not refined, we will continue to lose vast amounts of capacity (currently calculated as 361 hours annually across all the teams) due to rework within each of the processes, and our new team members not experiencing an optimal start through a substandard induction, which over the last 12 months, new team members rated their induction experience as 4.3 out of 10.

Problem Statement Example Two

The **Application processing team** have experienced a significant backlog of applications for the last five years where applications are often sitting in a queue for 3–5 months before they start to be processed. This creates poor customer experience and impacts on timely revenue collection and claims management. The third-party agents are not happy with the long delays, and they are advising their clients to submit their applications 2–3 months early.

From recent measures of performance over the month of October 2025, we know that:

- The length of time the applications are with the teams for processing (from allocation to the end of processing) is 1,341 minutes, which is 2.794 working days.
- The actual processing time/capacity used by the team to complete the application averages 37 minutes.
- Rework rates experienced are 46%, meaning that the application is delayed by 6.31 working days on average waiting for the customer to respond with the required information. Our team loses on average 19 minutes setting up the request for more information (which is 51% the time to process an average application).

If this process remains unchanged, rework would likely affect between 850–900 applications annually – significantly affecting the customer experience through longer processing times and costing the team 277.1 hours per year (875 applications x 19 minutes, which is the processing of an extra 449 applications).

IMPROVEMENT INITIATIVE PLAN ELEMENTS

A one or two-page plan should cover:

- a name for the improvement initiative
- a date and version number of the plan
- a process description – what the process is for, and the first and last process steps to define where the improvements are being performed

- the problem statement
- work that is in scope and out of scope as part of this initiative
- how this improvement initiative relates to strategy
- the owner of the process/service performance that will be improved through this initiative
- the initiative champion/sponsor who both champions and funds the initiative
- the initiative leader who will lead the team in their work (and note if there's anyone mentoring them)
- who the team are and the capacity they are committing
- list the metrics (key performance measures) to be used to monitor and measure the process performance. These measures are often new because the previous measures didn't properly capture the performance of the process. This can be added to the process description field.

Tips for Building and Using Improvement Initiative Plans

Plans should not take a huge amount of time to produce, outside of capturing and inserting the data. Even with defining the team and determining their capacity with their leaders, the plan should be less than a day to build and should be short enough that the team can read the plan swiftly (almost) every day to make sure they stay on point and their work is exactly what was articulated as **in scope.**

An important part of a good plan is making sure that what is in scope is very narrow. Too often teams scope the work far too wide, which causes delays and poor outcomes against expectations. Start small. It's important to put almost as much as you can as **out of scope.** Out of scope doesn't mean it's not important, it just means we're not going to do it now and risk diluting the team's focus on what is important and delay early benefits.

The appetite to widen the scope during the initiative as new and related problems are discovered isn't unusual, but **scope creep** will suffocate an improvement initiative, so fight against it, like the success of the improvement initiative depends on it, which it does.

For example, if you look back at the second problem statement example, the likely in-scope elements will be reducing the occurrence of rework and updating the application form – as the reasons for going back to the customer are identified and potential solutions may focus on improving the application form to prevent these issues from occurring. And as the team study all the reasons for the rework occurring, they will likely discover a host of other issues in the process that aren't related to the scope of the improvement initiative. It's important the team maintains focus on the purpose so other problems need to be noted and parked for later improvement initiatives – unless they are so crucial as to move the team's focus, which is a call for the sponsor to make.

Either way, the team needs to be working on one thing at a time and not absorbing others, which will stop scope creep.

If, at this point, your team doesn't have enough data to complete a problem statement, know that that is common. It likely means the process isn't properly viewed with good measures. Leave the unknown elements and metrics blank – these blanks act as placeholders of statements of performance in the plan and signify areas to be investigated and determined during this stage. However, ensure all necessary data is collected before moving on to answer the question in the next stage: why do we have the current level of performance?

Value of Improvement Initiative Plans

Plans can save a team a lot of time and effort by allowing them to assess the likely benefits of an improvement initiative and determine early on whether the problem is actually substantial enough to warrant capacity for a solution.

Many improvement initiatives are cancelled straight after the construction of the plan (and specifically a data-rich problem statement) and they can also be cancelled after capturing performance baseline for the same reason. This is often due to realising the size of the problem, once scoped and with data, is far less than initially thought, or the return on investment is too weak.

There's a number of reasons to have a plan, including:

1. **Finding a sponsor:** A well-articulated plan provides an overview of the problem, the value of fixing it, and the team's

capability to address it. This plan serves as a pitch to attract a sponsor who can support, invest in and remove any roadblocks for the improvement initiative. A dedicated sponsor will be a crucial ally for the success of the initiative.

2. **Ensuring consistent understanding**: Great consistent understanding and agreement across the team, including the sponsor, of the scope of the work and who will be involved.
3. **Maintaining team focus**: A plan – if referred to often (and you'll want to build that in the team dynamic) – helps provide a constant focus across the team of the purpose of the team. Often, as we look to make an improvement, we find other related elements that need to be improved, too, and they can become distractions. Regularly reminding the team of the plan helps to keep the team focused on the core objective of the improvement initiative.

CAPTURING BASELINE DATA

All good change needs to be based on knowledge. We have to move from changes being based on 'I think' or 'I feel' to 'we know'. We need to ensure that change is made on the solid foundation of data and knowledge over assumptions and opinions.

> 'It ain't what you don't know that gets you into trouble.
> It's what you know for sure that just ain't so.'
> Mark Twain

Insights From Good Data Capture

The knowledge we'll get from good data capture and analysis will answer these questions:

1. How are we currently performing?
2. How does this performance relate to and meet what our customers need?
3. Why do we have the performance level that we do?

The first lens is to see if you actually understand how you are currently performing. Do you have all the right measures that you need to see a full picture of performance? Are all the errors and rework and cheats (the things you do that are not good but are shortcuts to meet targets) being captured? Do you understand your rework in terms of frequency and the pain that it causes the team each time it occurs? All this relates to making sure that you have the right measures to monitor your performance against, and that you are measuring the performance and monitoring it as frequently as needed. If you are doing all this, you can then say that you know how you are currently performing.

The next point is to determine the alignment between how you are currently performing – your outputs and the efficiency of those outputs – and the alignment of those outputs to the needs of the customer. This alignment is often referred to as the capability of response, which measures how fast and effective you are in meeting the needs of your customers. This capability represents your outcomes.

You've been told a problem exists – great. And the team has decided what problems are going to be fixed and who will be the core team working on the problems. Now that you have determined which problems you are going to work on, you need to ensure that you have captured data to establish the baseline performance of that process or process step – how you are currently performing. You don't have data yet – you captured some estimates of the data, how often the problem was occurring (frequency) and its impact on the organisation and the customer (severity) earlier to help decide which problems you'd tackle first, but now you've defined the scope of the improvement you need the actual data. Data that means we know about these problems rather than what we feel or think that they are. And we need to know two key elements: how often does each of the problems occur, and when they occur, what is the consequence?

Capturing the data not only provides these two key insights (and initially proves whether or not the problem actually exists), it also helps us understand the problem much better, which means that we will more likely generate a solution that will work. The better we understand the problems we face, the more likely the solution to address the problem will design itself.

The reason why we don't capture all the actual data first is that we don't need it for the decision making and it would take a lot of time to capture it for all the problems – when we will only start by fixing a few. Now that your team have selected what few but vital problems to fix, your team need only capture the precise data for those problems because:

- The data will provide a baseline for your performance of all key metrics – how frequently the problem is occurring, and when it occurs, what is the impact on the organisation and customers. Certainly, by understanding the frequency of the problem, you can start to determine the root cause for the problem.

- You will have a baseline performance that you can test any potential solution to see the actual effectiveness of it. You will be able to determine the positive impact of that solution. Any improvement, of course, becomes the new baseline from which you would look to improve again.

- You will be able to articulate the benefits of the solutions, which essentially will be the difference, in any number of elements, between the performance you experienced before and the performance you experience now.

- Perhaps most importantly, capturing data on the performance increases the team's awareness and understanding of the reasons why you have the performance that you do and will better inform the solutions they will later develop.

It might be folly to argue that collecting data is fun or easy, as often it is neither, but make no mistake, it is essential for the efficacy of the designed solution. Data collection is crucial, but I can't sell it as exciting. Data collection is perhaps the single most boring step in this whole process, but because the process of improvement is linear, our ability to perform the next step in making improvements depends on the quality of the execution of the previous step.

Because of this, data capture is arguably the most important step to get right for the quality and effectiveness of the solution.

We also need to be patient during this step. We won't just be collecting data, we'll be learning a significant amount about the problem, which is crucial for solution development later. As we are capturing the data, we will better understand the impact of the problems on both the customer and your organisation, and with this better understanding there can be an increased sense of urgency to fix the problem, which occurs well before we understand the root causes of the problem(s). You need to be patient and properly understand the problems and the root causes before defining solutions. Being patient means not jumping to solutions that, through a limited and inaccurate understanding of the problem, won't have the impact you'd like them to have – accompanied with the sunk costs of implementation.

Set Up the Data Collection

It's important that data collection is done with minimum disruption to the work. Make sure that the data capture is designed so that:

- only essential data directly related to key performance metrics is captured. Ensure the team calculates the exact amount of data needed for the insights required
- data integrity by capturing information in a clear and consistent manner is maintained. Avoid discrepancies in data capture to prevent the need for extending the process of data capture.

It's crucial to regularly review data capture during the process to ensure its integrity. This helps identify and address misinterpretations, errors or inconsistencies early on.

How Much Data to Capture

There are formulas available for calculating the right sample sizes, which you can easily find on Google or YouTube by searching 'Calculate a sample size' for a how-to video. For specific formulae and explanations and a prompt to use in an AI tool to calculate sample sizes, refer to Appendix 7 on sample size calculation.

You do need enough data for the integrity of insights leading to the development of effective solutions. To ensure a consistent and reliable understanding of what's happening, you can use formulas to determine the size of the sample data needed to represent the performance of the entire population. However, a practical rule of thumb is this: When the values in the captured data become predictable, meaning you and the team can confidently anticipate or predict the next set of data values – and you're proven to be right with the capture of that data – then you have likely gathered enough data to form a comprehensive view of the process performance and have a good degree of resolution to detect improvements in performance when comparing future performance data to baseline we are capturing now.

Once you have reached that point, you are ready to analyse the data. As much as the data capture was boring to do, this is the exciting part. We get into performance forensics here – working out exactly why we have the level of performance that we are currently experiencing and all the factors that contribute to it.

Determining What Data to Capture

Developing short and succinct data statements can help clarify what data you specifically need – to reduce wasted data capture. Fill the gaps in this statement to ensure you're getting the right data, with the purpose of designing the data capture to understand the root causes of your current performance:

> **We need** [what data] with **the detail of** [detail, stratification] **so we can understand** [what is it we need to know]

Here's an example of a data statement:

> **We need** to collect data on Contact Centre calls/emails received related to applications. We need **the detail of** the themes of each request that comes through to the Contact Centre relevant to applications, the frequency of these themes, the time it takes to resolve, and where the request gets redirected to resolve. We need this information **so we can understand** the main issues our customers/external stakeholders are facing, how

117

often these issues are being raised, the time it takes to resolve, who these issues are getting passed on to, and whether the teams receiving the referrals once passed on by the Contact Centre are able to action these requests themselves or if they must be referred further.

And another example of a data statement:

We need data on how frequently an application is submitted with incorrectly declared information. **We need to understand** how long it takes from the time the team member starts the assessment of the application to when they make a final decision. **We need the detail** of how long the team member is spending assessing the application and the time spent waiting for internal and external additional information and/or an external response. This **will help us understand** processing and wait times spent identifying how often supplied information is incorrect and help identify solutions to reduce the number of times this occurs.

Simplified Data Capture

Data capture during the baseline stage can take a lot of time. Of course, we are capturing two levels of data – how often the problem occurs, being a measure of frequency, and when it does occur, what its impact is.

Data capture need not be arduous. It should be easy for those in the work to capture the data as they perform the work. Don't make it arduous by capturing data that would be nice to know – think purposefully about what you need to know and capture only that initially. If there's value in capturing other elements of data later, then do that after you've helped make life easier for the team that's capturing the data, so they themselves see and have experienced the value in doing so.

Generally, measuring frequency is often much easier than your challenge of measuring the impact. Measuring frequency is a lot more binary; you're counting how often something does or does not happen and that's easy to distinguish, determine and count.

But measuring the severity of the impact can be often far more difficult. For example, if you are measuring how much capacity is lost performing a piece of rework, and that piece of rework is worked on over a number of different times for different lengths (think of work being picked up, then put down, and then picked up again later) it can be hard to capture all of those events to have a cumulative understanding of the capacity lost.

Here's a tip: because we are looking to address a root cause, and the root cause drives the frequency of the problem occurring, what we can do is capture the frequency data, and while we're capturing the severity data, which might take much longer to capture, we can analyse the frequency data and start to determine root causes and the solutions to address the root causes rather than waiting until we have the severity data before we start to determine root causes.

Severity data gives us a complete picture of the problem's impact, contributing to our understanding of the improvement's benefit realisation. Initial insights into benefits emerge after the pilot stage, where the solution's impact on reducing problem frequency and impact is assessed. Since the pilot stage is still distant, there's ample time to collect severity data if necessary, so we can split our data capture into two parts – frequency and severity. First, when we have frequency, we can get into root cause analysis while we still continue to capture data on severity.

Tips on Data Collection

Here are some quick-fire tips for making sure that your data collection efforts yield the best results:

1. Pilot your data collection. When you know what data you're looking to collect, test how to collect it. That might involve getting a sample of historical data, or having a team collect new data. You'll learn a lot running a pilot about how you can refine your data collection before you go big and try and collect all the data you need for your calculated sample size.

2. When piloting data collection, involve enthusiastic team members willing to participate. Emphasise the personal benefits

of accurate data capture – as the reduction of the problems that your improvement initiative team are trying to solve will directly help them and ensure a blame-free approach to understanding current performance levels. This supports obtaining precise data to reveal process challenges, aligning with the principle of continuous improvement.

3. If those collecting performance data weren't already part of the improvement initiative team, then they are new stakeholders in the improvement – treat them as the crucial stakeholders they are by keeping them in the loop and informed, especially of the data and insights you are getting from their data collection work. Share the full picture of what the data is looking like. The more people wanting to see positive change from this improvement initiative you are leading, the better.

4. Check the data collection every day, both what the data is telling us and the integrity of the data collection. Perform this check while you receive and compile data (ideally daily), especially from those team members who are newly capturing data. The reason to check the data daily (at least initially) rather than every week is if the collection isn't going to plan, such as someone isn't correctly capturing the data, you will know early on and only lose the data for a day, as opposed to losing a week of data capture.

5. Make sure that the data being captured actually relates to the insights you need for the problem you are looking to solve. Sometimes we discover the data we think we need isn't providing us the insights we need about the frequency or severity of the problem. Also, test that the data is what you need to know as opposed to what you want to know or is nice to know. By capturing just the data you need, and with the correct sample size, you won't overburden the team with data capture.

6. Make sure that your team design a process to collate the data as easily as possible from those in the work capturing the data – meaning that data capture is as easy as possible for those capturing the data and that the process doesn't unnecessarily soak up their capacity or interfere with their work significantly.

NEXT LEVEL OF PERFORMANCE INSIGHT

You are most likely going to need to establish new measures to capture new data and properly and comprehensively understand how you are performing and why you are performing at that level.

Often, lead measures are missing and may have been discovered by the improvement team necessary to be captured. Your organisation is unlikely to be capturing the right data to reflect the performance of the process, especially from a customer's perspective, and if it is, there are likely integrity issues with the data – meaning that the data might misdirect the design of the team's solution.

The way in which you are performing needs to be compared against your purpose. So, the measures that you'll capture your data by need to comprehensively reflect purpose.

If we are only measuring how long a process takes to perform, are there not measures of quality we are also missing? And those measures of quality might cover two elements: what we need as an organisation internally, and the performance that our customer needs of us.

Do our measures capture the customer echo – the experience of the customer and what our customers think about their experience that they might share with us and others – and rework that might occur from that experience? Do our measures capture all our incidences of errors in this one process we are looking to improve, and the negative reverberations of that performance throughout the organisation?

Performing the rework is only half the problem – not hearing it so your organisation is susceptible to having to perform the rework over and over again is literally a commitment to waste.

We need to think holistically about the measures we are capturing to make sure our baseline shows a comprehensive view of our performance against our purpose.

In Figure 6, we see how things that go wrong in the process, affecting the customer, produces a negative customer echo. The small black dots represent problems in the process, some ultimately affecting the customer, such as bad service or product defects.

Most customers (light grey dots) have a positive experience, but problems in the process lead to errors and problematic customer experiences. The customer echo sometimes results in rework for the organisation, (marked by an additional black dot), in the process – hearing about and then fixing the problem.

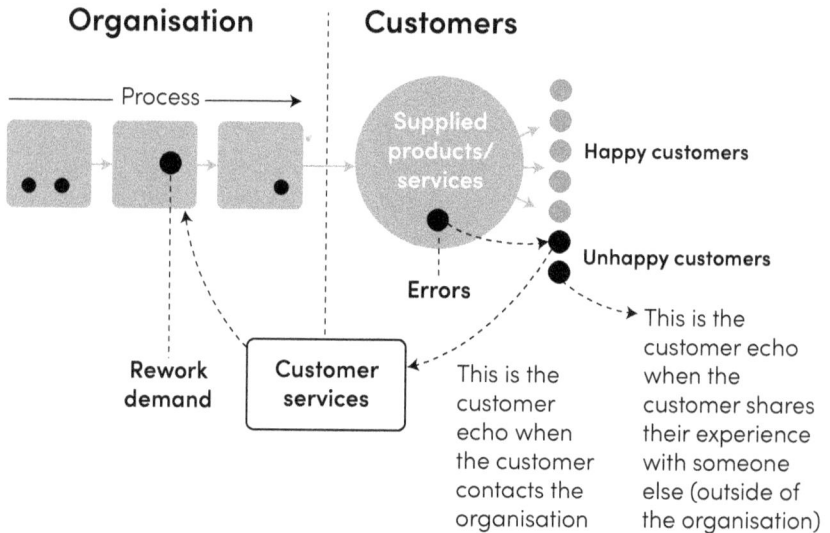

Figure 6

Understanding Operational Definitions

There's a concept that we need to be conscious of to help with ensuring the integrity of the data when we capture it. Operational definitions are precise definitions of how we will specifically capture the data to ensure the consistency of each data point is captured similarly – this is especially important if we have a team collecting data.

If we want to understand how long it takes customers to exit a plane after it lands, and we get our team at various airports to capture that data, we'll want to be clear and prescriptive with how that's done.

If the above is the only instructions we offer, we are likely to experience some significant data integrity issues resulting from the loose and imprecise operational definition of capturing: *how long it takes customers to exit a plane after it lands.* If there are integrity issues in data capture, our view of performance becomes blurred instead of clear. An example of what might blur the data is what 'landed' means to each of those capturing data. While one person might think it is when the wheels touch the tarmac of the runway, another might feel that it's when the plane has finished the taxi to the gate, and another, when the forward door is open – each of which starts capturing data only at that point. Combination or comparison of the data can't be affected because all that data is incompatible from being captured with different operational definitions.

Conversely, if the team had an **operational definition** like this, then those integrity issues would be alleviated:

> We will be capturing data on the time it takes for passengers to leave a flight once it has landed. The time will be recorded in minutes and seconds elapsed from when the plane lands – the first moment that all the wheels of the landing gear are simultaneously on the tarmac of the runaway, through to the moment when the last passenger has first stepped on the gate airbridge from the forward door of the aircraft.

An operation definition to aid data capture and the integrity of that data is only correct if it is precise, it is well understood and is strictly adhered to by all involved capturing the data.

VISUALISING THE PERFORMANCE DATA

You'll likely find that different team members are capturing only certain measures meaning that they will have a limited view of performance, so it's crucial to compile and share this data across the entire team and stakeholders. The best way to do this is by visually representing the performance of these measures.

There are a number of graphical techniques that can be used to visualise the data, including insight into the variation of the performance of that measure. You need to go further than just looking at averages (which might only be offered in a pie chart or line graph), you want a nutritionally rich picture that shows process performance variation and capability.

Capability is essentially how capable we are at meeting the expectations of the customer and putting it in numeric terms. For example, is our capability such that we meet customer expectations 100% of the time, 50% of the time, or only 10% of the time? When we don't meet expectations, how much are we missing by in actual terms?

We want to be able to show that, and not by showing the data. Showing the data is a mistake as it is often overwhelming. Instead, we want to visually represent the rich story that the data tells.

Keep it simple with graphical representations of data. Pie charts and line graphs aren't often useful in terms of being visually rich with information, but I would suggest the use of either:

- box and whisker plots
- histograms
- Pareto charts
- control charts.

Read more about these charts in Appendices 10, 11 and 12.

Visualisation of the baseline data supports and offers the opportunity to compare the baseline data to the other important factors, enhancing the capture of baseline data.

The first factor is for root cause analysis of the current performance. You can understand and detect the root causes of the way your processes and the systems around them are set up to give you the performance that you have now. Pareto charts and control charts can help with this.

The second critical element of a baseline is for testing the solution in a pilot. With the baseline, you will be able to determine the performance of a solution during the pilot of that solution. And when you make further changes to the solution during the pilot, again with the baseline, you will be able to determine the effect of those changes. Box and whisker plots are helpful in showing the performance differences between the baseline performance and that of the piloted solution.

The third critical element is benefits realisation. After you have run a pilot and tested and proven the effect of a solution, and that solution has been implemented to give you the new levels of performance, benefit realisation can be determined between the baseline and the performance you are experiencing now. Without a baseline, accurate benefit realisation would almost be impossible and certainly a lengthy and expensive exercise to determine.

CHECKING IN WHERE WE ARE

Let's take a moment to check in on the steps we've navigated so far. Here's a snapshot of the start of Loop 1, and where we are up to:

1. We began by enhancing team dynamics.
2. We captured and mapped out problems to visualise where they occur in the process.
3. We added preliminary data capture for each problem to differentiate the impact of each problem.
4. We determined the inter-relationships between the identified problems.
5. We selected the problems to fix first and determined teams.
6. We captured the overview of the improvement in an Improvement Initiative Plan, including data on problem frequency and severity:
   i. if data is lacking or lacks integrity, create new measures for accurate capture.
7. We established a baseline to understand current performance, which is crucial to support us in understanding the effectiveness of our solutions, both in the piloting and embedding of those solutions.

THE PROCESS OWNER AND SPONSOR'S ROLES

Now that we know how we are performing, we've got the first solid insight to offer the wider team and stakeholders on what we have learnt about the performance of our process.

Now is the perfect time to ensure we have a couple of roles in place and acknowledged. For the process owner, we'll need their permission to make the improvements to the process when we are at that stage. The sponsor is who supports this work, funds it, and knocks down any barriers that affect the work.

Here's a quick overview of these two significant roles.

The Process Owner

Every process, whether existing or to be built, requires a designated process owner. If a process owner needs to be found – whether it's through someone new joining the team or an interim arrangement – use this guide to help your team determine who best fits that role. Additionally, use this guide to better define the roles of current process owners. As a reference, these are some of the core roles of the process owner:

- Acts a central point for:
  - ~ conversations about the purpose of the process
  - ~ receiving all feedback for changes/improvements that need to be made to the process.
- Makes sure that there are no gaps in the process, that the process is seamless.
- Ensures there are safeguards in the process to reduce errors, rework, risks and issues.
- Ensures there are good performance metrics that show the performance of the entire process, both for the team and customers/stakeholders and who (individual or team) is capturing the performance data, who they are sharing the performance data with, and how often.
- Makes sure everyone is ready prior to any process improvement going live and everyone understands their role in the process and all training, guidance material (like checklists) and documentation is done – and that a pilot of the improvement has been conducted.
- Is primarily accountable for the performance of the process to be understood by stakeholders and drives improvement of

the performance (which is what the improvement team will help with).

- Manages and signs off changes and improvements to the process (and is the only person to do so) and ascertains the impact of changes to one part of the process, to other parts of the process and end-to-end performance.

- Makes sure there are regular reviews of the performance of the process to improve process performance.

The Sponsor

Sponsorship is a vital role with a significant impact on the success of any improvement initiative. The sponsor is usually a senior leader in an organisation that has the budget and influence to support the improvement initiative, clears all the roadblocks for the team to perform and is the key stakeholder for the team to update regarding the progress of the improvement initiative.

The sponsor also serves as the improvement's main advocate and collaborates with the improvement initiative leader to secure necessary resources for success, including helping with the ongoing needs of the improvement initiative team.

Communication is another critical aspect of the sponsor's role. It can be challenging for the improvement initiative leader to access upper management, so the sponsor can support the communication of the initiative's scope and objectives to all stakeholders, to both senior leadership and the wider organisation.

Ultimately, the improvement initiative sponsor is responsible for success. To achieve this, the sponsor must mentor and support the improvement team. A crucial coaching area is issue escalation, where the sponsor becomes the focal point for issue management, barrier removal and decision making when the improvement initiatives leader's influence and authority is exceeded.

The key elements of the sponsor's role are to:

- attend sponsor learning and coaching session(s) prior to having become a sponsor

- understand the purpose of the improvement initiative and key concepts for the initiative
- own the outcome, the result of the initiative
- track the initiative progress
- track the work of the team members and ensure and support their development
- support the team and break down any barriers for them
- attend all catch-up meetings run by the improvement initiative team
- provide focus and drive for the initiative and support the team
- assign/select and approve a dedicated resource for the initiative and ensure that the committed capacity of the team to perform the improvement initiative has been made available
- act as a vital link between the improvement and senior leadership by communicating updates and results of the improvement initiative
- be accountable for the work and the benefits both during and after the embedding stage
- park solution thinking or investigation of any issues that are out of scope of the initiative
- ensure a reasoned approach has been applied to the initiative
- keep the conversations and decisions focused on the data and what is known
- facilitate the making of a decision to continue working on the initiative into the next stage, either fully or with provisos, or worst case to rework elements of the current stage.

CHECKING IN WITH THE PROCESS OWNER AND SPONSOR

This section guides the sponsor and process owner on key points to discuss during catch-up meetings. These discussions involve updating the sponsor on progress and seeking endorsement and support for the next stage of the improvement initiative. While further informal updates are likely to occur for good stakeholder engagement, the following outlines the significant points for updates.

The stages and purpose for these catch-up updates with the sponsor and process owner are:

1. At the end of the 'Understand the current level of performance' stage, if not already done, share the visual representations of performance data and insights of the current level of performance with the sponsor.

2. Early into the 'Develop and pilot solutions' stage, if not already done, share the discovered root cause, the solution designed to address the root cause and the high-level overview of what a pilot is likely to look like, for the endorsement and support of the sponsor to now set up and run the pilot.

3. At the end of the 'Develop and pilot solutions' stage, share the results of the pilot, the impact of the solution to address the problem, and seek endorsement to start to plan the embedding of the solution in the wider organisation.

4. Early into the 'Embed proven solutions' stage, share the full **embed plan** for the sponsor's endorsement. This is significant because with the sponsor's endorsement, the solutions will be embedded throughout the wider organisation (or as the plan pitched suggests).

Figure 7 (overleaf) offers a visual representation of these stages. The questions that need to be asked by the sponsor at each catch-up update are covered later in this book in these sections:

-   questions for sponsors to endorse the pilot
-   questions for the sponsors to start the embed stage
-   sponsor approval to embed the solution.

These questions also provide a good guide for the improvement initiative team, helping guide them through the specific elements of their work in each stage.

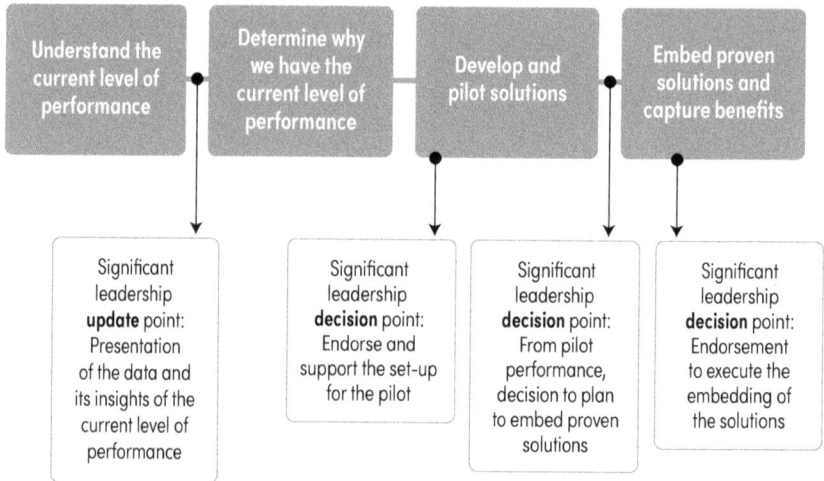

Understand the current level of performance	Determine why we have the current level of performance	Develop and pilot solutions	Embed proven solutions and capture benefits

Significant leadership **update** point: Presentation of the data and its insights of the current level of performance	Significant leadership **decision** point: Endorse and support the set-up for the pilot	Significant leadership **decision** point: From pilot performance, decision to plan to embed proven solutions	Significant leadership **decision** point: Endorsement to execute the embedding of the solutions

Figure 7

Update One: Presentation of the Data and Insights of the Current Level of Performance

For this update, the team will present the baseline performance data. The team then advises the sponsor that their next task is to understand the factors contributing to this current performance level, determining the variables, levers and root cause(s) that provide the core opportunities for improvement of performance. There are no set questions for this update to the sponsor and process owner – let the conversation around the data naturally flow.

CHAPTER 5

Determining Why We Experience the Current Level of Performance

Once you have baseline data of current performance, you need to understand the reasons why you are performing at that level. The purpose of this stage is to gain a comprehensive understanding of all the factors that together give us the current level of performance for better solution development.

With knowing these factors, you'll better understand:

- the differences in degrees of impact of the individual factors to our performance, and
- a better and wider array of what our solution(s) might entail through a better understanding of all the factors in play impacting performance.

Crucially, you'll know which of the factors are most likely root causes of your performance. Root causes meaning that they are the single reason for a stream of things that (and in our context, negatively) impact performance.

The key part of your performance data analysis at this stage is finding and determining the root cause or causes of the level of performance you experience.

ANALYSIS OF THE PROCESS PERFORMANCE DATA

After capturing nutritionally rich process performance data, the next step is analysis to interpret the insights it offers about your process performance. We are looking for variation of performance – as within these fluctuations are the contributing factors to that very variation. The root causes of these factors, which produce that very variation in performance, offer you the solution for consistency in performance.

Let me be clear about why variation is a reliable indicator of poor performance and something that we'd look to eliminate. Situations with high variation (and high variation being undesirable) can look like this:

- Times when there are no queues and other times when there are very long queues.
- Differences in response times for the customer – sometimes promptly, sometimes extended.
- Inconsistent decision making or evaluation within a team – something one person would approve for a customer another team member would reject.
- Variation in production by volume (all products that should be the same having differing levels of content) or count (should be 12, but sometimes 11 or 13 are packaged) or other measures (all size US 9 shoes are slightly different sizes).
- Things not being done properly – where each time something isn't done properly is a variation from the standard, leading to complaints and rework.

Variation Through the Lens of Special and Common Cause

There is often wide variation in the performance of our processes and it's important to understand the extent and the nature of that variation because it shows us where we can improve. The more variation we have in a process, the poorer performing the process is.

Take the variations of waves of demand, for instance. They make it more than tricky to plan your workforce and capacity effectively. And when it comes to vast variations in customer experience, many customers experience sub-optimal interactions. This may require rework or, worse, lead to losing customers. For repeat customers, the variations in their experiences means a lack of consistency, which can be unsettling, further impacting their satisfaction.

Reduction of variation in products is also crucial. When your products exhibit high variations, for instance, if a product states that the customer is purchasing 500 grams, variations might result in supplying 450 grams, short-changing them, or providing 550 grams, affecting your margins and setting unrealistic expectations for the next purchase.

Variation is a process evil.

Variation is not good, and you'll want to significantly reduce it. The size of the variation corresponds to the extent of its impact, with greater variation leading to poorer and more costly process performance or significant impacts on the customer. The nature of the variation is determined by the source of the variation. Is the variation from a one-off, significant or attributable event, or is it a ubiquitous part of your process?

For example, if you run a bottling plant and measure how much liquid you're putting in each bottle, the differences in the amount of liquid in each bottle is the natural part of the process, what we term **common cause variation**. However, if the amount of liquid is now reading zero for bottle after bottle because a mechanical failure has knocked the bottles off the conveyer belt before they are measured, then we have what's called **special cause variation**. Special cause is often referred to as attributable variation as the data can be attributed to a specific (special and unusual) event.

Whether it's special or common cause, it's variation, and any variation is counter to the performance we are training to obtain and needs to be guarded against or at least reduced.

Too many teams readily dismiss data because it doesn't look right, or they think (rather than know) that it has come about as a special cause situation as opposed to knowing exactly what was the special cause that caused it. More often than not, the data captured of your performance actually reflects your real performance. And it's that data, that performance, that needs to be addressed.

You cannot disregard any performance data unless it occurred for a special cause, and you know exactly why it happened, with the assurance that it almost certainly won't happen again (perhaps because you've implemented mistake-proofing measures – we'll discuss mistake proofing later).

We'll apply root cause analysis to determine the reason for and then to solve (by significantly reducing if not eliminating) the variation.

ROOT CAUSE ANALYSIS AND THINKING

We need to engage your teams to focus on root cause thinking when they are looking to solve problems.

Think of it as process forensics. When root causes are understood, leaders and their teams make insightful and informed decisions about the right countermeasures to expend their energy on. Conversely, when a team rushes to solve a symptom without knowing the root cause, the danger is there's wasteful use of their capacity and resources on a solution that proves to be only partially effective.

> ### The single largest reason why teams fail to solve a problem is they don't out-think the problem.

Trying to fix problems without knowing the root cause is tantamount to trying to reduce the rising sea level by eating all the fish in the sea. Sure, the sea level will decrease, but the fish in the sea weren't the reason for the sea level rising, so were not the root cause for the problem, which means sea levels, though initially dropping with the 'solution', will continue to rise.

All energy used to deal with symptoms of problems is incredibly inefficient, if not ineffective and wasteful. We must always park the impulsive jumping-to-solution, to instead determine and understand the whole chain of events which occur – purposefully right back to the root cause. Outside of knowing the root cause, then we can only look to alleviate a problem.

There are times and occasions where we would look to solve symptoms, but we would rarely knowingly choose to solve symptoms over root causes as a preference. Solving root causes means reducing the existence of the problem, whereas solving symptoms means the problem still exists at the same levels, we've just reduced the impact of it when it does occur. What we want to do is solve the root causes so we can reach a new level of performance and free up the capacity in the organisation, capacity that is often otherwise lost in alleviating the symptoms of problems.

Where possible, fix problems at the root cause rather than treating the symptoms, as only addressing the symptoms will result in continued manifestation of the problems. Whatever you choose, it's more so about a conscious and deliberate application of the energy in your organisation rather than jumping to a solution.

Differentiating Between Root Causes and Symptoms

The pain of a problem can be measured in two ways: how often the problem happens, and when it happens, the impact on the organisation and the customer. When we reduce the impact on the organisation and the customer then we are reducing a symptom. But when we reduce the frequency of the problem, then we are starting to address the root cause, which is more often the preference.

Think of it as this analogy: there is an issue with a particular intersection where there is frequent low speed car versus pedestrian incidents. Thankfully there aren't major injuries, but there are a lot of accidents on a weekly basis where pedestrians are suffering bumps, bruises and abrasions. What we're tasked with is coming up with solutions to better protect pedestrians.

If one of our solutions is to wrap all pedestrians in bubble wrap before they cross the road, then we need to have a team there ready to wrap people up, so they have a 40-centimetre coverage of bubble wrap all over their body. Perfect. And there is a team on the other side of the road to unwrap the pedestrian and retrieve the bubble wrap once they have safely crossed the road.

What we discover through piloting this solution is that there is the same number of accidents, but the injuries are less severe. What we've affected is a solution that takes care of a symptom of the problem. Reducing the *severity* of a problem means reducing the symptom of a problem.

But, if we come up with the solution that has significantly reduced the *frequency* of the incidents taking place, then we've addressed a root cause for the problem occurring in the first place.

So, here's the rule: by reducing the frequency of the incidents, we know we're tackling a root cause, whereas by reducing severity, we are only reducing a symptom of an incident.

Tools to Help Determine Root Causes

If we don't know, or choose to fix, the root cause, that doesn't demonstrate a lack of understanding, it often shows a lack of courage. Often, it takes courage to find out why a problem is happening – finding out why a problem is happening exposes a number of previously hidden ugly truths about why we have the performance that we do.

Finding a root cause implores us to use the same deep thinking each time – there's no mystery to it, root causes are all found methodically the same way though, of course, some root causes are easier to find and discover than others.

A solution can be informed, or not. Root cause identification prevents 'fixing' a symptom and helps us focus on identifying the root cause of a problem. We need to find the root causes to better ensure that our solution is informed. It's the quality of the solution that shows the level of understanding of the problem.

The 5 Whys Tool

The purpose of the **5 Whys** tool is to probe below the surface and the symptoms of the problem to get to the root cause of an issue. As a root cause analysis tool, it helps us to understand why a problem occurs with the specific objective to then develop the right solution to reduce the frequency of occurrence (which is when we know we have a root cause) rather than simply reducing the impact of the problem – the impact being the symptoms of a problem.

The benefits of using the technique include:

- it's easy to use, engages people and encourages teamwork
- it can be used alongside other problem-solving tools and techniques
- it helps to quickly separate symptoms from the root cause
- it enables critical thinking of the problem(s).

How to Use the 5 Whys

It is a simple technique that involves asking the right questions, particularly using 'why' questions to determine the root cause of a chain of events which is causing the issue we want to resolve.

Although this technique is called the 5 Whys, you may find that you will need to ask the 'why' question fewer or more than five times – five is just a nominal number. The technique is simply to ask why something happens enough to get to the root cause or the start of the chain of events.

Often, problems are felt in one process step, but their root causes are usually traced back to an earlier step. For example, in a contact centre, customer complaints may be experienced there, but the root cause will almost certainly reside in an earlier event like product creation or a previous interaction with the customer, such as a poorly worded application, where customers often supply the wrong information, and that isn't picked up until after the application has been submitted and the application is being analysed.

As you will be looking to eliminate or reduce the root cause, this technique could be used like mapping a process with flip chart paper, sticky notes and marker pens capturing the elements as you move back through the events, from the symptom to the root cause(s).

By asking *why* an event occurs, and then why that subsequent event occurs, over and over, continue the process until you get to the root cause.

Here are some examples of the 5 Whys technique being used:

Example 1

The customer's coffee was served too cold and they complained.

→ *Why was it served cold?*

There was a long time between when it was made and when it was given to the customer.

→ *Why was there that time gap?*

Because it was left sitting on the serving counter.

→ *Why would a coffee be left sitting there?*

The waiters only know a coffee is ready when they see it on the serving counter.

→ *Why do the waiters have to look at the serving counter?*

There's nothing to alert the waiter the moment when the coffee is immediately ready.

Root cause discovered for customers getting cold coffees, and we now have a good basis for a solution.

Example 2

We are having to dedicate a person full-time to clear our customer inbox.

→ *Why full time?*

Because the inbox is being flooded with emails.

→ *Why is the inbox flooded?*

Because the inbox is being used incorrectly – 33% of emails are out of scope.

→ *Why are so many emails out of scope?*

Because our contact centre doesn't have the information they need to support the customer queries and are forwarding on the queries as emails.

→ *Why doesn't the contact centre have the information they need?*

Because there's no consistent way that general notes are being captured on customer applications by our agents, which is read by the contact centre and relayed to the customers, which, often, the contact centre can't do, so they raise at request for support via email.

The root cause is the contact centre not consistently getting the information they need.

The 5 Whys is a simple technique that can help you quickly get down to the root cause of a problem. However, it won't solve the root cause and other problem-solving tools will likely be needed for solution development, testing the solution and embedding a proven solution – all of which we'll cover.

When you are asking 'why' a number of times in quick succession, be careful to use tact and patience – some people can find it confrontational or challenging, especially if they have been doing something for a long time that is just fixing or hiding a problem. Setting up the right team dynamic and environment for the 5 Whys technique is important for these reasons.

Staying on Track With the 5 Whys

For root causes, you really have to dig deep. Here's an example. You're on a maintenance team for a building that's washed down with a solution every day. This solution reacts with the concrete, resulting in gradual weakening and erosion over time.

So, you need to reduce the impact of the solution that you use to wash the concrete. The reason why you are having to wash the building so frequently is because the building must look pristine, and most of what you are washing off is bird poo.

Here's the trick – most organisations at this point think that they understand the root cause, and that is the solution they have reacts with the concrete, so their answer is to go to market to find a solution that doesn't affect the concrete.

But we know that this reduces severity of the problem, not the frequency – so it can't be a root cause. This is where teams can get derailed from the 5 Whys technique. The frequency is the need to wash the building every day, so by applying the 5 Whys tool we can drill down to find out that the reason why we have a lot of bird poo is that there are a lot of spiders that the birds are feeding on. And why we have a lot of spiders is because there are a lot of bugs. And the reason why we have a lot of bugs is because of the lights on the building that turn on at dusk attract the bugs.

Make sure that the questions focus on why the problem occurs rather than how we might mitigate the problem. This means we'll more likely find the root cause. For example, if we were to look to reduce the impact of a washing solution causing deterioration of the surface we are washing, rather than ask, 'What is the reaction between the solution and the surface that's causing the surface deterioration?' it is better to ask, 'Why do we have to wash the surface?'

Understanding the root cause allows us to develop a solution that deters bugs from the building. This means we only need to wash the building monthly rather than daily, and yes, with a product that is also better for the concrete.

Here is where we are landing with this point: make sure that you and your team properly drill down to the root cause. You'll get a massive return on the time invested to properly do that.

THE IMPORTANCE OF DATA TO DETERMINE ROOT CAUSES

Let's delve into the importance of knowing the frequency of the problem *as part of the data capture of current performance*. By knowing the frequency, you gain better insight into what the solution needs to be, thereby supporting the efficacy of the solution to tackle the root cause.

You own a café. It's a large café, with a big team and great customers. Consider this scenario: when the waiting team carry a tray of drinks to a customer's table, you experience a 1% occurrence of all the drinks falling to the floor. Take a moment to think about what the reason for this problem occurring could be.

Got that reason in your mind? Good, now...

Facing the same issue: your waiting team is dropping drinks 50% of the time while loading the tray before reaching the table. What could be the reason for this problem occurring at a 50% rate?

You likely have two very different reasons for the very same problem because of the variations in the frequency data associated with the occurrence of that specific problem.

And that's why data relating to frequency of a problem is a crucial insight to understand the root cause of a problem. The impact of a problem won't likely tell you the root cause of a problem, impact will tell you what it means to your organisation and your customer when the problem occurs.

Focus solely on this principle in the first loop. As we introduce elements in the second loop, aim to enhance, not diminish, this fundamental principle.

TEASING OUT THE PAIN POINT DATA TO DETERMINE ROOT CAUSES

After determining the pain points that are in scope to be improved in your process, and the inter-relationship between the pain points and the baseline data of the frequency and impact of the pain points (already determined), you now need to discover the root causes for these pain points to design the solutions.

And here's the gap between the pain points and determining the root causes: we need to capture the data that helps us determine the root causes.

Step one is: what is the data that we need to capture that will show us the various levels of performance outcomes, and the factors that contribute (as root causes) to those various levels of performance outcomes? This data is different from the initial data we captured to understand which problems we'd focus on first – now we know where we are focusing, we are capturing far more robust data to serve as baseline performance of the specific areas we are looking at.

You might or might not already have that data on those elements at this stage. If not, you've not missed a step in the process, but we do need to get this data to test the impact of our solutions and to understand the benefits as well as what we are looking to do now – determine the root causes.

Often, the data of performance will provide us with a number of questions that we'll need to ask to determine those root causes. For example, when there is a significant pain point within the process, we might capture data on or related to that pain point, such as:

- the various speeds that that part of the process is performed – from the time of the initial and the last step of the process we are studying, and
- whether or not rework occurred in that process step, or the significance of that rework.

By having this data, we can start to determine the right questions we need to answer to determine and understand the impact of the root cause (or various root causes) on the performance.

Sometimes the data itself will make the root causes evident – where we have data on all the factors that contribute to the performance. Think of it this way, we have data on an athlete or a number of athletes that run one kilometre each day with the key performance metric being how fast that kilometre was run, and the other data we have is:

- how physically and mentally recovered the athlete is before the run
- the time of the day, weather conditions and temperature for the run
- the clothing (running kit) and shoes they wore for that run

- the nutrition and timing of the eating of that nutrition prior to the run
- the amount and quality of sleep the night prior
- the athlete's mindset immediately before the run
- the warm-up – which warm-up exercises were used and for how long/number of reps
- whether or not a pacer (buddy runner) was present.

With this level of data, we might find we have irrefutable evidence of what more significantly contributes to the best results – being the fastest kilometres run. That's helpful. These insights mean we can more consistently have the athlete run the kilometre faster – meaning less variation in running times.

Sometimes we don't have data on the individual factors that contribute directly to the performance data we have, so we need to determine the questions we need answered to discover and understand what those factors are that influence performance, and the individual impact of those factors.

Another example of this would be all the reasons we need to return to a customer to get further information for their application. All this is rework, so we need to understand where the rework is coming from:

- Which questions in particular are customers having issues with understanding or not supplying the right information?
- Are we asking these questions with the right language? Is it easy and worded for our customers to understand without industry lexicon?
- Are we asking these questions at the right time in the process?

The questions might be behaviour based – meaning the way that teams choose to prioritise and process the work. For instance, if there are handovers in the process between teams, where work is handed from one team to various other teams for their input, and then received back by the original team, and the data shows differences in performance time and work quality during these steps, we can ask the teams specific questions to understand the reasons behind these variations and through the data, such as:

- When the work is handed over to you, does one person in your team perform the work or many?
- What could be supplied to you and your team to process the work better/faster?

It is the answers to these questions, through the analysis of the data, that will help determine the root causes for the current performance.

CHAPTER 6

Developing Better Solutions

This stage aims to develop reliable solutions which, when validated through pilot testing, produce tangible benefits. The end of this stage is defined by having those proven, high-quality solutions ready to embed into your work.

THE DEVELOPMENT OF SOLUTIONS

Once you understand the root causes of problems, your team can start to build solutions that will purposefully address them, knowing that it is those root causes that fundamentally impact the performance of the process. It is the adherence to these crucial principles that supports the significance of the solutions when:

- it is based on data, and
- it addresses a root cause, and
- you know how it will impact and benefit customers.

In this stage, we will look to develop those solutions and prove their efficacy by how much it changes your original levels or performance, which is what we will look to pilot. It is the baseline data we originally caught that will enable us to determine the performance of the solutions we are piloting. Only once solutions have proven to significantly improve performance do we look to invest time, team capacity and energy to implement and embed them.

Have the Right People Develop the Right Solutions

Let your team, rather than you or an external consultant, discover and shape the solutions for testing. Teams are more invested in their own ideas, making change management smoother. When teams who are in the work create their improvement ideas, they are more likely to adopt and test them successfully. This differs from having one team, or a consultant, who have developed a potential solution working to convince the team in the work to adopt and apply those ideas.

In continuous improvement, I'd suggest that a consultant's primary roles are to aid in problem discovery, help define the full impact of the problem when others have been too busy to notice, facilitate the integrity of the problem-solving process, and build the capability of the team. Team cohesion often matters more than the idea's quality for effective problem-solving and implementation – the team should still develop the solution, even if it's not thought of as perfect.

Empowering the team to develop the solutions and prove the effectiveness of the solutions through a pilot means we are effectively taking the strategy to front-load the change management aspect of embedding proven solutions. Too often change management occurs when one party has developed an idea or solution to a problem and tries to coerce or convince others to adopt that solution. That takes a lot of time and energy. The change management component is significantly reduced when teams develop their own solutions. And if there are other teams who perform similar work and can also adopt the same proven solution, then that team who developed, piloted and proved the solution can share this, as peers, with other teams.

Good Solution Development

Up to this stage, we've undertaken steps to make sure the solution is not determined before the problem is properly understood. It takes discipline to adopt the strategy of comprehensively understanding a problem before starting to solve it. It seems to me that we have an inherent mindset to jump to developing a solution way too soon – and that's something that we need to be conscious of and resist the urge to do.

'If I had an hour to solve a problem, I'd spend 55 minutes thinking about the problem and 5 minutes thinking about solutions.' Albert Einstein

Jumping to solution is natural but not effective as there is obvious inherent danger in having a solution that doesn't fix a problem. Worse than that, of course, is an expensive solution that doesn't fix a problem – that's career denting stuff.

Jumping to a solution can manifest as designing solutions that only resolve the symptoms that come from a broken process. Back to our leaky boat analogy – that's effectively choosing to find a faster way to bail out the water over plugging the leaks in the boat.

We need to adopt the mindset that there is nothing faster than doing it properly and getting to the root of a problem. Anything else is a poor shortcut, likely meaning having to rework the solution again later – if you are lucky enough to have a second chance.

Ensure the Customer is Central to the Solution

Whatever the solution is that you develop, make sure that your team knows how it will impact the customer. It might be a solution designed to be positively impactful for the customer directly, or it might be a solution that you don't know how it will impact the customer and suspect that it won't likely improve their experience but are assured that it won't negatively impact it. In that case, make sure your team have set the right metrics in the pilot that they can monitor the customer experience.

Either way, if it is positive or neutral for the customer, we need to know, and that's what we mean by making sure that the customer is central to the solution – knowing the customer impact is one of the core components.

We must also understand the holistic impact on the customer, considering scenarios where a solution may seem negative in isolation but proves overwhelmingly positive in the broader context.

Here's an example of that situation: as part of an application process, our solution might mean we are getting better and clearer information from the customer at the start. So, the impact of the solution means it now takes a customer on average four minutes longer to fill out the application. That is just the impact of this one element of the solution. However, when we consider the overall effect on the customer, those additional four minutes of capturing information now could potentially decrease the likelihood of needing to return to the customer later in the process for the same information. This could save the customer up to 20 minutes of their time.

Additionally, having to go back to the customer to get extra information meant the processing time of the application increased by an average of five days. So clearly, while this solution increases the customer interaction during the application stage by four minutes, holistically it is much better for the customer.

Consider having customers involved as part of your solution development for two reasons at least: firstly, though customers won't solve the problems, they will provide crucial insights into the impact of the problems that will help determine the root cause (for example, the way that they interpret a question on an application might prove to be the very reason why the organisation is not getting the information it needs). Secondly, those customers who played a role in addressing the problem are likely to be more receptive to participating in piloting a solution. This is ideal, as involving customers in any pilot is crucial for the understanding of the performance of the solution.

Solution Development Tools

What we are looking to do at this stage is develop ideas of what the solution could look like now we have a good understanding of the problem and the root causes of the problem. Let's focus on how to improve the solution that addresses root causes of the problem.

Brainstorming and Anti-solution Thinking

Brainstorming is about setting up a conducive environment for the generation of ideas. The keys to good brainstorming are:

- Keep it short and sharp. Many ideas will further launch off the ideas of others, so instead of brainstorming for five minutes straight, brainstorm for two minutes, share the ideas and then have the team brainstorm for another two minutes, share ideas again, and then a further minute.
- There are two main types of brainstorming, popcorn brainstorming, where people shout out ideas (and the scribe has to potentially capture them), and silent brainstorming, where the team think of and capture ideas individually and share with the group. Both have their merits, but I personally lean towards silent as everyone gets to have a say. Having some music on during the silent brainstorming helps too – it fills the unnerving silence.
- It's about one thing only – idea generation. There is to be no idea evaluation during idea generation. Strictly enforce this, otherwise one person's absent-minded critique of the ideas of others will rapidly shut down the environment and the appetite for some to be vulnerable enough to suggest crazy ideas. Brainstorming is mining – you'll have to go through a huge number of ideas to find the few gold nuggets. Facilitate the volume of ideas and the nuggets will come.
- If the team need energy to start the brainstorming process, start with **anti-solution brainstorming** rather than brainstorming. Start with answering 'How do we make this problem worse?' For whatever reason, perhaps there's an inventiveness when it comes to destruction that we innately have, as teams usually

have little trouble coming up with a vast array of ideas of how to make something worse. Once you've done that then you have the material to flip that question on its head and ask, 'How do we stop these things from happening?' You could use popcorn brainstorming for anti-solution and then silent brainstorming for (good) idea generation.

Brainstorming Resources

Resources you'll need for brainstorming are sticky notes, whiteboard markers (one for each of the team) and a good, clean wall space. Sticky notes will more readily stick to most walls, and especially glass, than to a whiteboard. Here are some tips on using sticky notes:

1. Get the team to use a marker rather than a pen so they can be read more easily from a distance.
2. Write just one thought on each sticky note so they can be moved and grouped as needed without having to be divided.
3. Remove the sticky note by peeling it across the pad, not from the bottom to the top. When you peel from bottom to top, the glue side tends to curl, making it less likely to stay attached. Peeling from one side to the other means the sticky note will stick better and flatter against the glass.

Popcorn Brainstorming

I've found two effective ways to facilitate popcorn brainstorming, but like anything, adjust the techniques to suit you and your team.

For the first method, ensure the team members each have a pad of sticky notes and a marker. Over a period of time, which might only be two minutes (the facilitator will time and provide a 30-second warning before the time lapses), the team simply shout out their thoughts and write them down (one thought per sticky note) as they shout it out. The reason they shout out their thought is it reduces replication, so others don't write the same thought. It can also stimulate someone else in the team to think of something slightly different, and to capture that. After the time is up, the team individually take turns to post all their sticky notes on a wall so they can share what they've written and remind the team what was captured. This is helpful if you're looking to do two fast rounds of popcorn brainstorming because effectively at half-time, when the team are individually sharing their ideas with others, it can stimulate further thinking for the second lot of two minutes of popcorn brainstorming.

The other method is to have people simply shout out ideas and one or a number of scribes capture the ideas on a whiteboard. This is generally more challenging for scribes and facilitators because they have to manage the capturing of thoughts of the team and likely won't be able to add their own ideas. In comparison, the first method mentioned above means the team themselves are capturing their thoughts and are still sharing them vocally as they capture them. You'd look to use this second method if you sense there are not too many ideas among the team, or they need help to stimulate their thinking.

Silent Brainstorming

The technique I use for silent brainstorming is to make sure that each team member has a pad of sticky notes and a marker pen. They need to know they have a set period of time to capture all the ideas that they can – one per sticky note.

The facilitator sets the timer for a length of time, usually two or three minutes. As a tip: I often have music playing softly in the background during that time to act as some white noise. Before the team starts, it is important the facilitator makes it clear that if any of them exhaust themselves of ideas before the time is up, that they don't talk – the key is that it stays silent, so others aren't being distracted as they capture their ideas.

At the end of that time (I often provide the team with a 30-second warning so they can capture their last couple of ideas before the time lapses) the team then take turns to individually stand up and present those ideas. It is important during this presenting and sharing process that they don't spend time justifying the ideas and that they are literally just reading out what is on their sticky note and keeping it short (a five-second explanation per sticky note) and to the point. We are not evaluating the ideas, we're trying to stimulate ideas, which is a principle that the facilitator will need to reinforce during this brainstorming process.

Don't Look for the Perfect Solution

Often, when we delay implementing 'better' for the perfect solution (which doesn't exist), it's really a form of procrastination and is under-pinned by a lack of courage. Never wait for the perfect solution. If your team have a solution now that is better than what was in place and it positively affects a root cause, take it. Take better every time.

This is only a short section in this book, but the impact of this single point is huge. It is crucial that the team know that we are not looking for perfect – we are looking for substantially better. There's a world of difference between the two, especially in terms of impact. Looking for substantially better gets improvements done earlier, whereas looking for perfect stagnates the whole improvement process, more than likely, with fiery debates in the mix.

Continuous improvement is about continually closing the gap between how we are currently performing and where perfection is.

A BETTER MINDSET FOR SOLUTION DEVELOPMENT

Too often teams become unstuck because they focus on developing a perfect solution, unanimously agreed on across the team. We can't know the quality of a solution until it is tested. What they should be focusing on is not developing perfect solutions, but developing *what could prove to be a solution* to be tested in pilots. It might sound like a subtle difference, but the effect of each approach is very different.

Frequently, teams define a solution as a fail-safe improvement rather than what it should be to actually enable progress – an idea likely to prove to be successful and needs to be tested.

Having teams focus on things to be tested to understand the impact is much faster than having a team reach a consensus on a solution. This mindset quickly enables progress to test and understand the value of their collective ideas. Of course, the more the ideas for improvement are based on the data of performance and thorough understanding of the problem and the root causes of that problem, the better the likelihood of a significant positive impact of the solution being tested.

We don't need consensus across the team that what is about to be piloted will prove to be a solution, and further, not all of the team need to agree that a specific solution should be piloted – as that would reduce the number of pilots that would run and inhibit the discovery of what does and does not work as a solution. To determine the value of a solution, the focus needs to be on enabling potential solutions to undergo a pilot.

If the testing of a solution is ensured to be safe during a pilot, the team (or a portion of it) can proceed with testing. The performance data from these tests will reveal the extent to which the solution works and whether the improvement is significant.

In essence, this approach aims to bypass lengthy discussions on the potential success of a solution and instead focuses on efficiently setting up elements for testing. It's like the saying 'the proof is in the pudding' – understanding how something works by testing it, rather than engaging in discussions about the untested solution's efficacy.

Achieving a balance is crucial, ensuring the design of what to test in a pilot is complemented by careful consideration of how to conduct the test. Teams too often expend considerable energy seeking consensus on solution design. You need to lead the shift from the focus of debating the potential success of a solution to determining how to pilot it to find out.

Tip: The effect of change is not measured by its size but by its measurable impact. Small adjustments can yield significant results. Regardless of size, changes should be assessed by their impact on reducing pain points in the process, such as the frequency and impact of events causing a loss of capacity. If even a small change significantly addresses this loss of capacity, that's the true measure of its impact.

153

Testing the Proposed Solution Addresses a Root Cause

You'll already know this: a simple test for knowing if your solution positively impacts on the root cause is if the solution reduces the frequency of a problem occurring or increases the rates of success. If so, the solution is targeting the root cause – so it is a good solution. It won't be a perfect solution, as it almost certainly won't absolutely resolve (meaning reduce to zero) all of the issues, but as long as the solution has proven to affect significantly better performance, then that solution is good to implement.

Conversely, if the frequency of the problems or the success rate continues, but the solution instead improves by reducing the impact to the organisation, then you haven't taken care of a root cause but have instead found a solution that improves the symptoms and the impact of the incidents. That's better than having no solution, but certainly not as good as having a solution that works on the root cause.

How we can test, and thereby know the efficacy of the solution, is through running a pilot.

PILOTING SOLUTIONS

Piloting is used to prove if the designed solution works and can often be the first opportunity to understand the estimated benefits that this solution will provide.

As has been mentioned, running a pilot must involve the customer component. To fulfil this means that:

- you understand the solutions impact on the customer, and/or
- the customer is involved in the testing of the solution in the pilot itself, and
- you capture the right data during the pilot, so you know the holistic impact on the customer, which is central to the efficacy of the developed solution.

Only when the pilot proves that the solution is effective and provides considerable benefits do we look to implement the solution. And that's the core value of running a pilot; you get insight on the impact of the designed solution before dedicating more resources to implement it organisation-wide. Having the right measures captured during the pilot is crucial for this.

Also, good benefit realisation practice is to ensure that you have captured the necessary baseline data to know the effectiveness of any solution that we are piloting. I would like to make a final point on an often-misunderstood aspect of the purpose of pilots. As much as pilots are used to prove the efficacy of a solution, they can be used more widely than that to simply test a thought, a new way of doing things to see what we can learn. So, we might find ourselves testing something that we don't believe to be a solution, but *we do believe we will learn something vital from*. It's crucial that we think of pilots offering this width of application because running pilots helps us transition from how we're currently performing to how we can perform better, whether we are testing a solution, or simply testing an idea where there's going to be a valuable learning experience, aiding future solution development.

A New Lens to Look at Ideas and Potential Solutions Through

I was supporting a team who were debating the merits of an idea, but they were having the wrong debate – instead of discussing how they could trial the idea, they were discussing the likely outcome of the idea, as if it could be predicted. It can't.

I was able to get them to agree to test the idea, not by convincing them it was a good idea, but that trying the idea was a good thing to do.

One of the greatest consequential costs to your organisation is that of good ideas being lost. Too many good ideas are dismissed, killed off before their benefits are known. Losing good ideas means lost revenue, lost opportunities to decrease expenses and a higher turnover of quality staff who are far more likely to disengage with an organisation which isn't moving as quickly as they are to make improvements.

Free up your organisation to know the value of the ideas your team are generating. Here are some rules I've developed when facilitating a team to make sure good ideas don't die early:

1. There's no good reason to have *everyone* agree to a good idea.
2. We only know what a good idea is when we actually test our ideas. (Sure, make this step as methodical as you like.)
3. We don't need everyone to agree to test an idea.

Support your organisation's growth by fuelling a culture to courageously but properly and safely test ideas.

Explaining and Defining Pilots

Launching a solution into a process comes with inherent risks. Running a trial or pilot enables the improvement initiative team to mitigate the risks that are exposed and understand what the real value of the solution will be when it is permanently implemented.

A pilot is the trial implementation of the identified solution, or the proposed design, on a reduced scale. The purpose of a pilot is to test the solution under real world conditions to verify design assumptions versus actual performance.

Setting up and running a trial or pilot is a complex and often intensive piece of work, but it's crucial to providing insight into the effectiveness of the solution before implementing it across an organisation.

The elements which contribute to a robust and effective pilot plan are:

- a clear and concise documented purpose and scope for the pilot
- set pilot success and evaluation criteria – state what would constitute a successful pilot of the solution, such as 'reducing the occurrence of errors by 40%'. This will help manage expectations and perceptions
- a data collection plan, as collecting the right data will provide crucial insight on the effect of the piloted solution
- potential problem analysis and risk management plans, i.e. what is likely to go wrong if there is a failure? What actions will we then take? How will we decide if we need to stop the pilot?

These questions apply to both preconceived and unforeseen circumstances

- a verification plan and review, i.e. planning time to review how the pilot went against the established evaluation criteria
- a communication plan, including who to consult with before the pilot, and who to inform after the pilot
- a schedule and workplan to set up for the pilot. The workplan will include the training needing to be done for the participants to support the pilot and the wider workplan. Team members need to be well trained.

BENEFITS OF A PILOT

The key benefits of running a pilot are to:

- test the solution without committing the entire organisation, which mitigates the risk of unforeseen and unintended effects
- gather insight into the likely failure points of an organisation-wide implementation of a solution. Although high-quality planning will reduce the occurrence and severity of failures, it's unlikely to eliminate all failures, so a pilot will help to identify failure points and any unintended consequences of the solution
- optimise the solution's design so risks are reduced and the effectiveness of the solution is increased further before a full-scale roll-out
- validate benefit estimates of the solution
- get organisational and stakeholder buy-in by demonstrating the success of the solution or giving assurance of improvements made to ensure future success
- offer the opportunity to evaluate the effectiveness of measures used to monitor the process, as having good measures is critical for ensuring the success of our processes.

Differentiate between the features and the benefits of a solution being piloted. For example, part of the improvements might be a new visual board for team stand-up meetings. Having a visual board, as a feature of the pilot, isn't in itself a benefit, but how the visual board is used is – as is the resulting impact on the team through the usage of the visual board – is the benefit. The visual representation and daily focus on performance data means that we can improve our performance fast in, for example, reducing negative customer experiences – that is the benefit that comes from the visual board.

Whenever we talk about benefits, we should also mention risks. Risks associated with the solution we are piloting should be regularly reviewed, updated and risk status reported to the benefits owner, improvement initiative governance and key stakeholders of that benefit where appropriate.

COURAGEOUS PILOTS

Sometimes we need to consider courageous piloting – knowing what you're prepared to find out during the pilot rather than delaying the pilot for what's perceived to be the perfect solution. After all, the pilot is what will tell us both the performance of the solution *and* offer crucial insight of how to improve the performance of the solution. What that means is, appreciating that you won't be in a position to pre-determine all the results of what you're about to pilot before you pilot, so you choose to demonstrate enough courage to know that there are some things you are prepared to find out during the pilot.

Too often teams delay pilots until what they perceive are the perfect conditions. Perfect conditions are few and far between, if they even exist at all, so it is often better to courageously pilot potential solutions in imperfect current conditions rather than delay. After all it is a pilot – we are looking to test something in normal conditions.

DETERMINING WHICH SOLUTIONS TO TEST DURING THE PILOT

There can be a bit of debate and conjecture on whether you should pilot all your solutions separately to understand the impact of each solution, or pilot them together. It simply comes down to whether or not you need to know the impact of each of the solutions separately.

If you don't need to know the individual impact then you will likely pilot the solutions together, where the overall result is more important – especially so if the solutions are complementary and none individually will have any negative effect.

For example, if you are looking to improve your personal energy levels and you want to pilot two improvements, one each around sleep and nutrition, then you can pilot them independently to understand each of their impact, but conversely, in making the decision that it's not about them separately but about their impact on improving energy levels, you might run a pilot with better solutions around sleep and better solutions around nutrition simultaneously to understand the net effect that those solutions will have on your energy levels.

Solutions that need to be run independently of each other would only be done if there's purpose in understanding the individual impact of each of the variables (solutions). In this case, for speed, your team might run one solution with one group of customers and a second solution with a second group of customers, and potentially both solutions with a third group of customers. This approach provides you with an opportunity to understand, if you need to, the individual impact of each solution while running the pilots simultaneously, saving time.

BUILDING THE PILOT TO TEST SOLUTIONS

Here are the elements that you need to consider to help build and run good pilots.

Determining How Long to Run the Pilot

A fundamental reason for running a pilot before launching a solution organisation-wide is often there are people that are reticent about supporting the pilot or are blatantly dismissive of the proposed solution to be piloted, and the pilot itself is a solution for those emotions.

The fact that you're conducting a pilot indicates a test of the solution's effectiveness before its full implementation. This means that even if some individuals in your organisation are hesitant to adopt the proposed solution, very few should impede the testing process through the pilot phase, which becomes your strategy. You want to clearly communicate to stakeholders that instead of an immediate implementation, the focus is on piloting the solution only, which will alleviate many worries.

Now that you're looking to run a pilot, there are a few factors to have in mind when you set the time period for running it. A healthy pilot needs to be long enough to capture a minimum of four natural cycles of the process. If process data shows the average cycle lasts about seven days, then we would look to run the pilot for four cycles of that, meaning a pilot of 28 days-plus.

Running a pilot for four cycles provides our team with sufficient opportunity to test and even improve the solution at least a few times during the pilot. It could look like this: the first cycle is simply about ensuring that the pilot is working properly – those in the pilot are following the new solution to make sure that it is being tested properly. The second cycle might be the opportunity to see if there are changes that can be made through the insights of the performance data – if there is something that can be improved or adapted in the pilot. We can also look to make minor improvements to the solution at the end of the third and fourth cycles.

Further, by running a pilot for the length of four cycles, that helps take into account that each cycle is the average time of the natural process. Some of the solutions we might be testing are to help take care of the longer incidences of the process, so even though the average process time might be seven days, some of the longer experiences in our baseline data might be 14, 15 or 16 days, and the solution being tested might specifically focus on alleviating or eliminating those longer examples. Again, this is why a minimum pilot duration of four cycles should be considered.

You need to be clear about how long you want to run the pilot for and what will be the start and finish time of the pilot. As a quick tip, the finish date needs to be defined in terms of what 'finish' means – the date you complete the capture and compile all the performance data to then make a decision whether you:

1. Continue the pilot, so it starts to become the new process standard.
2. Make further changes to the pilot while you continue the pilot, or
3. Decide to go back to the previous process – essentially pre-pilot state (this would only be considered if the pilot proved to significantly negatively impact performance).

But the key point is this: the finish date of the pilot is not (and should rarely be) defined as meaning that the team automatically reverts to the previous process if the pilot is proving to be very successful. That risks being incredibly disruptive for the process, the teams facilitating the process, and potentially the customer experience. The end of the pilot is a decision point where you validate the performance of the solution and decide on the path forward once you have the data and the full view of the performance of the solution during the pilot.

Don't think of the finish date, though it is defined, as a hard finish. The finish date might reflect the point where you can thoroughly and properly review the impact of the solution – more than the date on which the pilot stops. It might be a case of the pilot working so well you want it to keep rolling – essentially as business as usual.

The start date is equally important, informing the stakeholders and the team involved in the pilot plan what preparation and training needs to take place when, prior to, and in relation to the start date.

Determining Measures for the Pilot

Validating the pilot will be the performance of the solution, or the insights gleaned from the testing of an idea. Before the pilot, we also need to determine:

- What data *you* are collecting: convey the metrics being measured and how frequently you will capture the performance metrics during the pilot, who is responsible for capturing what data, and who (stakeholders) it will be delivered to and when.

- The pilot success criteria: state what metric or performance level reached will determine the success of the pilot – how you determine whether the solution is effective. For example, the success criteria might simply be: Reducing the number of occurrences of customer queries by 20%.

As a quick tip, if you and the team think you can reduce customer queries by 40%, don't make that level the success criteria. The success criteria is what validates the solution – think of it more as a minimum level of acceptance of the solution. So, in this case, though we might think pre-pilot that we can reduce customer queries by 40%, we'd only adopt the solution if it reaches a minimum of a 5% improvement. So, the success criteria might be set at 5% or 10%. Certainly, it could be a case of thinking to under-promise and over-deliver, but primarily we are setting and conveying the threshold of which the resulting performance of the solution in the pilot can be deemed to be better, or to be dismissed and the solution not adopted.

Ensure that your team has prepared to capture the pilot performance data needed to holistically understand all the improvements and the benefits of the solution(s).

Teams typically tend to go wrong in setting and measuring the success of a pilot in two ways:

1. The team doesn't temper the expectation that the solution won't be perfect – that it won't absolutely take care of all problems in the process. The solutions need not be perfect, (perfect meaning that the solution(s) solves **all** instances of the problem), as long as the solution offers a level of performance significantly better than what is currently being experienced, then that solution is successful, and in turn, it becomes the new baseline on which to build further solutions on. This is our 'better is good principle' in action. If we have better, and we have proven that we have better, then implement that. Always take better.

2. The team do not properly predetermine the exact measures that need to be monitored and captured during the pilot to

provide insight on the performance impact of the solution being piloted. The only measures needed (as teams usually overburden themselves with too many metrics measures) are to capture changes of the process performance that the solution is looking to improve, and any other elements of the process performance that we can't risk having slide backwards with a new solution. That might include overarching measures of quality or end-to-end timeliness of the process. Measures for the pilot have to include the impact on the customer – or at least the **Voice of the Customer** (VoC).

Key Elements in Pilot Design

These are the key elements which need to be covered to underpin a comprehensive pilot plan:

1. Pilot team:
    -   list of team members involved in the pilot
    -   define their roles, including the involvement of customers (all or a sub-group).
2. Pre-pilot set-up and preparation:
    -   bullet-point list of actions required for pilot preparation
    -   identify action owners
    -   include document creation, training sessions, pre-communications and customer contacts.
3. Potential pilot issues:
    -   summary list of anticipated issues and risks
    -   outline contingency plans and roll-back strategies for significant problems
    -   specify conditions warranting a roll-back of the pilot.
4. Communications and stakeholders:
    -   list stakeholders to be informed during the pilot
    -   specify required information and performance metrics to monitor the pilot
    -   define communication frequency and methods (personal catch ups, email, short video summaries) to deliver the information and performance overviews to the stakeholders.

5. End-of-pilot plan:
   - develop a plan and outline activities for the period between pilot completion (and the data analysis at that point) and solution embedding
   - considerations for transitioning from the pilot to the next phase – scaling up from a smaller pilot group to the wider team
   - address the roles of pilot participants, such as how they might continue or support the piloted process between end-of-pilot and embedding the solution.

Tip: When using customers in your pilot, select those friendly to your organisation. The pilot won't run perfectly. Honest and candid customers aid in making informed improvements and have the integrity to keep the performance of the pilot in-house. Just as crucial as choosing the right team members, the selection of the right customers is equally significant.

Pilot Planning Tool

If you would like to begin developing a pilot plan, or better still, a number of pilot plans across a number of teams, I suggest you set up a session with all teams involved and ask them these questions with the recommended time limits on the questions to write down their answers, which can later be transferred to their pilot plans and save a lot of time.

The team won't get all the questions completely answered, but it will serve as a great starting point for them in a very short space of time – about 45 minutes – and can reduce procrastination. For any question they can't fully answer, they should just note it as this provides them clarity on what to focus on in building the pilot plan.

Utilising the pilot template can help ensure that the teams are properly prepared for their pilot. These questions serve as a fast start in the development of pilot plans.

Question 1: As a team, you might have a number of solutions that you can run a pilot for. You have two minutes to agree on the solution(s) you are going to test in your first pilot.

Whatever you agree, the following questions relate to that or those solution(s).

Question 2: You have two minutes to name the pilot. Make sure the name, though short, meaningfully captures the purpose of the pilot.

Question 3: You have three minutes to write down (in a few sentences):

- the purpose of the pilot
- the solution or solutions being tested
- the root cause of the problem.

   Tip for the team: One sentence could suffice, for example: the purpose of the pilot is to improve the problems of x by testing our solution of y which looks to address the root cause of z of the problem.

Question 4: You have three minutes to list all the benefits you expect to see from the pilot and accompany each benefit with the metric you'll measure each with.

Question 5: You have two minutes to determine the pilot success criteria. First, determine the level of success as a percentage change you think you'll experience for each of the metrics/ benefits you are capturing, and then where you'd set the percentage as the pilot success criteria.

Question 6: You have three minutes to determine if:

a. you have captured baseline performance data to accompany and to compare to each of the metrics you've captured in the previous two questions
b. if not, what baseline data needs to be captured before the pilot is run?

Question 7: For each of the metrics/benefits you are capturing; you have three minutes to determine how you will collect the data in the pilot:

- What is the high-level process to capture the data? Is there to be a difference in the collection of the data of the pilot from that of the baseline, or will it be the same?
- How often will you capture the data?
- Who will capture the data or what team will capture the data?

Question 8: You have three minutes to list everyone involved in the pilot team – capture their name and their role in the pilot.

Question 9: You have two minutes to list those people that are not part of the pilot team, but as stakeholders, need to be informed about pilot progress.

Question 10: You have two minutes to list potential issues that would cause the pilot to be stopped.

Question 11: You have three minutes to pick and focus on the most likely issue and determine the high-level steps to stop and roll back the pilot.

Question 12: You have three minutes to list/bullet point all the other things that need to be considered and completed before the pilot can start. Things like:

- documents that need to be produced to support the pilot
- training planned and conducted for which teams
- communications, release dates
- customers that need to be contacted prior to the pilot.

To see the template for the full pilot plan, where the team can later hone their answers from the above, see Appendix 4.

GETTING THE SIGN-OFF FROM THE SPONSOR TO RUN THE PILOT

Before the pilot goes live, have the sponsor and process owner approve the pilot plan and commit to supporting it as needed, especially during the pilot phase.

Questions for the Sponsor

The questions in this section will help the sponsor fulfil the purpose of the meeting, which is to feel comfortable with and endorse the pilot and will help the sponsor to:

- understand the purpose of the pilot – what the team are looking to learn and what data will be captured
- understand the degree of impact on capacity in the process with the running of the pilot and over what period of time that capacity will be impacted
- understand that the pilot is ready to go and the improvement initiative team and those with roles in the pilot can be unleashed to run it now
- be assured that the pilot will be run safely.

This approach provides a suitably light but necessary and comprehensive approach to endorsing the team to start the next stage: running the pilot.

Remember, continuous improvement takes courage, and that means letting some things go. By the time of the pilot endorsement, there will much detail about the improvement initiative that you won't know because you've shown courage in your leadership to let the team get on with the work – so all you need to know is that the team have determined the root cause through good data capture, the solution addresses the root cause, and there is a focus on the benefits to our customers at the core of the solution.

Questions for Sponsors to Endorse the Pilot

The sponsor should pose these questions when approving the pilot, and the team should prepare to address them during the endorsement meeting. The sponsor isn't required to ask all these questions if they believe the criteria for endorsement has been met.

Because these questions add value and help the improvement team and the sponsor know what is being worked on during the stage and what needs to be done to ensure they're doing the right things in that stage, I'd suggest that both the team and the sponsor have and prep for these questions, not only for the catch-up to approve the pilot, but also early on to assist with the design of the pilot.

Purpose:

- What's the purpose of the pilot, the solution being tested and the root cause of the problem?

Data/information:

- Have you captured baseline data or does the baseline data already exist? And is that baseline data comprehensive enough that we can compare it to the insights and performance of the pilot which you will supply me (as the sponsor)?
- What are the benefits you are expecting to see from the pilot and how will you measure each benefit(s)?
- What is the pilot success criteria? What level of success as a percentage are you expecting for each of the metrics/benefits you are capturing?
- How often will you capture the data and what data will be interesting for me to be across and how frequently? What insights of pilot performance will I be supplied and how frequently?

Operational aspects:

- Who are the other stakeholders that are not part of the pilot team but need to be informed about pilot progress?
- What are the potential issues that you will monitor, which would stop the pilot if they occurred?
- Is there anything else that you need to set up? What support do you need from me or others for this pilot to be successful? (This question must be asked.)

- Are the full team running the pilot ready to go right now, so we can start the pilot at the first opportunity?

Sponsor tip: When leading a team or owning a process, avoid suggesting opposing or alternative solutions during this stage. Instead, enquire about the team's chosen pilot to gain a deeper understanding of their decision and the underlying reasons. This supports the culture we want to build. Frame your questions to explore potential solutions considered and assumptions that may have adopted or rejected based on captured data. Remember, the purpose of the pilot team might be either to solve a problem or to learn something to help later solve the problem. Focus on assisting the team in identifying what they aim to learn, the data they will collect, and ensuring the safe execution and evaluation of effects on capacity over time.

Tips for Running a Pilot

- Don't ever skip a pilot! The safety and insights a pilot offers before full implementation of a solution can't be overstated.
- Piloting some solutions early is better than a significant delay so that all solutions can be piloted together. Decide which solutions are in scope to be piloted now – solutions that are out of scope will be tested later, rather than holding up what is in scope to be piloted now.
- As the improvement initiative leader, make sure you have little to do during the pilot, so you are free to monitor the performance and do what is needed when it is needed. Despite the thoroughness of the planning, surprises requiring swift action will happen. This is effectively a monitoring role, and your capacity needs to be free for those who need it and issues that need to be resolved.
- Define and widely convey success criteria before testing the pilot to clearly express and manage expectations.
- Capture data daily initially in the pilot, especially if your team are depending on others to capture performance data, so you

can test early on the quality of the data being captured and make improvements to the data capture.

- Conduct daily performance reviews and updates of the pilot with the team. Consider those stakeholders who you might include in the reviews and updates.
- Your focus is piloting the solution to test the impact of the solution, not initially how well the solution can be adopted and embedded through the wider organisation. The first focus is to make sure that the solution works, so make sure you pilot it with people who understand and can test the solution – a handpicked team to be part of the pilot is absolutely fine. At this stage, you are not testing if everyone in the organisation can adopt the solution, making the pilot unnecessary hard while you're still testing whether the solution works. Your first step is to understand that the solution works, so pilot it with the most appropriate and engaged team first. When you know that the solution works, then your next challenge in the embed stage is to determine how to embed the solution across the entire organisation.
- Remember to celebrate a pilot that meets its success criteria. A good pilot reflects a lot of good work that has been done.

POST PILOT

Having run a successful pilot where the team have produced a proven, high-quality solution(s) ready to embed, you need to celebrate that, at least with the core improvement team that have produced this result. Here's what else you need to do post pilot to prepare to embed the solution.

How You Know if You Have a Solution

You know that you have a solution only when:

1. It is proven to be working better than the previous level of performance, and

2. You understand why it works better – why the performance
   has improved.

The solution's superiority is established through comparison to
the previously captured baseline of performance. The capture of
your baseline will prove to be pivotal for gauging the success level
of the piloted solution. By measuring the new performance against
this baseline, we can accurately assess and prove the solution's
effectiveness.

You understand why it works better as you don't want your
improvements to come about because of luck. The more luck plays
a role in a successful pilot, the more likely you'll experience varied
performance in any implemented solution after the pilot; simply,
luck won't last. That's why it is crucial that we understand why the
solution works better, so we have the insights about what it is that
we need to control to determine the beneficial outcomes.

As much as we can, we want to understand the levers of
performance, that is, all the factors that determine performance,
which the solution in turn addresses. If something is better and we
don't understand why, we might choose to keep it in place, but by
not understanding why the solution is working better opens us up
to risks and consequence. The risk being that performance may
unexpectedly regress or collapse, and that we are not likely able to
hone the solution for better further performance.

Because the solution piloted has proven to be successful – and
you know exactly why it has – you can now build a plan to embed
the solution.

Decision Criteria for Post-pilot Implementation

Since you have already determined the success criteria for the pilot,
stakeholders tasked with deciding whether or not the pilot becomes
standard practice will find it easier to make that decision at the
end of the pilot. This helps maintain focus on the initial reasons for
conducting the pilot in the first place.

Not having predefined decision criteria and performance
expectations for the pilot increases the risk of the improvement

initiative team grappling with a broader range of ideas and conjectures about what the pilot should have addressed. It also opens the possibility of others, particularly those dissatisfied with the pilot, measuring its success against their own criteria.

Both these situations leave what might prove to be an effective solution vulnerable to being dismissed solely for personality or political reasons.

We can only (sensibly) embed a solution when we know that we have a good solution – and the pilot offers us that insight. Here, we look to formally review the performance of the solution in the pilot with the sponsor and the process owner, and if the pilot has proven to be successful, we can start to plan how we embed the piloted solution(s).

Questions for the Sponsors to Start the Embed Stage

These are the questions for the sponsor, indicating their endorsement of the pilot results (i.e. the solution) and seeking approval to initiate the planning for embedding the solution. The focus is on obtaining the green light to commence the preparation for the embedding stage.

- What were the results of the piloted solution, and did you meet the pilot success criteria?
- Did the solution address a root cause?
- What were the benefits for our customers?
- Did you experience any unexpected benefits or any dis-benefits?
- What is the general plan to embed the solution and training requirements, and over what period of time?
- What are the risks of embedding this solution to the wider team or organisation?
- Is the process owner across all the benefits, dis-benefits and risks of embedding this solution? And do they approve of embedding this solution?
- Now that the pilot has ended, what is the plan for the application of the solution and the team that was involved

in using the solution in the pilot between now and when the solution is embedded?
- When would you suggest that we start to embed the solution?
- What help is needed from the senior leadership team?
- What help and support do you need from me to support your planning of the embed stage?

Embed Plan Template

Once the team have approval, they can move swiftly into planning how to embed the solution. The purpose of the embed plan is to capture and plan what is needed to transition the solution from the pilot stage to embed the solution throughout the organisation. This plan is focused on enabling that transition.

Once this plan is built, it is shared with the sponsor to endorse to start the final stage of the improvement initiative, which is the embedding of the solution in teams or throughout the organisation.

A full template can be found in Appendix 5, but here is a quick overview of the core components:

- **Training plan**: who will be trained and when, and what are the resource requirements of that training?
- **Continual tracking** of performance data to ensure continuous improvement of performance.
- **Visual representation** of the ongoing process performance.
- **Continual tracking** of benefits realised.
- **Stakeholder updates of this performance data and benefits:** which stakeholders will be updated with what information and how frequently?
- **Ongoing ownership and handover:** what else do you need to do to hand over the new process to the team and the process owner?

Once you have approval of the pilot success and you can start to plan to embed the solution you can move to the embed stage. There are a couple of challenges in the embed stage you need to determine, including how you are going to scale your solution if others outside the pilot team need to adopt the new process.

You also need to ensure the integrity of the new process, meaning that you design the process as well as you can to ensure that, as much as possible, it's incredibly easy to follow and perform. The more that a good process is consistently performed across a team, the more consistently you'll have better process performance and the less variation the team and the customer will experience, making life easier for all.

CHAPTER 7

Embedding Proven Solutions

The purpose of this stage is to properly embed the proven solutions and, in doing so, set an environment where the team, with their continuous improvement capabilities and new behaviours, can monitor (knowing what the performance should look like) and improve the performance of the newly improved process.

During the embedding stage, the ownership of the improved process is transferred to the process owner, as well as the capturing of the ongoing benefits of the improved process and the onus to find future improvements to the performance of the process.

What we are aiming for in our improvement initiatives is an outcome where each time the team receive work to perform, they know the process – the best (known) way to perform that work. With the in-built support and safeguards in this process, the team (working in the process) can feel that they can consistently and confidently produce good work, fast – and feel in control of their work. It is these components that we want to embed to complement the devised solution.

The focus of embedding (proven) solutions is to transition the successful practices discovered in the pilot to become the new norm. For the wider team, we are looking to embed the better process so they, too, can experience:

- fluency over frustration
- progress over procrastination
- performance over problems.

This stage is about embedding that proven process so we can, as we follow the process, safely trust that the process is providing us better performance and making life easier for our team and our customers.

IMPLEMENTING CHANGE

Improvement initiative teams can frequently make the mistake of prematurely thinking they've reached the finish line with a proven solution via the pilot, leading to a risk of failing to properly embed that solution. Teams could over-celebrate, assuming their solution is successful, and may then take their eye off the ball, believing they have completed the journey. Crucially, it is the most impactful work that begins at this point.

Until now, the improvement in performance was more a vision. The pilot phase has successfully proven this vision, but it is during the embedding stage that we truly realise the substantive benefits of the solution.

The good news is that your team has already completed a significant portion of the work required for the embedding process by developing and proving the solution's positive impact in the pilot phase. This proactive approach has front-loaded much of the necessary work before reaching the embedding stage.

Unlike teams that develop a solution and immediately move to embed it, your team, having piloted and validated the solution, faces a less challenging embedding stage. While there's still substantial work in this stage, entering it with the momentum gained from the successful pilot and armed with performance data significantly streamlines the embedding process.

At this point, the focus shifts from the initial vision to the transition. A vision holds little value without the ability to execute a successful transition. Developing a solution and proving its efficacy marks the initiation of any continuous improvement initiative.

176

The next, and more significant level of benefits begins with the implementation and embedding of the solution. The crucial tasks involve getting the solution adopted and maintaining the commitment to continually monitor performance for the sole purpose of further improvement.

Change Management

A great and effective concept to use with change management is $E = Q \times C$, a concept introduced to me by George Lee Sye (Lee Sye 2022), where the effectiveness (E) of the improvement initiative's implementation of the solution = Quality (Q) of the solution × Commitment (C) of the people to that solution.

I love this because it rightly points out that a huge component of the measure of the effectiveness of a solution is its acceptance, that people are willing to perform it and are committed to it. With no acceptance as commitment, the effectiveness of the solution is also nil.

Change management takes work, but how much work it takes can depend on a few vital variables. One is a principle that we have already discussed – having the right people develop the right solutions. When we think of change management, at its core (in our process improvement context) as the effort in affecting a team to absorb a new way of performing their work, it is far easier for teams to adopt the new practices that they have determined and developed themselves. That's why the principle of having the right people develop the solutions is so important. Additionally, when we're looking to embed solutions across the wider organisation, we have that team that developed the solutions share the solution with their peers, which is also advantageous.

We should be aware of other factors, like regional parochialism, where reluctance to accept ideas from one region may arise not due to the quality of the solution or necessary regional adaptations, but simply because of parochialism. It's surprising that such a factor exists, but it does.

If this might be a challenge for your team, there are ways around it, such as bringing someone from other regions on-site to either be trained in the solution to then convey back to their team or involving the other team earlier in the improvement initiative as part of the problem definition and solution development.

Another variable is showing and sharing the improvement data. Anything implemented will be judged and discussed, with or without the element of data. People will infer, judge and convey their opinions so it's important to share the facts of performance improvement early. Communicate to the stakeholders when they can expect the first performance data – the sooner the better – how frequently, and to whom that performance data will be sent. Then, of course, get that data out on time with a commentary sharing the interpretation of the data and comparison against what was experienced previously. Failing to provide performance data may lead to speculation and conjecture. This data will be the first full and accurate view of performance.

In messaging, as it was with the pilot, reiterate that the solution is not there to resolve all incidents but reduce the number of incidents or the severity of the incidents when they occur, or both. Again, this helps set the right expectations because otherwise the wider team will determine their own success criteria, which they will measure the perceived performance against. If the performance they perceive is less than their success criteria, there will be disappointment and a perception of failure. If we don't establish clear success criteria for the embedded solution – reflecting our experiences in the pilot – teams and individuals might fall into binary thinking that the solution worked perfectly, or it failed (which they might actually want to see).

This tendency becomes pronounced when there's a bias against the solution, leading them to consider it a failure if it doesn't completely resolve the problem. Unfair assessments of your team's solution complicate the task of gaining commitment from the wider team. To tackle this, it's crucial to proactively present performance data and a commentary on how it measures up against the pre-set success criteria. The evaluation of the solution's effectiveness will be judged, so it's about pre-empting any premature assessments with actual performance data.

As well as informing your wider organisation of the improvements and the effectiveness of those improvements, also inform your customers. If your team have made customer-centric improvements, convey to your customers the improvements you've made on the back of their feedback. This offers a number of benefits:

1. The customers know that they are not only valued but that your team has actively listened and responded to their feedback – this serves as validation for their input.
2. You are checking in that what you've done has manifested as a difference for your customers. There is a chance that you have done a whole lot of work in the organisation to improve their experience, but you need to know that they feel it. If they haven't, then nothing has changed in their mind, and the key reason they're considering stopping being our customer remains.

As you capture and convey the performance of the implemented solutions to the team and customers, the next step involves validating and articulating the benefits through the element of benefit realisation.

Sponsor Approval to Embed the Solution

Once the detailed and comprehensive plans for the embed stage (initiated at the end of the pilot) are developed, your next step is to have the sponsor understand and endorse the embed plan, providing guidance and support for the team's execution.

Here are questions for the subsequent review with the sponsor (and process owner) to secure their approval, marking the final checkpoint before full implementation:

- What are the high-level elements/tasks of the embed plan to be performed, and in what order will they be performed (such as: documentation, training, tracking of benefits, etc.)?
- What is the detailed timeline for embedding the solution, specifying the start date? This should encompass:

- ~ the training plan, outlining who will conduct the training, the resources required, and the scheduled training sessions
- ~ the mechanisms in place to track and monitor the ongoing benefits derived from the improvement
- ~ how this plan will ensure the improvement is continually improved by the team (in the work) who now owns the improvement.
- What metrics did you measure in the pilot that you should embed to continuously monitor performance? How will you know if performance drops below the new expected performance levels?
- What are the ongoing measures of performance to ensure the ongoing integrity of this solution?
  - ~ How often will they be reported on to stakeholders?
  - ~ Who will receive the reported performance? (Stakeholders being updated.)
  - ~ How will the measures of ongoing performance be visually displayed?
- What are the risks of embedding this solution to the wider team or organisation, and how are you monitoring those risks?
- Which stakeholders will be updated with what information and how frequently through the embedding of the solution?
- What else needs to be done to hand over the new process to the team (in the process) and the process owner?
- (After the decision, if yes, to go ahead and embed) What do you need from the senior leadership team to help you with embedding this solution? What help and support do you need from me for this embed stage?

As a significant step, when you have the go ahead to affect the plan of the embed stage, simply start to embed the solution as per your plan.

That above sentence is probably the single most important one in this whole book. Up to now, we've effectively made no change to the organisation. Now, we have the go-ahead and are starting to make a change that we know, through all the previous stages leading up to here, will be effective.

There are a few key things that the improvement team will likely experience during the embed stage that they might not have during the pilot stage – and that the team need to be aware of:

- The one-in-a-thousand events that didn't happen in the pilot (simply because of the size of the pilot) will more likely happen in the embed stage.
- You will likely be dealing with a lot more people in the embed stage than were in the pilot – so it will demand more energy. This is a tough stage made easier through knowing that you have a proven solution that can work and the data to back it up – that will help with change management – and the easing of it.
- Because of this increased workload, make sure that the team are refreshed and ready to go before this stage starts.
- Take your time with planning at this stage as it's even more important because of the one-in-a-thousand events.
- Like you did in the pilot, make sure that the improvement initiative leader is free during this stage to monitor the progress and performance of the embed stage and has capacity to deal with unexpected problems, which will likely and naturally occur.
- You have the sponsor on board to help. Remember, their key role is to remove barriers and clear a path – that's still their role and the help you'll likely need.

Embedding Change With the Right Measures

By this stage, you and your team have a lot of insightful measures of performance. The measures were starting to be developed as you mapped the process and captured performance on steps in the process, and the measures were refined through the pilot stage to holistically understand the performance of the solution.

Now, as you embed the solution, the question is: what measures from your pilot need to continue so the performance can be continually improved? Determine what those measures are, who will capture them, how they will be displayed, who they will be sent to, and how frequently they will be captured and updated.

The truth is, there is no finish line. And that's the right mindset and why we continually improve. Setting up the key measures of performance, which we've discovered through the improvement process and homed in on in our pilot, will help provide the crucial insights of where to continuously improve.

Represent these performance metrics on a visual board and distribute on a mini dashboard – both for the team in the work to see and the stakeholders of the process performance.

Simply determine who is collecting which performance data, who is converting that data to build the visual representation of the performance, who will send out the mini dashboard to the stakeholders, who will update the visual board with the visualisation of the performance data, and how frequently all this will be performed – build the whole dynamic and anchor it, perhaps by setting reoccurring reminders in the calendars of task owners to perform these actions.

Tip: Ensure your dashboard includes a blend of measures – some from the pilot and some new ones. This mix is crucial for supporting team behaviours and ensuring the dashboard data accurately reflects current performance. For example, if the dashboard shows chargeable hours, consider also measuring the accuracy of hour capture. Monitoring how well the team inputs chargeable hours (which might not appear on the dashboard) provides insights into the integrity of the data for performance metrics related to chargeable hours.

POST-IMPROVEMENT AND EMBEDDING REFLECTION

In this stage, post the embedding of the solution, we look to review how we did, what we can learn (for the next loop) and how we'll capture the ongoing benefits of this improvement and further improvements made by those in the process.

Session: Review the Improvement Initiative

The purpose of this session is to glean insights as a team of what we can learn from this improvement initiative for the next one. It aims to cover a spectrum of elements, ranging from the dynamics and capabilities of the improvement team to the development and quality of the solution, and the performance of the embedding of the solution. The goal is to identify the team's efforts that warrant repetition in future initiatives and strengthen those aspects of the initiative where there's scope to improve.

There are four main questions the team should ask themselves:

1. What did we set out to do? (Or: What were we trying to achieve?) Note: There will be a number of things in this list, it won't just be one element.
2. Did we do it? (Or: Did we get it done?)
3. What was the difference? (Or: Why did we not get it done?)
4. What would we do differently next time? (Or: What did we learn?)

This shouldn't be a long session – something that could and should be knocked out in about an hour. The team are not hunting for a myriad of aspects, more the vital few than the trivial many, as the value is about determining and analysing those aspects that were priorities and making sure we can perform better the next time round.

Here's the process, illustrated in Figure 8:

1. *What did we set out to do?* List all the activities, events and levels of performance that you set out to achieve. You are capturing these points high-level, so you could capture them on sticky notes (using these helps with understanding the space you need when you've captured all the elements, and then I might use a whiteboard to post these and capture the answers to the rest of the questions) or straight onto a whiteboard.
2. Once all the elements are captured, go through each element individually, answering the three further questions in succession:

a. *Did we do it?* You might simply give one of three answers: it was completed, it was only partially completed, or it wasn't completed at all. The labels I use are: Did it, partial, didn't do.

b. Capture what was the gap between *What did we set out to do?* and what was achieved for that element. If the element was completed, then you have nothing you need to add to this element – you achieved what you set out to do. Conversely, if it was only partially completed or not at all done, this is where you capture why that happened – and that is the lesson learnt.

c. Lastly, capture *What would we do differently next time?* – especially for those elements where you didn't meet what you set out to do. Also capture some detail here on those elements you did set out to do and you did achieve. What you're capturing are the vital reasons why it happened, so you know what you should replicate again in the next improvement initiative.

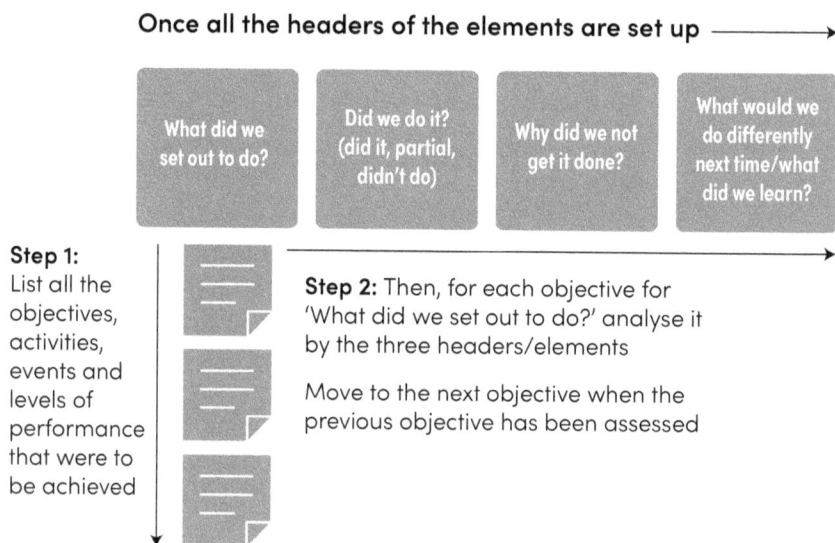

Once all the headers of the elements are set up ⟶

| What did we set out to do? | Did we do it? (did it, partial, didn't do) | Why did we not get it done? | What would we do differently next time/what did we learn? |

Step 1: List all the objectives, activities, events and levels of performance that were to be achieved

Step 2: Then, for each objective for 'What did we set out to do?' analyse it by the three headers/elements

Move to the next objective when the previous objective has been assessed

Figure 8: The review process in action

184

Stakeholders could be included in this session, but I usually run it with the core improvement team so we can be relaxed, candid and honest (as this session is primarily about building their capability) and then share some of our insights later with some stakeholders as needed. An idea could be to run this session out of the office/offsite if it will help the team dynamic and make them feel comfortable.

This is an important learning experience for the team, so a comfortable environment for them to discuss lessons learned is important, as is running this session as early as possible after the process has been handed back to the process owner, so the experiences are fresh in the team's collective memories.

BENEFIT REALISATION

There might well be some appetite to capture and articulate benefits of the improvements that you have experienced. Reasons could be to understand the impact of the improvement made, or to use the improvement story to support and enthuse a wider adoption of continuous improvement in your organisation's culture.

The benefit realisation framework should be central to the justification of the celebration. For the purpose of ongoing continuous improvement, we need to be able to comprehensively capture and articulate the benefits of the work being done.

Why a Benefit Realisation Framework?

The purpose of the benefit realisation framework is to ensure that all positive changes made to the processes and systems are captured and expressed. Benefit realisation frameworks provide us with the opportunity to capture and demonstrate the good work we do – articulated consistently across all projects and process improvements.

The intention is to demonstrate clear links between your organisation's continuous improvement and improvement initiative activity and the benefits experienced by our customers and team as well as the resultant benefits contributing to your organisation's strategies.

Specifically, the framework:

- demonstrates improvement initiatives are delivering outcomes for your organisation's customers
- cements the implementation of good performance measures and monitoring
- improves your ability to show examples of how your team's work has improved customer experiences
- develops continuous improvement practices and capability in your organisation
- helps fuel and sustain a culture of continuous improvement of performance across your team and the organisation
- establishes current state assessment processes that are comprehensive and robust, so benefits can be accurately measured against quantifiable data.

The purpose of this framework is to support your organisation's approach for identification, measurement and articulation of benefits that are delivered as a result of your organisation's work. For a list of key terms in the benefit realisation lexicon, see Appendix 9.

High Level Path of a Benefit Realisation Framework

Our opportunity to capture improvements in performance as quantifiable benefits can only be done with an established current performance baseline, against which all improvements in performance will be compared.

It is crucial for comprehensive benefit realisation that a current performance baseline is captured early on – before any improvements are made.

Benefits are better understood during a pilot of the improvement(s) with the resulting data of performance experienced during that pilot. The capture of performance data post the solution implementation needs to occur on a regular basis – the benefits being the difference in performance from the baseline performance and current performance.

And crucially, benefits need to be publicised to justify and support the change and energise further improvements. Continual improvements that provide benefits need to be part of any organisation's culture.

Aligning Benefits With Strategy

Whatever improvement you are about to launch into, it is best to check and know how it will align with, and contribute to, your organisation's strategies or values.

It's also important that you capture *all* the benefits that come out of an improvement. The following primary measures table provides a comprehensive list of all the improvements that might be available to capture (see the *Examples of elements of primary measures* list).

Often single improvements will have at least two benefits – and it's important that all benefits are captured to reflect the improvement. For example, improving resource and capacity needed to affect the process not only shortens the processing time, but reduces the number of times customers are calling for a progress update (which is a better customer experience), and the resources needed to update the customer. Simply put: improving processing time of customers' applications will be a primary benefit, and a secondary benefit will be a reduction in customer calls to find out how their application is processing.

Refer to the following list to review all potential benefits. Ensure that you capture these benefits for your project or initiative. Additionally, utilise the provided example in the table to map the benefits associated with an improvement, ensuring a comprehensive identification and capture of all potential benefits. Consider these lists as a tool to check verify that every benefit for any improvement initiative has been thoroughly identified and documented. I say every benefit, but likely, the benefits you do capture and prove will only be a subset of all the real benefits – there will be benefits that will be felt by the organisation or customers, but not captured or substantiated. Whatever your team captures will be the minimum benefits – less than the actual benefits.

Setting up a Template to Capture Benefits

Customise your own template (adding to the lists) to include the core values and strategies of your organisation to assist the team in capturing benefits. The template will assist the team to make sure that they are comprehensively capturing and conveying the benefits – not only the positive impact of the benefit, but how it relates to the values and strategy of the organisation.

If the team finds greater motivation towards the organisation's values rather than its strategies, allow them to express the benefits in alignment with these values. If there are other audiences who prefer the benefits to be articulated differently – such as how they support the strategy – let the team focus on expressing the benefits in relation to organisational values initially. Afterward, perform a translation to showcase how these benefits support the organisation's strategies if needed for other stakeholders.

It is important to note that the benefits will inherently align with the strategies, which the team will confirm during the development of the problem statement when they ensured that resolving the problem would align with the organisation's strategy. However, be intentional about who performs this translation and when – if needed. If it doesn't align with the team's enthusiasm for making changes, consider assigning this task to a more suitable party rather than burdening the team initially.

Primary measures:

- Reduction in customer waiting or queuing time.
- Improved customer experiences.
- Reducing rework.
- Reduction of risks and incidents.
- Reduction in working time.
- Reduced wastes (and costs of).
- Building knowledge and capability across your organisation.

Examples of primary measure elements:

- Reduced customer processing and waiting time.
- Reduction of frequency and/or the severity of incidents.

- Changes in quantifiable customer satisfaction rates or staff engagement rates.
- Reduced time and effort for customers to comply with requirements.
- The number of customers impacted by the improvement.
- Reduction of queue waiting times and numbers queued.
- Increased first contact resolution rates.
- Reduction in the number of hand-overs in a process and subsequent reduction of error rates or improvement in speed.
- Fewer incidents of rework (avoidable contacts) for customers.
- Value of capacity (staff time) saved.
- Comparative savings of a new channel for customers over traditional channels and the uptake of the new channels, such as self-service.
- Reduced rework/poor quality due to poor communication with our customers.
- Reduced rework demand – frequency of customers having to call back about the same issue and the amount of time they need to spend to do so, and the capacity soaked up of our team by having to handle the rework.
- Reducing variation of responses back to the customer.
- Improved cross team collaboration to support customer experience.
- Improved error proofing resulting in a reduction of errors and their consequence for our team and customers.
- Capacity gains within a team allowing for greater volume or quality of work to be completed.
- Growth in institutional knowledge.
- Reduced operational costs.
- New measures of performance and the driving of better behaviours.
- Improved and timely reporting for informed decision making.
- Building continuous improvement capability in the organisation.
- User performance and experience.
- Growth in cooperation between teams.

- Reduced number of complaints, time and capacity involved to deal with those complaints.
- Improvements that support our relationships with business partners and providers.
- Reduced reliance on contractors and outsourcing/increased team capability.

BUILD A CASE STUDY OF THE BENEFITS OF THE IMPROVEMENT

A case study is a document that captures the high-level benefits and purpose of an improvement initiative. One of the big benefits of using a case study is how it can be used to facilitate sharing insights that came from the improvement with other teams within the organisation, potentially energising them to make improvements themselves. They might even be able to use the insights to adopt the same improvements for similar benefit.

I would recommend that the case study is a short document – about two pages A4 size. I've noted below possible headings, what's covered in the content and where you have already built that content so it can be copied from the original source to save time. Your organisation might look to build a template for your case studies, and the template might include sections covering:

- **About the process:** short overview of the process – this information can be extracted from the *Process Description* section of the *Improvement Initiative Plan*.
- **The problem we faced:** short overview of the problem – this information can be extracted from the *Process problem statement* in the *Improvement Initiative Plan*.
- **What we expected to achieve:** short list (bullet point) the types of benefits the improvement team were looking to achieve. This information can be extracted from the *Expected outcomes* section in the *Improvement Initiative Plan*, and *The pilot success criteria* from the *Pilot Plan*.
- **How this work aligns to [your organisation's name] priorities:** list both the priorities and how this improvement

supports those priorities. This information can be extracted from the *Aligning with values* section in the *Improvement Initiative Plan*.

- **The solution we proposed:** Overview of the solution and bullet point the root causes that will be addressed by the proposed solution. Add the length of time the pilot was run for. This information can be extracted from the *Pilot overview* section in the *Pilot Plan*.
- **How it went:** fairly substantial section with data on the performance of the solution and comparing the performance against the pilot plan success criteria. Tip: annualise the benefits – what would the benefits look like over a year? For example: the performance in the pilot suggests that we'd save at least 2,230 hours of capacity across the whole team over a year. Capture benefits that were unexpected, such as the reduction of carbon emissions.
- **Ongoing improvement:** share the metrics that will be used to monitor ongoing process performance to enable insight to sustain the new levels of performance and make further performance improvements. Some of these metrics will come from the *What data are we collecting* section in the *Pilot Plan*.
- **Want to know more?** Add a section inviting any reader to engage with the improvement team to learn more about this improvement.

Of course, build the case study template to suit your needs. And if you have access to a graphic designer to take the look of it to the next level, that's certainly handy. If you're looking to build a video overview, do that, and I'd recommend you still build this document first to assist.

Tip: Keep the wording on the case study general and omit sensitive information, so you can share (and in case it is shared) with those outside your organisation, especially other teams in your organisation. If there are benefits that are sensitive, they can be covered in an internal benefit realisation document – of which a case study is essentially a sub-section of.

Celebrate Success

Celebrating success is important for the regeneration of energy in your continuous improvement movement. When good things come from making good changes, it goes without saying that people enjoy it, and they look for ways to make other changes to continue to experience good things. Even the acknowledgement of the positive impact of zero-valued improvements, such as the reduction of waiting days for the customer (which might be of no financial benefit directly to the organisation), is crucial.

Swiftly celebrate success to anchor continuous improvement. While positive changes in work are essential, pairing them with regular celebrations is key. Choose your celebration style, but make it frequent to mirror ongoing success. The principle of *Start smart* by producing fast improvements supports that.

Celebrating improvements is vital for change management, fostering engagement even among past detractors. During celebrations, showcase improvements and benefits with data, express gratitude and highlight behaviours that drove success.

> **Tip:** Use the opportunity of a showcase to convey behaviours that led to improvement and sustained performance, emphasising this in statements like 'Consistent performance of X ensures ongoing benefits like Y. And as a team, we're tracking what underpins the performance of X with measuring Z'.

Navigating Improvement Guilt

Leaders must be conscious that improvement guilt is a very real thing. Despite recent positive improvements in their team's processes, resulting in increased capacity and a more balanced workload, these improvements, where the team find they have more time for quality work, can also bring about an unexpected challenge.

In contrast to their previous overworked selves, team members might start feeling guilty about their freed-up capacity and feel like they are working less. Of course, they're not getting less done, but are simply handling their tasks more efficiently. The feeling of guilt can be unsettling for some, if not all of the team, given how different their experience is compared to when they might have had a backlog of work, and the intense efforts to manage that backlog over the previous months or years.

As leaders, it's essential to acknowledge these emotions and assure the team that they are performing better than they were before (you should have the data to prove this – and the team should see it too) and this efficiency is the expected result of the improvements – and that crucially, with this new efficiency, you now have options that weren't available before. For example, the increased capacity could be substantial enough to explore significant opportunities, such as transitioning to a four-day work week – performing the same work, for the same pay, over 32 hours rather than 40 hours.

PART III
LOOP 2

Loop 2 Map

Understand the current level of performance

1. Build the value chain:
   a. determine the good measures of performance for the steps of the value chain.

2. Focus and notice – what's going on in the organisation. Having insights and performance data on the things to improve:
   a. knowing from customers what to do and what not to do – a better understanding of customer insights
   b. capturing further improvement ideas from the team, from their experiences and validated with data.

Determine why we have the current level of performance

3. Facilitating Gemba – leaders being closer to the work.

4. Analysing the system around a process.

5. Better data analysis.

Develop and pilot solutions

6. Process improvement (with Lean, and other tools and concepts).

7. Good measures and the use of visual boards:
   a. do we have the right performance metrics? Refine the metrics we have: are they lead or lag measures? Are they driving the right behaviours?
   b. the third link – measuring three steps deep.

8. Better piloting.

Embed proven solutions

9. Post-implementation review (applying continuous improvement to improve your team's methodology).

10. Constant review of performance:
    a. dashboards
    b. sustaining the momentum of improvement, into the next loop.

A CALL TO ACTION

Welcome to Loop 2, your team's second venture through a continuous improvement initiative, designed with added detail to match the ambition to tackle more complex problems. Here, we'll further build the capability of your team, with new and complementary skills building on the capability established during Loop 1.

In Loop 1, the focus was on delivering a general understanding of improvement whilst primarily sustaining the appetite for a continuous improvement mindset in your culture. Now, with those successes under your belt, the emphasis shifts to providing your team with more opportunities to refine their continuous improvement skills. While Loop 1 was about getting something done, and done right, Loop 2 is about doing the right things even better and building the team's capability to handle much more complex problems.

Loop 2 is about refining our thinking to make sure what we are working on is purposeful and the appetite to improve specific elements is driven by data.

Energy and desire are often the base fuels for the adopting of continuous improvement.

In this loop, our challenge is to mature our capability.

We'll look to work to make life easier for ourselves and our customers, removing all those things that stop us from being the best we can be.

We'll challenge conventional wisdom, contributing to performance improvement apathy in your organisation.

We'll focus on being relevant in our conversations with data and using data as an assurance to the efficacy for the need to improve, reducing assumptions and opinions being expressed as reality, and the occurrences of anecdotal based changes.

We'll eliminate language where individual teams in organisations isolate themselves from the common purpose and their contribution with other teams to fulfilling that purpose – not 'they' but 'we'; many teams working together with one shared purpose.

We'll recognise that good enough is no longer good enough and evaporate the expression 'this is the way we've always done it' from our vernacular.

We'll build in good measures that drive the right behaviours, hunt out processes without intermediary and lead measures, and add those critical measures in because we can't look to improve what we can't see.

Loop 2 is about refining our thinking to make sure what we are working on is purposeful and the appetite to improve is driven and supported by data.

REVISITING THE METHOD

A good continuous improvement methodology covers four key steps through the improvement process:

1. **Understand** what the current level of performance is.
2. **Determine** the root causes for why we have that current level of performance.
3. **Develop and test solutions** that address those root causes, to improve the performance and prove that the solutions work through piloting and testing.
4. Implement and **embed the proven solutions** with better reporting to highlight the ongoing benefits.

Let's look at each of those steps in more detail for this second loop and your second time through an improvement initiative with this approach.

CHAPTER 8

Understand Your Current Level of Performance

What we'll term the **value chain approach** establishes better measures throughout the organisation's operations so you have a better idea of where you might go next to improve the whole end-to-end performance. Of course, you might engage a number of teams depending on your internal capability to support this and their appetite – still, go where the love is.

BUILD THE VALUE CHAIN

Now that the team have started to share insights, ask questions to look for improvements and cooperate with each other, let's leverage that with working together to make sure that we are all on the same page in terms of the purpose of the organisation and how we contribute to that, individually and collectively.

Encourage the team to collaborate and visually capture the sequence of events involving the customer. This representation should highlight the key components of your interaction with the customer, illustrating the steps that contribute to fulfilling the organisation's purpose. These steps represent critical stages in the customer life cycle, and if executed well contribute significantly to achieving the organisation's purpose. Typically, these involve about 4–8 essential steps and could be something along the lines of:

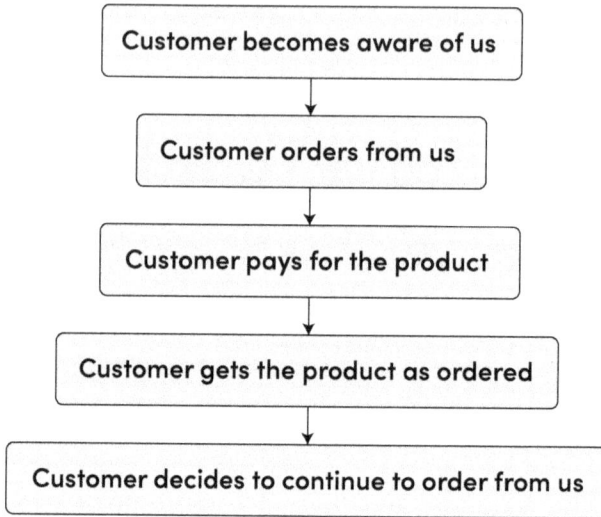

```
┌─────────────────────────────────────┐
│  Customer becomes aware of us        │
└─────────────────────────────────────┘
            │
            ▼
    ┌─────────────────────────────────┐
    │  Customer orders from us         │
    └─────────────────────────────────┘
                │
                ▼
  ┌───────────────────────────────────┐
  │  Customer pays for the product     │
  └───────────────────────────────────┘
                │
                ▼
 ┌─────────────────────────────────────┐
 │  Customer gets the product as ordered│
 └─────────────────────────────────────┘
                │
                ▼
┌──────────────────────────────────────────┐
│ Customer decides to continue to order from us│
└──────────────────────────────────────────┘
```

Of course, this is very high-level, there are a number of processes that sit under each of these five sections. But in this case, this number of elements is perfect for the high-level value chain that we are looking to capture at this point.

Building a value chain purposefully provides a focus on value work for our team, where we can then look to find, later, opportunities for:

1. Customer-centric improvements that gain new customers.
2. Customer-centric improvements that keep and support your current customers.
3. Internal process improvements and efficiencies.

Your organisation is free to define what it would like to refer to this value chain as – as admittedly, value chain is a bit of a clunky term. Perhaps it can be thought of as a process map of only the value-added steps from the customer's perspective. Once completed, and opportunities for improvement are identified within processes within the value chain, those process steps are added among and between the elements of the value chain to start to catalogue all the improvements being made in the organisation.

Tips for Facilitating this Session

Like mapping a process map, don't get tied up trying to construct a value chain that encompasses every single possible customer journey – that would likely both over complicate the value chain and also cause a lot of unnecessary discussion among the team. What you are looking for is to construct a value chain that is about 80% accurate for the journey of your customers, if not at least one group of customers, or one product or service your organisation offers.

Your team (at least some) will likely struggle to think of the value chain at this high level, and that's usually because they rate some of their tasks as being crucially important for the experience of the customer (and they would be likely right) and think that those tasks should be individual links in the chain. You'll know if you are experiencing this if the value chain is getting to be over about 12 steps long. If the value chain is becoming too long, one option as a facilitator is to continue to capture all the steps as they are being presented and then go through the value chain with the team looking to group similar and corresponding steps. Assure the team that losing that level of detail won't mean not acknowledging the steps, as we will assure the visibility of those steps in the next stage where we determine key measures.

Change the name of the tool that represents the value chain. I've called it the value chain and provided a definition, which is sufficient to begin with. However, we want the team to take ownership of it, so let them brainstorm and decide on the term or name they will use to denote the value chain specifically designed to represent the customer journey in your organisation. This is best done at the end of the session when the team better understand the concept and its application.

As the facilitator of this session, it's crucial to grasp the nature and objectives of the upcoming session. Being aware of the purpose of the next session (which, in this case, is to build the initial metrics for each of the steps in the value chain) will enable you to maintain the appropriate focus in the current session, ensuring that the outcomes align with the specific requirements for the next step in this process loop. Remember that there's Appendix 1 for additional facilitation tips and best practices.

DETERMINE THE GOOD MEASURES OF PERFORMANCE FOR THE VALUE CHAIN STEPS

This next step is open to a bit of conjecture; it's a bit of a chicken-or-egg scenario. Do we:

- keep working together as a team and better our cooperation among the team, but come up with some initial metrics that might not represent the customer's view, or
- start to get the customer's view now?

It is my experience that it's best to keep working together as a team for this leg of your continuous improvement journey, and how they can better work together to support the customer, though they might have an imperfect view of what the customer needs at this point. Some of your initial metrics (which is why we term them 'initial') will change and be adapted as your team gets an even better understanding of your customers later, but let's make a start now in getting your team to think about the customer and how they can work together to support the customer.

At this stage, your team should focus on customer-centric metrics and be open to making changes to their work that align with the organisation's goal of meeting customer expectations.

Build the Initial Metrics

For each of the sections of the chain, have the team decide on some key metrics you could measure your performance in that section of the chain by.

Having just one or two measures for each section of the chain is about right as a start, usually meaning that you'll have about 5–20 measures overall. That's plenty. It is often the case of less is more for the focus of the team.

Again, have the metrics displayed visually with the value chain. These are just the initial metrics so they will evolve as the team develops a better understanding of this principle.

If we use the previous value chain as an example, captured in the table below are the metrics for each of the steps that the team might come up with:

Value chain step	Metrics
Customer becomes aware of us	• Frequency and volume of queries from new potential customers • Conversion rate of queries to orders
Customer orders from us	• Frequency and volume of new customers • Number of orders received on time prior to cut-off • Quality of information in orders coming through/our ability to action orders without going back to the customer
Customer pays for the product	• Payments received on time • Accuracy of payment amount matching order totals
Customer gets the product as ordered	• Customer complaints • Positive customer feedback • Customers affected by out-of-stock items
Customer decides to continue to order from us	• Customer retention rate • Customer referral rate

If you are struggling with this stage, or if time is of the essence, just start and work on one section of your value chain that focuses on customer retention. For the reasons expressed before, there is no point spending precious time and energy trying to get new customers if your current customers are leaving you just as quickly. You'll continue to lose your current customers as well as leave your organisation vulnerable to losing the new customers you've spent time and effort getting.

Tips for Facilitating this Session

Teams may hesitate to suggest metrics if they're unsure about how to measure and collect data for them. It's important not to let the team blend these two concerns at this stage. The method of capturing data for a specific measure is a challenge to be addressed later. Keep in mind the principle of focusing on one step at a time. In this session, concentrate on developing the metrics that will offer the best insights into your performance within each section of the value chain.

When dealing with metrics in a section, consider the balance between the effort required to capture the data and the insights gained. Teams often generate more metrics than necessary, some being 'nice to know' metrics. If the effort and value of a metric are uncertain, it's usually best to omit it.

As the team captures data, certain metrics may prove less useful or insightful than initially thought. Keep it simple, try out metrics, and assess their value after gaining insights over several cycles.

*

In this second loop, a large element of understanding the current level of performance is through having a much richer understanding of your customers, which is the focus of the next chapter.

CHAPTER 9

The Customer

Previously, we emphasised the importance of your team actively selecting areas for improvement to establish a sustained culture of continuous improvement in your organisation. This means that the chosen improvements may not have had a significant impact on customers compared to other potential enhancements. Therefore, there is a need to heighten awareness of the customer and understand how the performance of our processes directly affects them.

This chapter aims to ensure that, if not already done, you integrate the customer deeply into your continuous improvement culture. It addresses how to accomplish this, emphasising the crucial enrichment of your understanding of current performance through stronger customer insights.

THE CUSTOMER ECHO

In every interaction between your organisation and the customer there's always (what I'll term) an echo – and you need to make sure you understand and glean the insights from the echo. The customer echo is everything that happens after each interaction between the customer and your organisation, and is what the customer thinks after the interaction, feedback via surveys or complaints, or rework. Most organisations are not aware of the insights that the echo offers, which is a massively missed opportunity. Organisations capture performance in terms of how long it takes to perform tasks for the customer, how much money is made from serving the customer, but not often the richness of the customer echo. And the echo is the comprehensive truth of how we are performing.

Customer echo can be in any direction, such as outwardly to their friends, colleagues, or posts on social media, but we'll focus on and refer to it as the reverberation of the customer's experience throughout your organisation, often resulting in rework for your organisation, the customer, or, more likely, both. Being unaware of, or ignoring the customer echo can lead to repeated situations like the following:

> **Team member:** 'ci lab, that's an interesting name. What do they do?'
>
> **Me:** 'ci lab helps organisations improve their customer focus and performance to make life easier for their customer. For example, if a customer fills out an online form for an appointment with the promise to be contacted with a confirmed appointment time, and then receives an automated email saying, "Please call us to make an appointment", and then the customer calls and has to provide all the same information again over the phone, and then that customer receives a confirmation email of the appointment with attached forms to bring to the appointment, again asking for the same details, I work with teams to become aware of that and work through changes to improve it. Fast.'
>
> **Team member:** 'Far out, that's insane!'
>
> **Me:** 'And interestingly, that's what I experienced before today's appointment...'

The customer echo is what occurs after every interaction we have with our customer. It's incredibly powerful information that is often ignored because capturing and using that information isn't built into the system as an action. Everything can be forgiven its first failure, but if the failure is allowed to repeat, that's literally intentionally building waste into what we do. Hearing the customer echo will highlight our failures.

When the customer interacts with the organisation, two crucial outcomes emerge from that experience:

1. The customer can't help but form an impression of how they feel about engaging with your organisation.
2. The customer makes a decision about whether they will choose to use your services again. The flexibility of this decision depends on factors such as competitor options or, in the case of a monopoly, the decision to continue using your services or not. This decision exemplifies the concept of the customer echo, where their experience resonates and influences subsequent choices.

Both those things are incredibly significant to every business and organisation, and they only happen when and where (think customer channels like contact centres) the customer interacts with your organisation. Many insights to how your organisation can improve lay at that connection point – where your organisation and customers interact – and your strategy must include improving that point. Those interactions (the customer echo) are absolutely gold for improvement insights.

WHY HEARING THE CUSTOMER ECHO IS CRITICAL

When your organisation interacts with the customer, and from every single interaction, everything after that moment is the customer echo. It offers us crucial insights to our customers and their thinking, which is why your ability to recognise, capture, interpret and act on the customer echo is critical to ensure your improvements are aligned to your customers.

If your organisation is not attuned to picking up the customer echo, then there is a void of insight about how your organisation is performing from a customer's perspective. Being attuned to the customer echo means you can learn more about aligning with your customers' needs and stay relevant to them.

If we don't properly capture the customer echo, it will still exist, but it will only exist with the customer.

Only the customer possesses a perfect understanding of how they feel about the interaction with your organisation. Obtaining this knowledge is crucial, as achieving customer-centric improvements becomes significantly challenging without it.

Recognising the importance of aligning your organisation and its work with that of the customer, the upcoming sections of this book will explore the crucial elements of:

- how we design the right measures that capture crucial insights of the customer echo
- how we determine and establish the behaviours needed to elicit fantastic customer service, then how we measure and monitor to support the right behaviours in our teams
- how we ensure brand incongruence – that the customer experience matches our brand philosophy
- how we facilitate and unleash the untapped capability residing in our team for improvements.

KNOWING WHAT YOUR CURRENT CUSTOMERS THINK

To turn your existing customer into a repeat customer, it's crucial to understand their thoughts. This involves recognising what they find great about your services, instilling confidence that you will consistently deliver to that, and addressing any aspects that are poor experiences. For the latter, you must have improvements in place to prevent recurrence, and convey this to your customer. Achieving both hinges on gaining pure customer insight.

The best way to know what your customers are thinking is to simply ask them: What do you think about the product or the service? Let me repeat this: Only the customer possesses a perfect understanding of how they feel about the interaction with your organisation.

FAILURE TO ACT ON THE CUSTOMER ECHO

Failure to act on the customer echo can result in a culture of apathy amongst your team that manifests as a lack of responsiveness, not being as dynamic an organisation as the customer needs, affecting your brand and reputation, not just for one customer but likely a swathe of customers, all culminating in customer evaporation.

Customer Evaporation

Customer evaporation occurs at the points at which a customer thinks: 'It's not me, it's you.' Customers may be lost, either as potential new customers or within our existing customer base, at four distinct points in the customer relationship:

1. Failure to respond to customer inquiries or keep potential customers informed, leading to disengagement, queue abandonment, or frustration from lack of updates on orders. Clear, simple and well-timed communication is important.
2. Challenges in delivering products or services, resulting in the need for offering or providing refunds. This failure not only results in lost sales but also potentially damages the customer's trust.
3. Failure to understand and meet customer expectations (ignoring the customer echo), leading to:
   a. not addressing problems promptly, including fixing underperformance that becomes known to others and reputational damage
   b. failing to encourage and support positive referrals from satisfied customers
   c. neglecting to gather and act on customer feedback swiftly.
4. Inability to transform current customers into repeat customers by maintaining connections, following up, seeking feedback and offering support.

Figure 9 chronologically illustrates the above key moments when a customer can choose to disengage from your organisation.

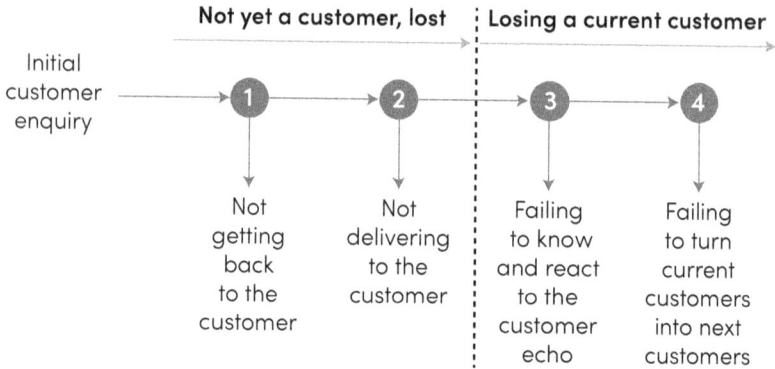

Not yet a customer, lost		Losing a current customer	
Not getting back to the customer	Not delivering to the customer	Failing to know and react to the customer echo	Failing to turn current customers into next customers

Figure 9

Let's look at that first point. The conversion of queries from potential customers into actual customers is crucial for all organisations. While some measure this as part of their customer conversion metric, it's important to recognise that the effectiveness of these metrics lies in the behaviours that deliver the results. One key behaviour that strongly drives customer conversion is answering the questions they put to us. Sounds simple, right? Too many organisations fail to answer customer queries properly, if at all.

As an example, if a customer poses three questions as part of their initial enquiry, providing answers to only two is insufficient. Customers ask specific questions because they believe the information is vital in deciding whether to choose your organisation. Unlike the Meat Loaf song: *Two out of three ain't bad*, it's more a case of two out of three is not good.

Consider if the three questions were:

1. Do you have the specific tyre (X) in stock?
2. What's the cost?
3. Can you replace it while I wait?

Each of these questions is crucial, and neglecting to answer any of them could potentially deter the customer from choosing your organisation. If the questions arrive through email, web queries or live chat, assume the customer has sent the same enquiry to other organisations. It's not just what you answer but how you answer, as they may compare your response to others.

A good way to answer (aside from providing all the answers to the questions the customer has asked) is to also provide the answer to the next likely question as well. Something like:

'Thanks for your query, Susan. We don't have that tyre in stock, but we can source it and if we order it today (by 3pm) it will be here tomorrow. The cost of the tyre is $79, and that includes fitting, balancing and taxes, that's the grand total. Yes, you can most certainly wait, it will take us about 30 minutes to get the new tyre on, and we have an area for you to wait in with tea, coffee and Wi-Fi access. Would you like to book in for tomorrow (Thursday) or Friday?'

Now, the trick is not just knowing that we need to answer all the questions customers ask, but how do we build this behaviour in the culture – that's where the benefit is.

Failure to Act as Fast as Your Customer

Improvements to your organisation's processes have to happen as fast as the dynamic of your customer's expectations or there's a gap in terms of what you offer and what your customer expects of you. (You'll remember Figure 3 on page 29.)

The velocity of which customer's expectations change, which I refer to as the dynamic, is different for each organisation. The key is knowing the expected velocity of change of customers for your organisation – and the best way to know when a change is occurring is through the insights that the customer echo provides.

One Bad Customer Experience is Really One of Hundreds

One common mistake organisations make is spending a lot of time fixing and resolving mistakes that have affected a customer and assuming it is an independent case of poor customer experience. Often, they fail to realise that this mistake is probably one of many similar mistakes stemming from other practices and the energy should be applied to those practices to resolve the prevalence of the issues affecting the customers at the root.

For instance, systems are set up in organisations to deal with the frequent problems of individual customers – the customer calls the contact centre with their problem and the contact centre deal with it, either well, poorly or somewhere in between. Where the opportunity is lost is because what in isolation looks like one customer complaint or one poor customer experience is actually one of a multitude of similar, if not exact experiences. And this is often missed by organisations because they don't collect the data on the customer experience, or the customer echo.

So, there's an imbalance between the amount of effort organisations put into fixing individual customer experiences over improving the practices, processes, or behaviours that cause all poor customer experiences in the first place.

What too many organisations suffer from is expending too much energy fixing problems as quickly and as well as they can as they occur and incorrectly thinking that this is great customer service. Rather, you also need to invest your energy in understanding and fixing why the problem occurred in the first place. You already know this as root cause thinking.

Alternatively, when organisations collect and compile the data on customer experiences, they see how frequently this problem occurs and that would become the impetus to fix it. However, because the stratification and culmination of the similar customer experiences aren't being compiled, effectively no change happens in the organisation to address that issue. The organisation is effectively unaware to where it can improve the customer experience and the organisation's performance.

Does Service Quality Reflect the Brand You Want?

A crucial aspect of customer experience is ensuring it is congruent with your brand's intended image. Whether your brand emphasises delivering the best, exceptional, friendliest, or most accommodating customer service, the customer ultimately determines if your organisation lives up to these aspirations.

Consider the example of price integrity, where offering fair prices is a key brand element. In situations like pricing queries at a supermarket checkout, customer misunderstandings can lead to embarrassment or, if the pricing is genuinely incorrect, significant effort to rectify the issue. Both outcomes represent the customer echo. Often, organisations fail to capture and act on it. For instance, if frequent pricing queries indicate customer confusion, ignoring this customer echo could result in continued loss of your team's capacity through fixing issues and increased customer embarrassment. Recognising and addressing the root cause, in this case, clarifying pricing, is essential for aligning actions with brand values. Organisations without continuous improvement will continue to have team members resolve pricing issues – wasting vast amounts of time and energy and providing a poor customer experience.

And just a note on the embarrassment of the customer; there are few moments as impactful on a customer as when they have been embarrassed. I'm sure we can all think back to a moment where we were embarrassed as a customer, and the sense of injustice and abject humiliation it caused. Too often organisations look only to reduce errors, defects or faults that impact the customer and there's something far more significant not often thought about. It's incidents in our processes that cause our customer embarrassment.

HOW TO CAPTURE THE CUSTOMER ECHO

Here are four ways that you can start to capture the customer echo.

1. Your Best Next Customer is the Customer You Already Have

Customer loyalty, as the oft forgotten two-way street, also means being loyal to the customers you have. Here's a valuable tip that is easy to implement and will provide crucial insights directly from your customers. Ask them the following question: What would be the single most likely reason that you would stop being our customer?

Maintaining a continuous improvement mindset is essential for staying relevant and understanding the evolving needs and performance expectations of your customers. This effort must be ongoing, considering the dynamic nature of customer needs. Unfortunately, many teams and organisations lack the appetite and commitment to thoroughly comprehend their customer's experience.

Customers freely provide vital insights, detailing what the organisation has done right (valuable information for replication) and what needs to be done right to retain their loyalty (new strategies to implement and error reduction). Remember, your next customer is likely to be someone you already have, as long as you understand why they chose your service in the first place.

Good service takes soul, effort and courage.

Focusing on Your Current Customers

A priority to pursuing growth is to focus on retaining existing customers by understanding their preferences and potential reasons for leaving. Focus on creating a 'pit of happiness' – an exceptional experience that not only keeps current customers satisfied but also captivates new customers.

Investing in customer satisfaction has a dual impact, resonating positively with both current and potential customers. This strategy is more effective than solely pursuing new customers, potentially offering subpar service that leads to dissatisfaction and evaporation among both new and existing customers. Once excellence is established, introduce new customers to this experience, optimise internal processes for scalability and to free up your team's capacity to support continued business growth.

Two (Further) Great Questions Your Team Can Ask Customers

The most valuable customers are the ones you already have. Retaining existing customers is more cost-effective than acquiring new ones, and customer evaporation undermines growth. Instead of focusing solely on efforts to recover lost customers, the emphasis is on preventing the experiences that prompt customers to leave.

What should be considered, then, as the first law of sustainability is knowing precisely what core customers need to experience and, equally, what not to experience. To inform how you harmonise your processes to produce better results for your customers, teams should ask customers personally and authentically:

1. What is the one thing that if we did it, or failed to continue to do it, would lead you to stop being our customer?
2. What is the key reason you choose us, specifically why you are our customer?

The answers to these two questions are critical because they tell us what we must absolutely keep doing (our vital competitive advantage) and what we need to make sure never happens. These insights hone what we need to improve in our processes – to ensure we provide what is needed and to error-proof against the occurrence of that one reason why our customers would leave.

Though only two questions, they'll likely provide richer insights than a customer survey, with the insights of most surveys being far removed from the customer's experience in the actual process.

Not many organisations ask their customers why they would leave, but it is a simple question that only your customers can answer, and it is critical, absolutely critical, for us to know.

Even if you have ruined things and that customer has decided not to return – knowing specifically why they won't return will provide you the opportunity to fix things with your current and next customers. Finding this out takes courage – but everyone loves to feel listened to. If you don't ask, you risk losing more customers and, here's the kicker, you'll have no idea why.

2. Traits You Can Incorporate to Improve Your Customer Focus

Let's say you have three options to understand your customer and in turn develop a solution for a problem that affects your customers. Let's play these options off against each other for their effectiveness to get pure customer insight – the very thing that you'd want to build any solution around:

1. Obtain valuable feedback by creating an environment where customers feel comfortable sharing candid opinions. Efforts to establish a trusting relationship are essential, as customers will only provide feedback on what they consciously remember.

2. Raw observation, such as watching or listening to customer interactions, provides an in-depth understanding of real-time situations. Improving actual situations as they occur is the goal, and direct observation is often more insightful than obtaining customer feedback and insights.

3. Experience the customer's journey firsthand by going through the process as they would. This approach simplifies understanding by putting oneself directly in the customer's shoes. Consider potential limitations, such as a small sample size, as personal experiences may not reflect broader issues affecting more customers. Guard against confirmation bias by consciously stepping out of your role and adopting the customer's perspective.

To gain a more objective understanding of the customer experience, it's recommended to use a combination of these three approaches. Each method provides unique insights that collectively enhance your knowledge.

3. Contact Centres: The Hidden Gold Mine in Your Organisation

Often, contact centres focus solely on reducing customer waiting times, overlooking their potential as a rich source of customer information. Let me share an experience of analysis of the customer journey across various channels, where we discovered a gold mine of insights. Specifically, we found a significant number of calls to the contact centre immediately after customers visited the organisation's website, providing a hotspot for valuable information. Handling these calls was extra work, with the website and app failing to offer what the customers needed – what we refer to as **rework demand**, which we'll cover in the next section.

By listening to these specific calls, we gained crucial insights into website development needs, eliminating assumptions and accurately assessing benefits before making improvements. This approach reduced the risk of wasted work and allowed us to understand which improvements would positively impact customers and alleviate pressure on the contact centre.

The analysis also revealed how the contact centre supported other channels, such as calls and messages following onsite appointments or previous contact centre calls. This information led to improvements that aimed to get things right the first time, reducing rework and costs and enhancing the overall customer experience.

Recognising the contact centre's role as a source of valuable insights changed perceptions within the organisation. Instead of being seen solely as a resolution-based entity, the contact centre became recognised as an agency providing crucial customer insights, monitoring performance, and driving continuous improvement initiatives.

This is reflected by a shifting view of the contact centre's contribution. Instead of handling customer calls and messages as the primary focus, it's rightly being regarded as a channel that reflects the performance health of various organisational processes. Consequently, many good customer-centric ideas originate from the contact centre.

4. Introducing the Concept of Value and Rework Demand

One effective way to sustain the team's ability to identify ongoing improvements, especially when dealing with customers, is to understand the concepts of value and failure demand. These terms originate from the systems thinking methodology developed by Vanguard. **Value demand** is the work initiated by customers, serving the purpose of the organisation, while **failure demand** refers to extra work resulting from customer misunderstandings (of which the onus is on the organisation) or organisational failures where something that should have been done wasn't, or wasn't done properly, causing rework.

To facilitate continuous improvement, it's recommended to allow teams to rename concepts, with the purpose of making the concepts more relevant to your team. For instance, a team renamed failure demand to rework demand, emphasising the corrective nature of the effectively extra work. Analysing performance involves identifying rework demand categories, frequency and impact on the organisation and customers.

Rework demand is a subset of demands placed on the organisation by customers that hinders capacity for purposeful work. Imagine an emergency ward in a hospital where 10 people are waiting for medical assistance in the accident and emergency ward. Of these 10 people, nine have the flu (value demand), and one person wants to purchase a hamburger. The person who wants to purchase the hamburger is in the wrong place, and dealing with them and redirecting them out of the hospital takes time and resources – that is rework demand. Of the other nine people that had the flu, one was misdiagnosed and accidentally released while being afflicted with meningitis. Later that day, they had to be rushed back to hospital in a worse state, now being even more of an emergency – requiring more medical staff and resources to help. This is also rework demand.

In both the hospital and contact centre examples, capturing rework demand is essential. This helps identify the right problems to fix, as rework demand highlights symptoms that guide improvement teams to the root causes. By reducing rework demand, you can free up organisational capacity and offer an improved customer experience.

Generating solutions that support a continuous improvement mindset is most effective when done by those directly engaged with the work and customers.

THE POWER OF CAPTURING THE CUSTOMER ECHO

Having a customer echo register or list is about the action and mindset of starting to collate all customer feedback. The register itself serves as a catalyst for the team to start to think and become conscious of feedback from the customers and potential customers who know why they haven't yet become customers. The purpose of the register is to capture and quantify each of the experiences or potential improvements that can be made for the customer.

Starting a Register of Customer Echo Insights

Establish a **Customer Insights Register** to capture customer experiences and potential improvement initiatives, where what is captured can be a catalyst for the improvement team to decide what to work on next after collating and ranking those insights.

Begin by creating a register for customer-driven improvements, collecting feedback from various channels connected with current and potential customers. Share this feedback with the team, emphasising the importance of collectively deciding on actionable items. If your organisation lacks such a register, initiate one that welcomes contributions from anyone within the organisation.

When instilling a continuous improvement mindset, focus on two core elements in this order:

1. Understand how your customer perceives the outputs of your processes – ensure you are providing what they need and identify any gaps. (A customer's perception is the outcome.)
2. Know how well your organisation is performing its processes.

These steps prioritise your customer's experience first, understanding how your products or services align with their needs. Subsequently, we then look to refine and improve processes to better produce that alignment between our products and services, and the customer's expectations.

The register can capture qualitative or quantitative data, such as customer sound bites or the frequency of known issues affecting them. Allow team members and even customers to contribute to the register. There's flexibility in defining the structure of the register, but the key is to initiate it with inclusivity for all organisation members to contribute any insights that offer valuable information. Once insights are gathered, focus on specific areas for improvement and consider adopting or discontinuing certain measures of performance, which we'll cover in the section on good measures.

WHO IS YOUR CUSTOMER?

To know and understand your customer, you must start by identifying who they truly are. This goes beyond mere labelling; knowing your customers involves adopting a holistic service-oriented mindset. This mindset helps your team uncover the extensive diversity of your customers, both within and outside the organisation.

Every time I'm with a team discussing who their customer is, I'm often left dazed by the ensuing debate. Countless articles, books and similar publications attempt to define a customer, and there will be more to come, all striving to offer a specific definition. I'm not going to offer a definition to avoid unnecessary debates. Instead of categorising customers and having terms like end-user, ultimate customer, primary and secondary customer, internal and external customer, let's just understand the concept of a customer, and simply apply that concept so we know who our customers are. Spend the energy more wisely by asking: What do we need to do to fulfil the needs of our customers? When we understand this, we better understand our purpose.

Our customer can be internal or external, someone requesting work, the person directly affected by the work, it is all about context of purpose. Customers are essentially anyone an organisation does something for in the fulfillment of its purpose. For example, a prisoner is a customer for the purpose of the penal system, which aims to rehabilitate. While I previously avoided offering a definition, this is more about presenting a concept: Where there is purpose in work there's a customer or customers. So rather than defining who is or is not a customer (which I'd argue, as the first step, is a fruitless exercise), instead determine the purpose of work and there you'll identify customers through the defining of purpose.

Understanding the customer is about understanding the concept of the customer, rather than attempting to articulate exactly who our single customer is – as this scenario almost never exists. Customers are diverse, and organisations (almost without exception) serve multiple customers. However, not all customers are equal; some may not be desired, like a disruptive passenger on a plane affecting others' experience. Customers have varying requirements, emphasising the plural nature of the concept.

Stakeholders, on the other hand, are not direct recipients of actions but are impacted by changes. Those working on the next step in a process can be seen as working for their customer, not their boss, who is a stakeholder with an interest in their performance. This distinction is crucial, particularly in the public sector with those who are ministers or hold portfolios.

Know the Customer Intimately

As much as we have a mantra that leaders need to be in the work to know the work and make good and informed decisions to support the team (and we'll talk more about Gemba soon – the practice of leaders being in the work), the same principle needs to apply with our customers; we need to be where the customer experience occurs. It is the customer experience that needs to be driving the work – that is, the improvements that we are making to the way that we are performing the work.

I'll reshare the example of the four team members based at an airport who observed and monitored the customer queue for two hours. Instead of actively servicing the queue, their task was to watch and take note of any occurrences that required improvement – this was a novel approach to gather insights for the first time. It would be fair to say that the team, all of them having worked in this queue for a minimum of 10 years, thought (I should say vehemently expressed) that they would see nothing new. I asked them to humour me and convinced them to do it anyway.

There's a huge difference between doing something and studying that very thing. When we study, we see – and we only see and learn when it, by and large, is a deliberate action. In removing themselves from the work to study what was actually going on, they (as you'd guess) saw a vast array of incidents that they had never seen before. This happened for two reasons, because they were studying the queue and because they worked at the head of the queue, which wasn't representative of what happened in the queue – as they had assumed. Now armed with these new insights, they gained a more intimate understanding of customer experiences and behaviours, which they would leverage to design better solutions. The outcome, in this case, was a remarkable 89% reduction in negative customer experiences.

Not to harp on about the hollowness of surveys but suffice to say that no survey would have captured the incidents they witnessed. Neither they nor their customers would have thought to mention what needed improving for their experience, certainly not the extent that it was experienced, specifically related to those incidents, if a survey or a focus group with customers was run.

THE COMPLEXITY OF UNTANGLING AND IMPROVING CUSTOMER QUEUES

To improve queues, we must address their root causes, as queues are symptoms of underlying issues. Adding more staff or enhancing the customer experience within the queue doesn't address these root causes. True improvement involves either reducing the reasons for queuing or significantly cutting waiting times during peak periods.

Understanding customer behaviour in queues and incorporating this knowledge into solutions accelerates the queue. This approach aligns with customers' natural behaviours, fostering a more intuitive experience rather than trying to manipulate or redirect them.

When considering queuing, it's essential to broaden our conceptual understanding. For instance, in a restaurant, queuing extends until the customer receives the first item of value that the business can charge for – not when they are seated, finally, at a table. Recognising queuing in this broader context provides more opportunities to enhance the customer experience and reduce queuing time.

Queues are not the problem, rather, they are a manifestation of a problem; queues are symptomatic of process performance and the capability to handle demand, especially at peaks. We can either manage the queues to improve the customer experience in the queues, and in doing so alleviate a symptom, or improve the process that is causing the queues – this is a root cause improvement. Queues show the occurrence of a bottleneck, and it's that bottleneck that needs to be improved.

Effectively handling queues is vital for customer satisfaction, as highlighted by David Maister who said in *The Psychology of Waiting Lines*: 'Once we are being served, our transaction with the service organization may be efficient, courteous and complete: but the bitter taste of how long it took to get attention pollutes the overall judgments that we make about the quality of service.' (Maister 1984)

Here's a quick checklist for areas to potentially improve the queueing process or experience:

- Ensure customers are well-informed and comfortable with the preparation process. This involves aligning preparation steps with the natural behaviours of customers, avoiding confusion and embarrassment in understanding the queuing process. For instance, customers, whether familiar or not, being supported to know exactly what to do with security procedures at airports *and* having those procedures conducive to typical customer behaviours contribute to a smoother and faster queue. Similarly, providing menus for customers to review before being seated at a table improves the customer experience and speeds up the ordering process once seated.
- Entertain customers during the wait to alleviate the perception of queuing. This can involve initiating service while in the queue or delivering service in segmented parts, breaking down the overall wait time. By doing so, customers find the queuing experience more enjoyable and less burdensome.
- Be transparent and communicate the duration of the queue, ensuring customers are aware of the time commitment. This transparency contributes to customers feeling that the

service is worth queuing for, emphasising the real value in the queuing experience.
- Your customers need to be assured that they are in the right queue, with what they need (nobody wants to queue twice), and that they won't miss out or lose out, alleviating anxiety commonly felt in queues.

Let me share an experience I had at an airport. After using the automated check-in machines and obtaining baggage tags, we queued for the baggage drop-off machines. The queue was longer than it should have been, and I noticed a lot of lost capacity – there were a good number of machines to drop off the luggage onto that were ready but idle, mainly because we had a bottleneck at the head of the queue.

The bottleneck was caused by an airport representative checking passports and ensuring customers had checked in and tagged their luggage. The queue stagnated because some individuals hadn't completed these steps – unfortunately they likely didn't realise that they needed to do this before entering the queue. This meant that these requirements were explained individually to each group at the head of the queue, stifling the queue and delaying others who were ready but couldn't use the idle luggage drop-off machines.

Customers in the queue, unprepared for the process, were unhappy to discover the additional steps after queuing – with these discussions further prolonging the waiting time for everyone. Every minute of discussion at the queue's head added a minute of waiting time for each person, resulting in 40 minutes of lost time for the approximately 40 people in the queue.

To address this issue, the key solution involves reducing the frequency (if not entirely eliminating) instances where passengers join the queue unprepared for the baggage drop. This would effectively dissolve the queue, ensure full-capacity use of luggage drop-off machines, enhance the customer experience, and simplify the representative's role by reducing rework demand.

*

In this section, we've focused on capturing a lot of data and insights on your customers, the customer echo, and simply how they feel about your service or products. This information serves as a vital starting point for a new loop of improvement, which is what we will now focus on in Loop 2: how do these customer insights support continual improvement of your products and services? Of course, it's not about just knowing the customer insights – it's also about acting on them to make informed improvements.

CHAPTER 10

Determining Why We Experience the Current Level of Performance

Once you grasp your current performance, the subsequent step involves understanding all the factors influencing that performance level. Some of these factors form a chain of events, beginning with the nucleus of the sequence – what we identify as the root cause. Identifying the root cause(s) is pivotal at this stage, as it enables you to understand the essential variables that have a significant impact on and can enhance your performance levels.

GET AWAY FROM THE SCREEN AND IN WITH THE TEAM: GEMBA

Gemba is the Japanese term for *being in the work* – being immersed in the work, where it is happening and leading from in the work rather than from outside of the work. Focus and notice. Focus on the right areas of the work and notice what is going on. It's about being uninhibited in having a clear and unobstructed understanding of reality, to be informed when aligning your team to deal with problems and challenges.

Don't have an open-door policy, have a be-on-the-floor policy.

As a leader, you should be involved with the daily stand-ups. If you aren't, the question is: are you focusing on the right work, or are you skipping daily stand-ups because they're not purposeful? If they're not purposeful, then they need to change to become purposeful for you and the team.

Being in the work with your team also helps build crucial elements of the relationship needed for continuous improvement – and specifically the fundamental element being trust. With trust, we experience a perpetuation of the sharing of insights, issues and problems that are often hidden from other levels of an organisation's hierarchy.

Think of problems and issues being well known on a horizontal plane but being distorted, partially or completely hidden to those on a different vertical plane of the hierarchy.

In Appendix 8, there's a great list of questions that leaders can ask of their teams to support their first venture into gemba.

IMPROVEMENT OPTIONS WITHIN A SYSTEM

In this section, we'll define the relationship between a system and a process.

As a quick definition, a process is a string of events of how we do a particular thing – what we do and the order in which we do it to get an outcome. A system is all the elements that a process is enveloped in, which impacts on the performance of the process. The system includes all the components that support, resource and affect a process.

A good process could be strapped with a bad system, or we could have a good system support a clunky process to occur – and both examples would provide reduced overall performance.

Because the elements of a system have the ability to impact the process, it's important to understand how the system could impact a process as we determine process improvements.

To offer a purposefully simple example at this stage which you can have in mind for the following sections, think of the process of making peanut butter toast. It's generally a simple process. We've the process locked down. And think of the desired outcome of that process – perfectly toasted bread (of your choice) with the right peanut butter perfectly spread. Here's how the system can impact the outcome: there might rules about which peanut butter you use, there's a chance that you'll be short a plate and/or a knife, that we need the toaster to be available and working and there's good power supply for it, that you've been supplied/have access to the right bread; there is a huge number of variables within the system that sit outside of the process and impact the outcome.

THINKING ABOUT SYSTEM

Think widely. Processes don't exist in isolation, they're part of a broader environment, a system. In the first loop, we looked at a process, or perhaps a step in a process, whereas now we consider the impact of the system – everything that contributes to the performance of the process. There are a number of elements far wider reaching and impactful that affect the performance of a process than just the way we execute the process steps, and the value of those process steps themselves.

Focusing solely on refining process steps may lead to significant improvements within the process itself but might not result in tangible enhancements to overall performance. This is because other factors existing in the broader system, within which the process operates, can hinder its performance. Therefore, it's essential to adopt a broad perspective aimed at improving the entire system, going beyond the mechanics of individual processes.

A process by itself is hollow. It is just a component of a system. Is it possible to make improvements to a process and find that overall performance doesn't improve? Yes – as it might be that you also needed to increase the capability and/or commitment of the team. When we are looking at capability or engagement, we are now thinking about components of a system.

Plus, what if you improve the process and the capability but not the measures causing specific behaviours? Should you expect performance to change? Perhaps not. This is what a system is – all the components and limitations of system performance need to change for performance to change.

What we are focusing on by looking at a system is the net effect. In essence, a process can be clean, but its system could pollute it, inhibit it, make the process hard to perform or set targets that lead to process deviation – all resulting in poor overall performance. While individuals engage with the process, the system, in turn, influences individuals. Ideally, we aim for a system that collaborates with and bolsters individuals rather than impedes them.

'Every system is perfectly designed to get the result that it does.' W. Edwards Deming

---

Examining a system involves identifying potential constraints on performance. The purpose of thinking about the elements of the system is that we can start to become aware of their impact as limitations on performance. Knowing the impact of these system elements will better inform the team to develop more effective solutions that address the root causes of the performance.

The system encompasses all players and factors that impact the performance and demands of our process. Here, as a starter, are some elements of a system which could be impacting performance:

- **Suppliers:** assess the quality of their support, contributions, reliability, and adherence to requirements.
- **Customers:** evaluate their requirements, behaviours, demands, and assumptions about your industry.
- **Equipment, IT, hardware, and applications and tools:** examine for workarounds, bugs, downtime, and the relevance of rules hard coded in the IT system.

- **Current processes:** assess the quality and inherent wastes in existing processes.
- **Performance metrics and measurement:** scrutinise measures and targets and the resulting behaviours they drive. Is there a consistent view about how much current performance can be improved between the team and leaders?
- **Team and leadership dynamics:**
  - ~ Culture, behaviours and beliefs: is there the right dynamic (especially in terms of cooperation within a shared process) in the team for better performance and continual growth?
  - ~ Engagement (including that of the leaders): is there good engagement (desire) for improved performance? And are the leaders engaged in the work? (Gemba)
  - ~ Capability, including leaders understanding the work and true performance:
    - · Does the system support/enable the team to work together?
    - · Is there capability in the team for good performance and to improve performance?
    - · Have the team been provided with the best training and support to do their work?
    - · Does that training include building continuous improvement capability?
  - ~ Organisational culture: assess entrenched behaviours and assumptions (including how everyone works; all on the same desks, with the same tools, working the same hours, onsite or working from home balance).
  - ~ Hierarchy and job descriptions: consider the current configuration of roles and responsibilities and how that affects the balance of workloads and the linear flow and order of work. This involves understanding that certain process steps must occur before others.
- **Organisational strategy, vision or plan:** is there anything in the organisational strategy, vision or plan that aids the performance of the system yet to be unleashed or is incongruent with and hinders the performance of the system?

- **System constraints and dependencies:** identify and determine if they are still appropriate, have been interpreted and acted on correctly (such as legislation and regulations).
- **Conventional wisdom and practices:** question and challenge entrenched practices limiting performance improvements and innovation.

Revisiting Challenging Conventional Wisdoms

The above list of elements of a system can be changed to improve performance. For many of these elements, they are calcified through conventional wisdoms, which limit our ability to challenge and change those system elements, arguing *why we can't* make the changes rather than employing the *why can't we?* mindset.

When we subscribe to a conventional wisdom that goes unchallenged, our system and its performance is being burdened with a challenge. We need to become consciously aware of and challenge those elements of the system that give us the performance that we experience. Those current elements, or 'settings' in the system, were defined well by Seddon when he referred to them as *System conditions* (Seddon 1999).

Highlighting system conditions means that we identify and become aware of those elements that determine the configuration and nature of the current system. By doing so, we open the door to thinking beyond the constraints of the system and conventional thoughts, paving the way for unleashing new solutions, reshaping the system to provide new levels of performance.

System conditions encompass all aspects open to questioning or deconstruction that contribute to the current level of performance. Identifying these conditions can be challenging as it requires a conscious effort to scrutinise habitual aspects that likely subconsciously impact our work. Deliberately considering the influential factors shaping our work, often subconsciously applied, overlooked or unchallenged, is a demanding but crucial task. Persistence and patience are key in the brainstorming process, which involves investing time, effort, thought and endurance to name and understand these system conditions.

Again, during brainstorming, refrain from evaluating the reasons for, or impact of, the system conditions as you name them; focus simply on capturing all conditions. After the brainstorming evaluate the potential disproportionate influence and impacts of the system conditions on performance if they remain unchanged. Take it one step at a time – the initial and challenging step is to compile and articulate the system conditions.

There can be a bit of a struggle wrapping our minds around the vast array of systems conditions that exist, so here is a good example of some system conditions that a team highlighted as their first step to determine and then to challenge the constraints of these conditions:

- need a degree to do this work well
- can't change the IT system we use
- checking reduces errors, so the more we check, the better
- need to be here for at least five years before one has enough knowledge to properly do the job
- only individual performance is measured
- only we can train ourselves – training has to be internal for the team by the team
- we can't provide advice to our customers, only audit them
- procedures can only be changed every six months
- we can accurately determine risk based only on transaction type.

The list is generic enough that as you read through it again, think of how you might challenge the condition, or identify how the condition might have a severe and negative impact on either the purpose, the team and/or the organisation.

BETTER DATA ANALYSIS

We've already talked about special and common cause variation (quick definitions are also in Appendix 10) and when we capture problems that we include the frequency and severity of those problems. Let's go further to share good principles of better and more insightful data analysis – principles that we need to be aware of to ensure that we don't make common mistakes in the interpretation of data, leading to poor insights, judgement, decisions and actions in response to that data.

Variation in Our Process

When we're analysing the performance data, one particular aspect we are looking for is variation within a product or service. Any variation we see reflects the instability of the process, which cause defects and problems that are not good for our customers, and this is why I say that *variation is a process evil.*

Experienced variation is contributed to by all the factors in the system, such as the waste in the process and the differing capability of our team and machinery. We attack variation through the removal of waste and strengthening our capability.

As customers, we don't like variation, we like consistency. Better than that, we like consistently good experiences. Whether it's short waiting times, getting two of the same item being exactly the same, or a flight without turbulence, we naturally like stuff healthy and smooth sailing.

Variation occurs when different levels of performance are provided to the customer. Some of those variations of performance are acceptable to the customer and others are not. With greater variation of performance is an increased likelihood of more undesirable customer experiences. The more variation you have in your performance, the more process evils you have. If you expect a delivery at 10am and receive it at 10.10am, that's probably ok. If it arrives the next day, then it's probably not ok for most.

You want to significantly reduce or even eliminate variation by your customer's definition and control your performance. Being in control of variation and thereby your performance, you have a solid, consistent foundation to further enhance performance, ensuring improvements in one area persist even as your focus shifts to address other aspects.

Simply, you're looking for variations in your data that tell you where to look to determine and understand the reasons for the variations. You want to understand how to replicate the good results, such as those variables that meant an application being processed quickly and properly, and conversely, how you eliminate the variables that meant a slow and poor outcome.

By embedding what provides consistently positive events and decreasing the frequency and intensity of unfavourable events, you can reduce process variation. This indicates successful efforts in addressing the root causes behind such variations.

There are many tools that can help with variation analysis, with one of the most instrumental being a Control Chart, also known as Shewhart Charts or Statistical Process Control Charts (SPCC).

Tip: Analysing process times often involves receiving spreadsheet data with start and end times linked to specific incidents. By identifying the specific applications that experienced delays, you can uncover common factors and then develop effective solutions. Similarly, this approach can be used to understand variables leading to swift application processing, facilitating the creation of solutions to replicate positive outcomes.

Getting Variation and Variety Mixed Up

Variation and variety are not the same thing. Variation is the differences in *the same* product or service, it's not the range of products or services offered. Your range that you offer customers is your variety.

You want to reduce variation, but not by attacking variety, making sure you are offering what the customer wants.

Here's an example of variation, variety and the impacts of capability affecting variation. You want to eat a vegan burger today, and as you check the menu, you notice limited variety with only two vegan options. You choose one based on the photo and ingredients, and the service is excellent compared to your last disappointing experience (that's variation). The burger looks close to the photo, indicating consistency (lack of variation), which is positive. Still hungry, you consider potato or sweet potato fries and desserts, which are all variety. Opting for a dessert, you find it looks nothing like the menu image and your serving is smaller (undesirable variation), especially since the price wasn't any smaller than on the menu!

Variety, which can be informed by the Voice of the Customer, is what we offer, variation is how we perform in providing it.

Perhaps you might be pondering if training your team to improve capability will reduce variation. Undoubtedly it will help – generally, the greater the skill and capability, the greater the ability to replicate performance with less variation. Further, improving someone's capability will also entail improving their autonomy and ability to make decisions in their work – removing what might be thought to be necessary elements of command and control. That should be appealing for organisations looking to adopt a culture of continuous improvement.

When Data Talks, We Must Listen

We need to be conscious of the fact that sometimes the data we capture, and the story it is telling us, seems incongruent with our expectations – and the danger is, because of that incongruence, we dismiss what the data is telling us.

We need to be conscious of this mindset; instead of seeking reasons to dismiss the data, we should focus on understanding why we have the data that we do.

It takes a concerted effort to be blind to our prejudices when we are looking to understand the story that the data is telling us and the insights that the data is offering us.

The data is the data because of specific reasons, and it is crucial to understand them. Within these reasons, there might be a new truth that we are not currently aware of. As a personal example, my mindset was centred around the belief that the more kilometres I ran in training each week, the better a runner I would become. However, there were consecutive weeks where I ran significantly fewer kilometres and, surprisingly, my race performances improved. Initially tempted to dismiss this data due to its incongruence with my mindset, I had to consciously switch my mindset to understand how I could achieve faster race times while training 'less'.

The Benefit of Good Data Analysis

We know about the sense of urgency we have to jump to solutions. What we need to be conscious of is the good analysis of the data that significantly helps us to determine the solutions. The better we analyse the performance data we have the more readily quality solutions start to become evident.

> Solution development doesn't start after data analysis;
> it starts through data analysis.

While people often want to jump to a solution, it is the trawling through the data to understand the story the data is telling us that provides the critical path to developing the right solutions.

CHAPTER 11

Developing Better Solutions

In this section, we're going to delve deeper into these elements to strengthen the team's capability for solution development by:

- introducing new tools, more advanced analysis and further considerations to develop better solutions
- developing better measures of process performance which drive the right team behaviours to support process performance
- defining the scope of the solution, ranging from fixing a single step in a process through to complex system improvements, while also addressing rework demand
- managing a vast array of solutions and determining how to rank and order potential solutions
- running better pilots with customers and capturing the initial actual benefits.

RANDOM WORD: ANOTHER TOOL FOR SOLUTION DEVELOPMENT

Random word is a unique solution development tool where you take any random word (the more random the better) and you apply it to something you might be developing, such as a solution or a product.

For example, with a team that was developing tyres, they wanted to see if there was something new or unique they could do so they picked a random word – duck – to stimulate their thinking. Because ducks come in a variety of colours, they thought about what colour they could bring to tyres, initially thinking about colour on the outside of the tyres. Then someone suggested bringing colour to the inside of tyres and then the conversation became about how useful that would be.

The idea became that there could be a thin layer of colour applied within the tread of the tyre, and when the tread reaches a point where it is worn away and safety is a concern, that colour starts to come through, alerting the owner that it is time to replace the tyres.

However, there was a concern that in doing that law enforcement would see the colours and that might mean our customers receiving tickets for infractions.

So, the idea then became that there would be two distinct colours for tyre indicators: one as a warning for the driver and the other to signify the minimum tread. These colours would be trademarked and unique to the brand. If a customer with the brand's colour returns for tyre replacement, they would receive a significant discount, creating an incentive for customer loyalty. This not only benefits the customer but also the business, as the discount is lower than the cost of recruiting a new customer.

You definitely need a strong and collaborative team dynamic to use a random word because you really are testing the bounds of thinking exploratively without criticism. Random words can also be used by individuals simply to twist, stretch and stimulate their own thinking.

MAKING IMPROVEMENTS ON VARIOUS LEVELS

Improvements are usually talked about generically, but let's understand the key distinctions between the improvements that can be experienced.

It's important to understand these distinctions because we can deliberately choose the improvement type to suit the maturity of the team.

Following is a table listing the types of improvements you can make in an organisation, listed in increasing complexity and starting from the simple and quick improvements based on little data through to deeply investigative and wide-reaching improvements.

What improvement is the most purposeful is dependent on the factors in a situation. In Loop 1, we had the tools to address rework, errors and affect process improvement (the first two rows in Figure 10, on page 244). Now, we are looking to build our capability to cover the other more complex elements of improvement.

Here is an overview of the types of improvements you can make and their impact, from fixing just a step in a process through to the whole system, including the process and the demand on the process:

- **Single rework and error fixes:** fixes a step in the process where rework occurs.
- **Process improvement:** looks at all steps in the process to ensure the end-to-end performance of the process is improved.
- **Demand analysis and process improvement:** seeks to not only look to improve the end-to-end performance of the process, but to reduce the rework demand and aiming to improve first time resolution/completion.
- **Demand analysis and system improvement:** includes full analysis of demand, and the system, everything that supports and restricts process performance.
- **Intervention, Demand analysis and system improvement:** integrates insights to understand and predict demand resulting from past demand. This enables you to proactively forecast and plan for demand, or perhaps reduce overall demand. For example, if data indicates the raising of an issue by the customer means a high likelihood of a related issue later, you then could aim to address them together initially to enhance efficiency and reduce costs associated with handling subsequent requests separately.

Fixing the ...	Means that we perform (white box) or do not perform (grey box)			
Single rework and error fixes	We make less mistakes in the process, there's less rework occurring within the process	Not cleaning the whole process end-to-end	Not reducing incoming demand to the process	No insight of inter-relationship between demands by individual customer
Process improvement	We make less mistakes in the process, there's less rework occurring within the process	Clean the process for better end-to-end performance and efficiency	Not reducing incoming demand to the process	No insight of inter-relationship between demands by individual customer
Demand analysis and process improvement	We make less mistakes in the process, there's less rework occurring within the process	Clean the process for better end-to-end performance and efficiency	Improvements to reduce rework demand	No insight of inter-relationship between demands by individual customer
Demand analysis and system improvement	We make less mistakes in the process, there's less rework occurring within the process	Clean the process for better end-to-end performance and efficiency	Improvements to reduce rework demand and improving system elements of process performance	No insight of inter-relationship between demands by individual customer
Intervention, Demand analysis and system improvement	We make less mistakes in the process, there's less rework occurring within the process	Clean the process for better end-to-end performance and efficiency	Improvements to reduce rework demand and improving system elements of process performance	Predict the value demand with greater efficiency to handle it and/or reduce frequency of subsequent value demand in this or related processes

Figure 10: Improvements – scale and nature of the possible improvements

Figure 10 replicates the text on page 243, showing what each approach does and does not provide.

Simple improvements to parts of the process might have served us well in Loop 1, but now we are looking at other inter-related parts of our operations for wider benefits in our work in Loop 2. Nothing in this table is a hard rule but serves to highlight the progress of maturity of performance improvement.

THE ROLE OF CULTURE IN IMPROVEMENTS

There is little point in changing a process when the new process will depend on adherence to some cultural elements that don't exist. For example, having forms that convey information from one team to another, but having a culture of sending through work between teams that is sloppy or incomplete. Without a culture of doing things right the first time, the form will only act as a channel or conduit to replicating the cultural issues being experienced. During solution development, determine: what cultural characteristics do we need to establish to get the most out of and support the improvements we are looking to make?

A culture strongly influences the engagement of a team. It is a good investment to spend time understanding how you can improve the culture and engagement of your team, which results in better performance. Too often, cultural norms of the ways of working are applied indiscriminately across the team. The team is made up of different people with differing reactions to stimuli. Start to understand what people need, including what working environments enable them to be the best engaged.

Let me come right out of left field on this one. I'm amazed that we don't (at least for some) bring the nature of a working day closer to that of a sports event. Too often, the larger populous trudge to work and trudge through their work. As a sporting event, where there's a strong focus on performance, we'd make sure our team:

- turn up early and full of energy, prepared with the right hydration and nutrition
- have a great (fit-for-purpose) warm-up

- collaborate as a team to know the strategies and plays for the day and how we as a team are going to affect those strategies
- are energised through music and/or the captain's or coach's speech
- are unleashed into the game
- know when the game is finished
- have a score to know how the game is unfolding, and how we did.

So many of these elements can be transitioned in our workdays. Why can't work be as exciting as sport? Why can't we be invigorated with the challenges of the day? Why can't we leverage the performance of being part of a team, working for each other for a global result rather than individual results?

Another Cultural Element

Without instilling a customer-centric continuous improvement mindset within teams after any organisational transformation may lead to the inevitable need for another transformation. Failing to continually monitor and eliminate the gap between what customers want and what the organisation offers, and providing that efficiently, will likely result in ongoing challenges and problems. Cultivating a culture of continuous improvement is essential for sustained success in effectively and efficiently meeting customer needs.

ADVANCED ANALYSIS TO FIND POTENTIAL IMPROVEMENTS

Let's delve into some more advanced tools, perfect for developing better solutions in Loop 2.

Using the Lenses of Lean

After you have developed a process map, you can analyse each activity of the process through a number of lenses and can categorise the value of each step to help hone your focus on where you can improve the process steps (if not removing them entirely) to remove wasted activities from the process and free up the team's capacity.

With knowing the nature of these improvements, you'll understand as a leader how likely and vital it is that changes will involve cross-team collaboration and cooperation. If (in reference to Figure 10 on page 244) an improvement is on a single rework or error fix, then it will more likely be enabled by a single team. For any improvements that are an end-to-end process improvement, or more significant than that, then almost certainly those improvements will involve two or more teams.

Analysing the Process Steps

Steps in a process can usually be categorised as one of three things: a step in the process that contributes to producing something of value to the customer (termed customer value-add), something that the business needs to do for the continuity of the business (activities like placing orders for inventory or issuing invoices are business value-add activities), or steps that are non-value-add.

Simply go through each process step as a team and decide if that process step is:

- **Customer value-add**: something that the customer happily pays for. If you didn't do this process step, then it would negatively affect the product or service that the customer expects and requires. This is a step that is performed right the first time (so does not include rework) to bring value to the customer, which they recognise and expect.
- **Business value-add**: something that is done to support the crucial running of and to sustain the business, and for the business to deliver customer value-add activities, or are required by contract, law or regulations, or for health, safety, environmental, ethical or team health and development reasons.
- **Non-value-add**: this is what we are looking for – work that soaks up capacity and resources and does not benefit the customer nor the business – as it doesn't meet the definitions

above of customer or business value-add. These activities simply generate waste. Non-value-add activities can be further categorised into one of the different forms of waste, usually referred to as the seven wastes, which we'll cover in the Lean section, next.

A quick note: Business value-add is sometimes referred to as business *non*-value-add because the term value-add is, for some teams, to be used exclusively from the customer value perspective. Know that these two terms can be used interchangeably. I prefer business value-add to help isolate what we are looking for, specifically having the team focus on non-value-add activities that offer no value to the customer nor the business.

In highlighting non-value-add activities in our analysis, don't get caught up in over-analysing if an activity is customer value-add or business value-add. I've experienced teams getting caught up in this debate if an activity seems hard to differentiate between customer and business value-add.

Avoid spending time on unnecessary debates, the focus should be on identifying and eliminating non-value-add activities within the process to increase team capacity. Whether the value-add is for the business or the customer doesn't matter (at this stage) because it is determined to be a type of value-add. Keep moving and analysing the process steps, looking for what the team agree to be non-value-add work.

When debating customer value or non-value, ask the customer if the process step is worth paying for. For business value discussions, explore the impact of removing the step. In short:

- If the team are confused whether an activity is customer value-add or non-value-add, ask the customer if it is important to them.
- If the team are confused whether an activity is business value-add or non-value-add, enquire with the business teams why you are performing that activity (the 5 Whys tool could help here).

The focus is always on the identification and then removal or reduction of non-value-add activities. Because of this analysis of each step in the process, you might discover quick wins, such as capacity lost in the team building reports that are no longer relevant to the stakeholders, which is non-value-add work that can be immediately stopped.

LEAN

There are not many methodologies I've specifically called out by name, but **Lean** is going to be one of them. It offers a very different and complementary mindset to the continuous improvement approach.

The Lean concept helps us optimise how we perform tasks, achieving greater efficiently and saving resources. If we are not performing well and there's lots of mistakes and rework, I'd suggest looking to remove those errors before we look at efficiencies in your performance. Once we've improved our performance and are consistently meeting our customers' expectations and standards, we can use Lean to determine how can we be more efficient in producing those consistent results.

Lean is particularly impactful now with a focus on reducing environmental impacts, both from competitive advantage and moral standpoints.

The Lean Mindset

Identifying the common wastes that occur in a process provides the opportunity to work the removal of those wastes into any solution you develop.

The seven fundamental wastes are:

1. **Transportation:** excessive movement of people, information or items, usually externally from an organisation's site.
2. **Inventory:** excess inventory on hand.
3. **Motion:** any unnecessary physical movement of people or relocation of information and items, usually internally within an organisation.

4. **Waiting:** customer queues and process bottlenecks.
5. **Overproduction:** producing more than what is needed, usually in terms of products, though can include anything, such as the production of reports that are not used for their insights.
6. **Overprocessing:** additional work over and above customer requirements (which can contribute to increasing customer queues, over-engineering of products).
7. **Defects:** things that have not been done, or not done correctly, and usually generate rework or defective products.

A helpful way to remember the first letter of each waste of the acronym TIMWOOD, which is the order I've listed them above.

Though all the wastes are likely to occur in a manufacturing environment, a service environment can also experience significant waste, primarily in the areas of waiting, over-processing, over-production and defects (as rework).

The 8th Waste

The 8th waste refers to an underutilisation of human resources, where part of someone's or a team's capacity and capability remain unused, thus failing to tap into the team's full potential.

The solution involves balancing the workload across the team, ensuring a faster process through having the right people with the right skills contribute to customer value-add activities at the right time. Not adopting a continuous improvement approach within the team culture hinders the unlocking of their capability to identify and resolve issues, representing a prime example of the 8th Lean waste. The primary aim of this book is to guide you in effectively utilising this 8th waste by building and unleashing your team's potential for making improvements.

Improving Organisational Efficiency and Reducing Hidden Factories with Lean

Removing wasteful elements of a process provides significant and numerous benefits for an organisation. The elimination of wasted energy enables an organisation to reduce costs and save time, which in turn can result in a more responsive and efficient team.

In my experience, there is always substantial waste in the **hidden factory** – the industrious efforts by your team to do something just below the surface (meaning unseen), which isn't related to the purpose of the process, but perhaps for their sanity, preservation or reputation. A sure sign that a hidden factory has been identified is when someone, seeing the full process for the first time, exclaims, 'We do what?! Why on earth are we doing that?!'

Hidden factories can be driven through extra work done by the team to doctor how their performance is being evaluated, to preserve their reputation. Don't skip ahead, but on page 266 is 'A cautionary tale', an example of that very thing, a hidden factory, activated by poor measures of performance in turn driving the wrong behaviours in a team. Awareness of waste, which will take courage, is the first step towards its removal. Lean is a great lens through which to view and raise awareness of embedded wastes, exposing the hidden factories.

Mapping a process and capturing data on the occurring wastes is an extremely cost-effective way to expose the hidden factories and the waste in a process. It also provides the team with the insight to make an informed decision on what needs to be fixed first and why and start to determine root causes.

APPLYING THE LENSES FOR IMPROVEMENTS

In this section, I've shared a number of crucial lenses for advanced improvement of processes. Let's better contextualise what order we should use these tools for the better impact. Here's the order by impact, with a richer explanation for the order to follow:

1. Reduce load/incoming rework demand on the team.
2. Remove non-value-add work.
3. Reduce rework and the occurrence of errors (with mistake proofing and checklists).
4. Balance workload and reduce handovers.

5. Improve visibility of performance.

Reduce the Load and Rework Demand

The first thing you might want to look at is the quality and quantity of the work coming in – to reduce the quantity and improve the quality before you refine the process that handles that work – and that is why we apply this improvement first.

Sometimes we have extensive control over this and sometimes we don't. In an accident and emergency department, the nature of incoming work can be beyond our immediate control. However, in cases where we handle standardised customer applications and various questions on those applications lead to customer confusion, there is a greater opportunity for us to improve the quality of incoming work. Of course, the more predictable and consistent the quality of work coming in (meaning we know what we will likely get and can prepare for it), the easier it is to process that work and the less likely rework will need to be performed, such as going back to the customer for clarification – with the customer's reply additionally becoming rework demand for our team.

Remove Non-value-add Work

As you analyse all the work being performed by your team in the process, some of the work you are performing may be simply wasteful and unnecessarily sucking up capacity. Before refining other steps in the process that will remain, remove those steps that you no longer need to perform now. The work or task may have had a purpose previously, but you might find yourself in a position where that purpose no longer exists. So, your focus becomes how to remove those tasks to make the process more relevant and to free up the capacity of your team. Often this might take the shape of unnecessary quality checks or signing off an activity before the work can continue.

Reduce Rework, Errors and Mistakes

Next, we can focus on minimising waste in the process and reducing the frequency of errors that lead to rework. Of course, any rework sucks up capacity of the team and stops them from working on other tasks. Rework and errors can be measured in two ways: how frequently they occur and, when they occur, the impact on the team and the customer.

By capturing initial data on error frequency and impact, we gain insights to develop solutions for error reduction. Comparing the new data against the original baseline allows us to assess the effectiveness of our solutions.

One way of reducing errors is through mistake proofing, and one of the tools for mistake proofing is using checklists.

Mistake Proofing and Checklists

Mistake proofing is used to detect and prevent errors from occurring, especially those that affect your customers. Mistake proofing could be preventative in nature, where it stops the error from occurring, or proofing in nature, where it detects an error that has occurred before moving on in the process. Mistake proofing can also be referred to as error proofing.

Mistake prevention and proofing comes in many different forms. The underlying principle of the tool is to support the process in such a way that it makes it significantly more likely for the team to produce a service or product without errors or defects.

Here's an example of mistake proofing: a coffee shop frequently serves drinks at the wrong temperatures. The coffees are consistently at about 90°C, while the green teas, which should be served at 80°C, are being served between 60°C and 100°C. The errors with the green teas occur because the temperature depends on the judgement call of the team member of how much cold water is added to the boiling water to get the desired 80°C. The team wants to reduce the errors occurring for the customer. Mistake proofing would be the use of a thermometer to test the temperature before the drink is given to the customer. Focus on mistake prevention over mistake proofing if possible, so better mistake proofing could be the use of a kettle that has a temperature thermostat setting.

Mistake proofing is an exciting tool for the team, requiring creativity to enhance process steps. Identifying when and why errors occur allows for effective prevention using mistake-proofing techniques. Prioritise mistake prevention, but when needed, implement easily piloted mistake-proofing solutions for quick results.

The Power of Checklists

Building a checklist offers quick wins for performance improvement of vital steps within a process, ensuring that they are done better and more completely with the aid of the checklist. The high-level steps to realise benefits through checklists are:

1. Identify issues and capture baseline performance data.
2. Leverage the principle that those in the work design the solutions to create a comprehensive checklist capturing all the actions in the order they need to be performed.
3. Form a team to pilot the checklist.
4. Pilot the checklist and gather new performance data and the benefits.
5. Once better performance is proven in the pilot, embed the checklist as a working practice.

Balance Workload and Reduce Handovers

Now that we've identified and refined the valuable parts of the work, the next step is to balance the workload of the work across the team. Sometimes you find when a process goes through a number of hands, some steps in the process demand minutes of someone's attention and some other steps demand hours from another person. If there is an opportunity to balance the workload, meaning moving tasks from one person or team to another to make sure everybody is equally investing the same amount of capacity into the process, this can significantly reduce bottlenecks from happening, which tend to occur when a few people are being overloaded. Balancing the workload across a team to perform a process means the whole process is performed more efficiently and completed more quickly.

Another option is to reduce the number of handovers in the workflow. If there's still value in having someone else or another team perform specific tasks, investigate building new capabilities into a team to eliminate the need for handovers. Any time we hand over work, it can slow down the process and introduce errors.

It's also crucial to assess *how* work is handed over. Properly packaging the work for the next person or team in the process ensures they can perform their tasks faster and with fewer errors because of the way it has been prepared for them.

While we are in this element, another good thing to do is to make sure that the right work is being performed in the right order, testing to see if there would be benefits in reordering the order of the work being performed.

Improve Visibility of Performance

One of the final steps we will look at is improving the visibility of performance to the team and potentially to the customer. The team members' ability to see how their work process is performing enhances their sense of influence on its outcomes.

After implementing changes to reduce workload, speed up processes through reduced rework and handovers, and reduce bottlenecks through balancing the workload, these improvements need to be made visible through capturing and displaying the new performance data and sharing it (and the benefits of the good work done) with the team.

Additionally, we'll look at how the performance measures influence team behaviour. It's crucial to ensure that these measures encourage the right behaviours rather than prompting shortcuts in the process to meet arbitrary timeframe targets, for example.

But remember, if customers reveal something new and purposeful, it should be incorporated. This approach considers both eliminating non-purposeful elements and retaining purposeful aspects critical for achieving the desired customer outcome.

In Figure 11, we see the five steps as a graphical representation of the approach to improve the process.

Current process

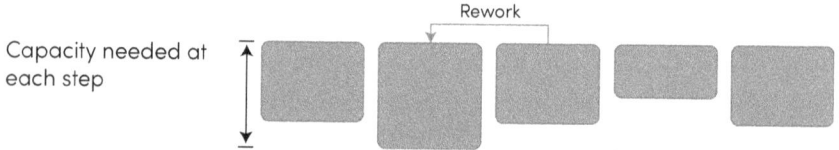

Step one: Reduce (rework) demand

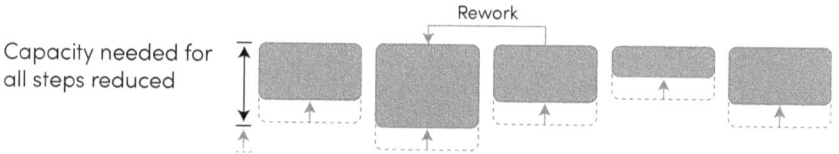

Step two: Remove non-value add work

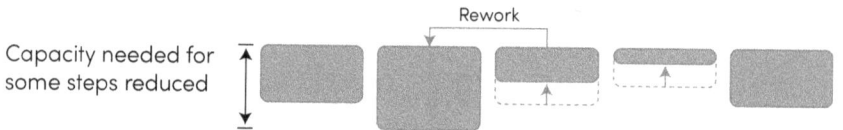

Step three: Remove (or reduce) rework

Step four: Balance workload

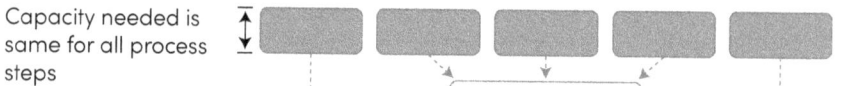

Step five: Improve visibility of performance

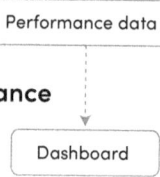

Figure 11: Diagram overview of all the elements of reducing waste and the order

GETTING CLOSER TO FIRST-TIME RESOLUTION

When the customer contacts your organisation (illustrated in Figure 12), there'll likely be one of three outcomes for your team member handling the query:

1. The representative can properly resolve the query in the first instance, which is the best-case scenario.
2. The representative can hand over the customer query to someone else to resolve it.
3. The representative does not fully resolve the customer query properly, which can lead to the customer contacting the contact centre again later, illustrated by the arrow circling back through as a second customer contact. Worse yet, the customer doesn't call back and stops being your customer.

We want to aim to reduce these last two scenarios as much as possible.

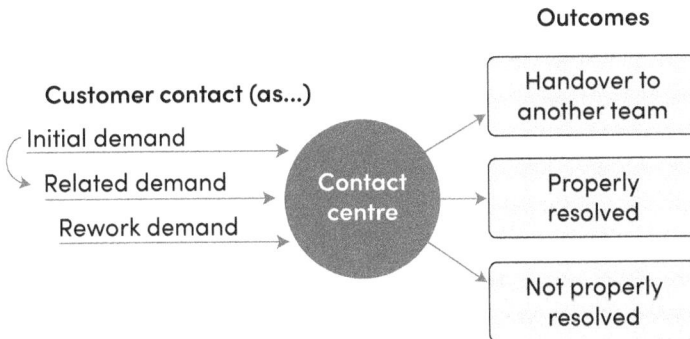

Figure 12: Customer contacts the organisation through the contact centre

If we overlay this scenario with the improvement lenses we have talked about, we can identify the order we can and should implement improvements:

1. Reduce rework demand coming back into the contact centre for any reason, which would likely have the biggest positive impact for both our organisation and our customer.

2. Reduce errors by applying mistake proofing to reduce:
    a. handing over the customer query to another team who are incapable of resolving it
    b. the contact centre mishandling the query, leading to an incomplete resolution where the problem is not fully fixed.
3. Build the contact centre representative's capability to handle a greater number of customers queries.
4. Build the measurement and visualisation of the vital metrics of:
    a. frequency of handover of customer queries and monitor the reduction of handovers
    b. frequency of the correct handover of customer queries
    c. frequency of first call resolution and the reduction of rework demand.

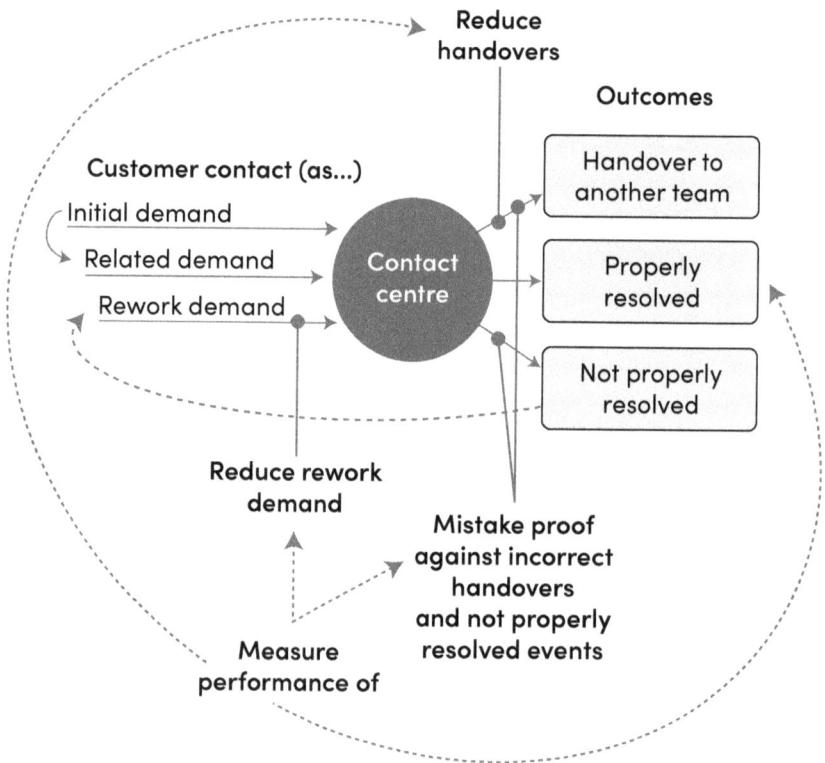

Figure 13: Where and how the improvements impact the customer contact experience

There's a great opportunity to reduce errors and customer handovers at the point where your organisation meets your customers and improve the first-time resolution rate.

By analysing data on customer contacts and the reasons for the handovers, you can identify areas to build the capability of the customer contact team for more efficient query handling. While complete resolution for all handovers may not be feasible, quick wins are possible. An example of this was when one team was handing over a part of an application to another team to assess and then return a judgement, with that team's assessment adding just over 120 days to the process. As the quick win, after two hours of training, that team was no longer dependant on the other team to review that specific part of the application; they could now perform the assessment themselves, reducing the processing time for 80% of the applications from just over 120 days down to one hour.

Additional data on the reasons for customers calling back helps us understand unresolved issues. Once we understand through the data why customers are calling back, we can collaborate with the customer contact team to address root causes and reduce rework demand.

Too often people think that this is a lack of diligence or capability of the person who took the call or the customer query. But often it's the lack of support and availability of information and system functionality accessible to the representative. Irrespective of what the reasons are, we need to find out how often those incidents are occurring and the root causes. We can then make an informed decision about how to reduce handovers and the frequency of incomplete resolves, thereby increasing your customer contact first-time resolve performance.

FACILITATING SOLUTION DEVELOPMENT WITH CROSS-TEAM COLLABORATION

Encourage cross-team collaboration by initiating the conversation with this sentence, allowing each team to contribute and fill in the gaps as they collaborate, so one team will suggest to the other that:

If you can [action/activity], then we'll be able to [action/activity], which will provide the benefit of [benefit that resonates for both teams/benefit that fulfils purpose].

One team proposes a collaborative agreement, specifying what they will provide and suggesting what the other team can supply. The mutual benefit derived from this collaboration should align with the interests of both teams and ultimately contribute to the overall success of the organisation.

This, of course, is the starting point of a negotiation to find the best way for the two teams to collaborate.

The essential element to running an effective improvement discussion with another team (so you can run a pilot with them – for example)

What they want

What you and your team want

Spend 0% of time here

Spend 0% of time here

Where **both** teams spend 100% of their time discussing

During discussions on improving team collaboration, it's important they stay focused on how their collaboration can produce outcomes beneficial for both teams and the organisation. This is the overlap of the Venn diagram above. Consider revisiting areas where you currently allocate 0% of your time, but only after establishing some goodwill.

Why have I mentioned this tip now? Because you'll likely find a good number of improvements that you'd like to make will involve the permission or support of, or coordination with, other teams. If others haven't been part of the analysis of the process, they will likely be in a different (and less informed) headspace. So, this is the type of conversation your team will need to have.

Cooperation First, IT Last

Continuous improvement will enable significant gains in processes before the need to automate them. Automating broken, unhealthy and over complicated processes is far more time consuming and expensive to do than healthy and well modelled processes.

Here's an experience I had of cross-team collaboration and cooperation: Four teams in the same region were receiving and processing equal amounts of the same application form but in four very different ways. An IT initiative looking to automate the process had four business analysts going out, one to each of the sites, to try to capture their processes requirements for a new system. Because the sites were processing the application so differently from each other, the customised requirements and modifications they would need to make to the system to accommodate each site were outrageously unwieldy.

We took a different approach to focus on collaboration and cooperation across the teams. We facilitated the teams working together to share how they process their applications and why they process them the way that they do. The teams were able to cross-pollinate their good ideas with each other. Rather than teams needing to perform their processes differently for regional differences, which didn't exist, the truth was some teams had discovered better ways of performing the process. They had previously either shared the idea with other teams and it wasn't adopted because it wasn't understood, or they didn't share the improvements at all, as there was no forum set up to do so.

The differences between the teams evolved over time simply because they were working in silos and weren't communicating with each other. They didn't need to communicate as their role was to process the forms, not process the forms *and* improve the ways the forms were being processed. Without that second hat, they weren't consciously looking for and sharing improvements. In one day, we were able to assimilate much of the four process differences into one uniform (and faster for most with the incorporation of benefits from others) process, ready to be automated if needed.

Don't assume that IT professionals would oppose this principle – in fact, they strongly support it. When coding a process, who wouldn't prefer a clean and well-defined process? It not only makes their work easier and more efficient, reducing the likelihood of mistakes, but it also significantly saves costs. More than anyone, IT professionals appreciate the benefits of cooperating to clean up a process before automating it.

IT, AI and Robotics

In my experience, it is worthwhile to prioritise process improvement over automation. Improve and streamline your processes before automating them to ensure you're automating the right things, cost-effectively and with greater success.

While there's significant buzz around robotic process automation (RPA) and artificial intelligence (AI), it's crucial to view them as tools to unleash your team's capability in improving how your organisation delivers to customers. These technologies empower employees to not only perform their more valued tasks but also to free up their capacity to enhance the work they perform, fostering innovation.

When introducing robotics and AI, focus on enabling your team to repurpose their capabilities for overall performance improvement, rather than solely pursuing cost savings.

Transitioning from menial tasks to innovative improvements is key for becoming a sector-leading, customer-focused organisation. The strategy should centre around unleashing team capability and capacity, with cost savings as a subsequent outcome rather than making cost-saving the primary goal of robotics implementation. To implement robotics effectively and relatively cheaply, the cleaner your processes are, the better.

So, what's the first step? Prepare your processes or steps in a process for roboticisation. Swiftly analyse processes to identify candidates for roboticisation and assess what needs to be done to clean and improve your vital processes. Good analysis will determine which processes need to be improved before being roboticised, providing immediate gains through this refinement.

Another crucial consideration is whether robotics and automation would accelerate the actual execution of the process or solely the movement of work from one process step to another.

Consider whether certain process steps are knowledge-based, involving evaluation and decision making, while others are transactional, where a file moves between individuals or teams. Distinguishing between these types of steps is crucial for determining the suitability and impact of introducing robotics and automation in different aspects of the workflow.

I have seen teams that have been incorrectly advised to invest vast amounts of money on the movement of work from one process step to another, but each of those process steps were heavily humanised knowledge-based steps. This investment resulted in merely accelerating the movement of files from one individual to another, inadvertently leading to bottlenecks without any actual reduction in the overall process time. Essentially, tasks were transferred more rapidly into the queue of the next step but did not progress any faster through it. The real bottleneck was the human-centric nature of these steps. Instead of enhancing the system's ability to transfer work, the focus should have been on enhancing the team's ability to efficiently execute their tasks, thereby addressing the true source of delay in the workflow.

The next natural step after we have improved the capability of a person to perform their work faster is to look to improve the capability of a team member to reduce the need to hand over the work to another, reducing the number of handovers involved in the process. With this approach, you'd also eliminate any back-and-forth movement of the work between the team. So that's why IT comes last; though crucial, we need to first focus on how we can enable our team to make better decisions faster.

GOOD MEASURES

To have an insightful and accurate view of performance, we need to develop good measures. Good measures should focus on the right elements of performance and support the right behaviours in your team for better levels of performance.

> Not being able to properly see your organisation's performance is like cleaning your teeth in the dark, with the tube of hot muscle rub next to the toothpaste. Sooner or later, you'll feel a heck of a burn you won't see coming.

Developing good measures is incredibly powerful, impactful and positively influential on establishing and effecting a culture of continuous improvement.

Good measures:

- ensure they drive the right behaviours, related to purpose
- place emphasis on incorporating lead measures, contributing to desired outcomes, rather than only having lag measures of outcomes
- provide a comprehensive and accurate reflection of performance
- are updated at the appropriate frequency, preferably in real time.

Think of these key measure ingredients this way: if we want to improve our body composition, I'm arguing that rather than only measuring our weight every day, we should focus on measuring the quality of meal intake before each meal and the energy we are burning with exercise throughout the day. That offers something closer to the right measures in the right place.

Why Good Measures are Crucial

Good measures provide us the crucial insight of how we are performing in what matters. It is those insights that enable us to make great decisions that manifest in making life easier for our teams and our customers.

Your reputation is not defined by your standards, your reputation is defined by your adherence to your standards, which becomes the customer experience and echo.

A quick note on the value of understanding and the inter-relationship between the voice of our customer, our purpose, and our measures of performance. The customer's voice defines our purpose, helping us define the right measures for our organisation. Understanding this three-way relationship is crucial for developing effective measures. Simply put: customer input informs our purpose, we enhance processes accordingly, and we create measures accurately reflecting our performance in meeting that purpose for customers. Here is an illustrated version of the synergistic relationship between the voice of our customers, purpose and measures:

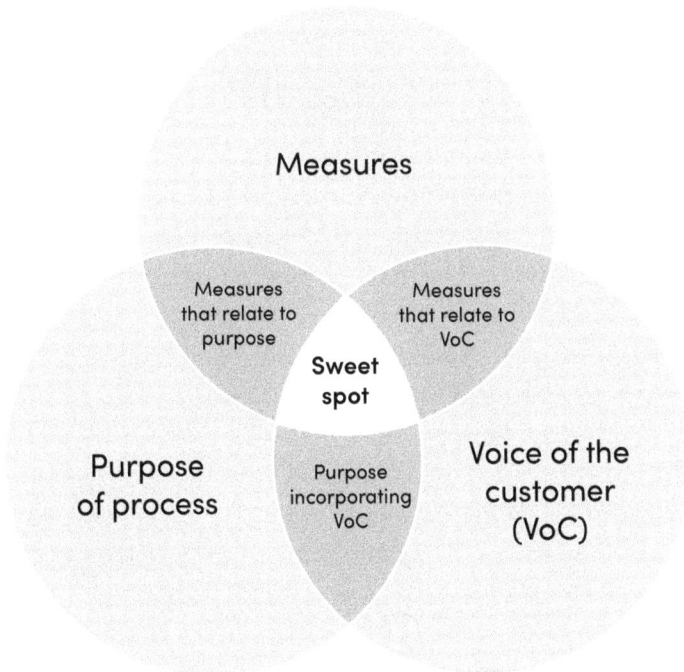

Measures

Measures that relate to purpose

Measures that relate to VoC

Sweet spot

Purpose of process

Purpose incorporating VoC

Voice of the customer (VoC)

A Cautionary Tale: The Toxicity of Targets

Measures are only suited if they are related to the purpose of the organisation and drive the right team behaviours to fulfil that purpose. In my experience, there is often a misalignment between targets, measures and the behaviours they drive and the purpose of the organisation. The current measures of performance may not be fit for monitoring how an organisation is delivering on its purpose or strategy, and if so, these measures do not deliver an ability to provide necessary insights to improve performance.

Improving the system, and the measurement of performance to thereby improve performance itself, is unquestionably sound and requires a joint effort in thinking between leaders and the team.

When leaders set targets, they could unintentionally shift the team's focus from system improvement to target achievement. This transition can lead to poor outcomes, particularly affecting the customer experience. Setting targets too frequently inadvertently absolves the need to think about improving the system.

Simply, working to meet a target and working to make improvements are two very different things with two very different outcomes, especially for the customer. Improving the system means exactly that – making things better. Better for the organisation and better for the customer.

Thinking about meeting targets over improving the system certainly opens the door to mischievous work as hidden factories. This is poor for the organisation, or the customers, or likely both because of the relationship they share, even in a public service setting where the customers have no other option.

Here's an experience with an organisation I helped, it's the cautionary tale I referred to previously:

An organisation had a monthly target to process 80% of applications within 24 days. If they hit 78%, the team has under-performed. Hit 80% or more and the team is going ok. The percentage (a measure of average rather than process variation) was the only measure of performance at the end of the month.

The behaviours that this target drove were:

- Without being supplied performance insight, towards the middle of the month, the team would regularly calculate how they were tracking in terms of the percentage of applications processed in 24 days or less.
- If they were tracking above about 85%, they would carry on and continue to calculate their performance.
- If they were falling below 80%, they would deliberately stop work on applications that had already gone over 24 days, because finishing them in that month meant they would be added to the performance data. They could afford to do this as the data didn't measure variations between the applications. Applications that were, for example, 26 days old around the 20th of the month were deferred for an additional 10 days until the start of the new month. This now resulted in a processing time of at least 36 days. However, the measurement focused solely on whether the application was processed 'on time' or 'late', without considering the actual time taken for processing.
- As another action, if they were falling below 80%, the team would start to cherry-pick those applications that would look faster to process. They would spend about 20 minutes analysing each application for the cleanness and speed that it could be processed. If it was determined that the application would be fast to process and would be done before the end of the month, then the team member would process it. If it was determined that the application was unclean and would likely take a longer than usual time to process it was put back in the queue for someone else to pull out later and analyse, losing valuable team time with that 20-minute assessment being repeated by another team member later. These 'longer' applications would be processed, but only when they were pulled under certain conditions: it was early in the month, or the target percentage was healthy enough to take a hit. If you were wondering where the team leaders were at regarding this hidden factory, they were also judged by the same target, so this behaviour was fuelled by them also.

As crazy as it might seem, the team were acting rationally, doing exactly what was being asked of them by the targets established by senior management – and to meet that set target every month – was their only measure of performance. How the team was behaving reflected a poor element in the system they had to operate in.

What needs to define team performance is not whether or not we hit a target, but whether or not performance is improving.

Meeting targets and improving performance yield different outcomes for organisations. Targets often drive unintended behaviours and consequences, contributing to hidden factories and the use of manipulative, short-term tactics. Ask yourself: What dubious practices does our team engage in to meet targets? These practices, whether visible or concealed, often exist when targets are set. To enhance performance without hindrance, it's crucial to measure performance effectively, without targets that are likely counterproductive to improvement. Instead, prioritise the right measures that drive desired behaviours. Would you prefer a team to expend energy meeting targets or focusing on core performance improvement?

Moving From Targets to a Measures Mindset

Not having targets doesn't mean that the systems performance isn't measured, nor does the absence of targets mean an absence of measures nor accountability. In fact, a focus on targets dilutes the view of the system performance because we are looking only at the (positive or negative) gap between the target and the performance, and not what we should be looking at, which is the changes in the system performance.

We need to see (and of course facilitate) continual improvement – that performance is getting better and better. All our thinking on the process and system is dedicated to making this happen by the whole team through looking at the levels of performance and understanding and acting on the root causes of performance variation.

Targets often represent lag data, determined at the end of a period, while good measures are live, current and lead data, continuously available to the team. Choosing the right performance elements to measure in turn drives the right behaviours in the team and enables a refreshed awareness and focus on improvement amongst the team.

For example, if we suggest that the primary measure of the performance of an economy is Gross Domestic Product (GDP), then what would that specific focus on improving GDP mean for the consideration of innovations in technology that support a better environment? Not a lot. A focus on GDP doesn't measure and thereby entice innovation and the development of sustainable practices. So that wouldn't be a good measure if innovation and sustainability is something we wanted to adopt.

Conversely, if we were to change the measure to be Sustainable Domestic Product (SDP), measuring the total production of sustainable products that have little, neutral or no negative effects on the environment, we can drive a change in behaviours, and more importantly, through those new behaviours, we would experience improvements and innovations, the impacts of which we can't even fathom now.

A significant element of continuous improvement is determining those measures that drive the right behaviours in our organisations and teams.

Revelations in innovation can be sparked by having revolutionary measures.

Investigate what measures could be adopted that drive cooperative behaviours between teams, and current measures that exist that need to be removed as they drive counter-productive and competitive behaviours, contributing to poorer customer outcomes. You might see that some of your current measures of performance are far removed from how you need to be measuring performance to be a customer centric organisation.

The lead measures need to resonate with your teams. We define what excellent customer service is and determine the behaviours that will contribute to that excellence, and then measure and monitor the prevalence of those behaviours, focusing on no other performance elements which do not contribute in this way. This approach ensures your team remains focused on the right behaviours, in turn delivering the right outcomes.

Determining and Developing Good Measures

Good measures are those that drive the right behaviours and culture within a team to drive the right performance, rather than arbitrary targets, which often aren't deliberately determined with team behaviours and culture in mind. Measures need to also focus on the root causes so that the right behaviours are established at the right point of the process.

For example, why measure how quickly we can rework a problem if we have determined the right behaviours that are the root cause for stopping the rework? Sure, keep the rework measure if it's important to someone, but not at the expense of, nor viewing it with the same importance as, the measure of the team performing the right (root cause) behaviour that prevents the rework from occurring.

Good measures are like a washing machine with a glass door, you can see what is going on as it is happening. For example, you can find out you have left something in your pockets and act during the wash rather than discovering the outcome after the wash.

Additionally, good measures significantly contribute to having a good baseline of performance – how we are really performing, right now. This is crucial for the benefit realisation of improvements made. Benefits can then be properly articulated and shared. There's little good in having done good work if people don't know about it and can't look to adopt the mindset or the solution themselves – like we discussed as a reason for building and sharing case studies.

What defines a good measure are metrics that provide accurate, timely and meaningful insights, enabling a team to act on the process to improve performance for the customer. These measures should continue to contribute to the ongoing reporting of benefits experienced through the solution.

Having better measures:

- drives the right behaviours that we know delivers the right performance
- enables better reporting and provides better insight of performance
- leads to more informed decision making on further continuous improvement.

Optimising Measures to Provide Better Insight and Drive the Right Behaviours

Frequently, organisations don't have the right measures to effectively reflect the real performance in a timely manner. Measures of performance might currently exist, but they commonly have these issues:

- They are measures of lag data, which provides a review of performance with no opportunity to improve the performance over the period they were measuring. For example, the average time to deliver to the customer over the previous month.
- They don't show enough of the process or performance of the system. The measures might be of certain points of a process, centred around some steps at the expense of a full end-to-end view, including that of the customer experience.
- The measures are not frequent enough, potentially measuring monthly what the team would really need measured daily to make timely adjustments to performance.
- They don't show variation of process performance. The more variation in the process where the more uniform outcomes should be, the more we need to see this in our measures. Measuring process performance as averages conceals valuable insights that would be gained from understanding the current levels of performance variation.

They drive the wrong behaviours, usually to meet targets. Teams become inventive, not in improving performance, but in manipulating work to meet the set targets.

The Components of Building Better Measures

Here are the components of building and embedding good measures that you need to be aware of:

- establish measures that drive/complement the right behaviours for quality and purpose of the work/process, and reduction of risk
- determine the right frequency of the measures to ensure you are making informed decisions about changes that need to be made related to the current performance (now and ongoing)
- ensure the measures provide the ability to benchmark performance and articulate benefits and value of performance improvement
- plan and perform the transition and training to the new measures – including the visualisation of those measures.

Measuring at the Right Frequency

Another element of establishing good measures is determining how frequently you check in on your measures. The positive effect of good measures driving the right behaviours for great performance evaporates when the checking in on those measures are likely too far apart. For example, if you have a process that might take 2–4 days as a typical cycle time, and your team are measuring that process performance monthly, the frequency of those measures is too far apart to see changes in that process performance.

There's a concept called the **Ten bucket rule** where the resolution of your measurement is helpful if it's a tenth of what you're measuring. This is usually applied to process variation, meaning that if some of your service offerings are often delivered 10 minutes late to customers, you'll measure your lateness by the unit of minutes, but it can also be applied to process length. If your process takes two weeks (10 working days) then check in on progress performance daily. It doesn't need to be strictly applied as a tenth, but it's a good idea to have it frequent enough that your team have enough time to be alerted to and resolve problems in the process to enable the performance to be where your customer needs it to be at the end of the process.

Applying this rule will also help you to:

- better see the amount of variation in the process by the right degree of resolution of the measures
- move from looking at performance through the lens of lag data (after the event) to looking at performance through the lens of lead data (as the event is progressing) so you can determine if work needs to be supported or expedited.

The (Possibly) Most Impactful Measure

One measure organisations all too frequently ignore is the reply rate to new customer first contact. This reply rate is crucial. Any new customer that has reached out with a query, or better still, an order, needs to be replied to 100% of the time. Anything short of that and you are haemorrhaging opportunity.

If we are only replying to about 80% of our customers, and from what I've experienced, that's all too common, then we are losing significant opportunities to grow the revenue, or service levels, of our organisations.

The Power of the Third Link of Related Measures

The third link in a chain of measures is the key to success. Instead of focusing on the result, focus on the critical elements that lead to success. Consider a BMX race as an analogy: winning the race is the ultimate goal (the first link), but to achieve that, you must ride faster (the second link). Riding faster involves various elements like pumping smoother and pedalling at the right time (the third link). Still, this isn't the final step; you need to address what's required to facilitate these elements, which becomes the fourth link, and so on.

In organisational strategy, the first link is the overarching goal (e.g. becoming an industry leader) and the second link is the broad approach to achieve it (e.g. selling more products). The third link, which is crucial, involves the specific actions to sell more products. Going further into the granularity of these actions (the fourth link) is where you delve into the details of how to execute the strategy effectively.

Focusing solely on the end result, like wanting to change body composition by weighing yourself daily, is insufficient. The power lies in concentrating on measuring and monitoring the right elements. This involves following a process centred around the third link in the chain, which ultimately is the 'how' we'll deliver the desired result. This approach ensures that measures defined in the third link define and drive the behaviours needed for the overarching tactic or strategy.

The third link is about conscious awareness of process. It's about not focusing on the result but focusing on the process to produce the result.

Focusing on the result does not deliver a better result. Focusing on the right process to deliver the better result is what delivers the better result.

The third link is the how – the right process to deliver the results. For example:

1. **Link 1:** What (say, improve body composition by shedding fat, increasing muscle mass and aerobic capacity).
2. **Link 2:** By (elements of better nutrition and working out).
3. **Link 3:** How (details of the plan of the elements).

We've talked about the 5 Whys (the multiple whys), this third link is the multiple *Hows*. While the 5 Whys tool solves problems, it is the *Hows* of the third link that determines how to affect strategy.

LEAD MEASURES FOR BETTER PERFORMANCE MONITORING

Moving from lag data to lead data is crucial for better performance insight.

Lag data only shows you the performance after it has occurred, when you have no opportunity to change it. In contrast, lead data shows you the performance during the process, so the team have an opportunity to adjust the performance before the result. Lead data shows you what the result is likely to be.

Hindsight is perfect. Lead data is the next best thing.

Setting up lead data capture requires careful consideration due to its potentially exhaustive nature. Consider capturing lead data if:

- it doesn't significantly add to processing time (and if it does, try to find a way that it will not)
- it adds to the intrinsic value of accountability
- it's not used as an employee performance monitoring tool (remember, performance reflects the system)
- it has customer purpose
- it has control limits and the team understand the laws of variation
- it's not used to expedite work through the process faster than other work over the improvement of the process itself
- it will be shared with the team in the work
- it will drive the right behaviours.

Regularly measuring performance at the right intervals is crucial for effective measures. Having great metrics won't help much if they're assessed too infrequently. If our process takes days but we're checking metrics monthly, we're dealing with outdated information, offering little value.

Think of it like sports; the score is available during play, enabling teams or individuals to adjust strategies in real time. They know the score and what it takes to win, unlike waiting until the end to discover the outcome, leaving little insight during the game.

VISUALLY CAPTURING AND DISPLAYING MEASURES OF PERFORMANCE

What drives your motivation? We often experience it in recreational activities – winning in a team, achieving a personal best, or simply pushing ourselves hard. Modern technology, like GPS watches and apps, provides detailed (and often live) insights of our performance. Most importantly, it provides the insights we look for, the knowledge we want about our performance, helping us understand both the result and the 'why' behind our achievements or challenges.

Now, considering the motivation that data provides us in sports through the insight it provides, why don't we implement the same approach in our work? Visual boards should be a home for detailed performance measures that energise us and our team and track and give feedback on how our daily efforts and improvements are yielding significant improvements. It's about tracking performance daily, seeing the impact of changes made and eagerly awaiting the data for the next day.

Data can motivate and enables us. So, why not build visual boards that excite your team, displaying dynamic and relevant data? Focus on what matters for customers and ask yourself and your team: What motivates us? What performance data do we need to see? Then tailor your boards to reflect these elements and you'll find more genuine and powerful sources of inspiration.

Building a Visual Board

A visual board captures all the insights that a team needs to be able to better perform their work. The visual board will likely include lead data of performance, with indicators of when the performance has reached a level where the team needs to intervene.

Here are a couple of tips:

- the construction of a visual board helps embed an improved process; building a visual board could be part of the embed stage as the improvement team hand over the improved process to the process owner
- add information to the visual board that captures work rhythms and important meetings (like a calendar reminder) and improvement initiatives underway – the things that need to be done by the team daily, weekly and monthly, being part of the work rhythm. Have those key elements listed on the visual board for checking at the daily stand-up meeting.

Want to know all about visual boards and how to construct them effectively? See Appendix 2.

A Quick Note on Setting up Stand-up Sessions

Stand-up sessions complement the visual board. The purpose of daily stand-ups (for no longer than about 10–15 minutes) is to better support communication, coordination, collaboration and cohesion across the team, especially while any improvement initiatives are underway, and to share progress with the team. Stand-ups establish a team dynamic (culture) of daily checking in of progress and a focus on delivery.

The purpose of this approach is to track elements of the critical steps:

- what needs to be done (and checking that there's nothing falling through gaps)
- when it will be done, and in what order
- how we are progressing – what's been completed and how completion is tracking against elapsed time
- being alerted to any barriers to delivery.

During the daily stand-ups, share a high-level overview of all the activities coming up, current performance, improvements being worked on, on-site visits and engagements, who is where (in terms of the team) during the day and the next day (on-site/off-site/day off), and upcoming important meetings and events.

Each person at the stand-up would have only one minute each to share that information – relative to them. It is important that everyone stays on point and shares what they need to for only a minute. Any extended discussions can take place after the stand-up with those that need to be involved.

Key measures of current performance (especially those that are customer focused) could also be shared. The team should offer (in their minute) their insights on:

- what they did yesterday
- what progress they are looking to make today

any barriers to progress and support needed with those barriers (this is extremely helpful for leaders and is why it's crucial that the team's leaders are involved in the daily stand-up as a priority).

It's important to keep this meeting valuable for all, focused and on-point to only information that supports the entire team. Information that's good for only one or two in the stand-up is then shared outside of the daily stand-up so as not to waste the time of others.

It's not unusual for all members of the daily stand-up to take turns facilitating it and making sure that everyone stays on point. Your team can decide if the stand-up sessions are open to all or not. Some teams have open sessions where anyone can come along, and they post a message like this on their visual board: **We hold stand-up sessions here for 10 minutes every morning at 9.30am – absolutely everyone is welcome to join us.**

Stand-up meetings are a great way to start the workday and provide the team with energy and direction at the start of the day. They improve the team dynamic to instigate a (daily) focus to getting the right stuff done, support cross-team collaboration and improve stakeholder engagement, as stakeholders can also be invited to the stand-up sessions. That said, find the best time for your team for the daily stand-up. I've experienced some teams getting the biggest benefit of having the daily stand-up in the middle or close to the end of the day (which changes the context of the three key points that they cover to be, for example: what has been done today, what will be done tomorrow, and what support is needed for barriers for tomorrow's work).

NEXT LEVEL PILOTS

Let's build on what we learnt about pilots in Loop 1. The key to improvement is not developing an extensive solution for a problem but developing a pilot. The reason can be because you have more skin in the game when developing a solution, more emotional inertia stopping the solution from happening, and much of what might be the basis of the solution might be ill-informed on actualities – opinion over data.

Often in trying to develop a solution, teams try to pre-determine what will work as a solution, and we are looking to then experience unanimous agreement to make the change that adopting the solution will entail. That's a tough task. An excessively big jump. In contrast, developing a pilot involves testing an idea with the explicit goal of learning from it – and in turn accelerating the development of the solution. Pilots have a lower threshold for agreement, making them less challenging and emotional than adopting and embedding a full-fledged (and yet unproven) solution.

Creating a pilot requires less effort and is safer to set up than implementing organisational-wide change, so it is less inhibiting and reduces procrastination and risks for those averse to change. It is the outcomes of the pilot that can grease the wheels for an easier (and better supported) change or save us from the implementation of something that proves to be toxic.

Here are some additional questions to address or factors to consider in the development of your pilot:

- Is the timing right or is there a compelling reason to delay?
- How can we ensure the safe running of the pilot? Consider costs, potential reputational damage, involving trusted customers, and addressing any risks, especially if lives are at stake. Clearly define how the pilot will be conducted and, if necessary, reversed before commencing.
- Be clear about what is and is not a showstopper for piloting a solution. We don't want to unduly delay the pilot by waiting for a perfect solution or the perfect circumstances to run the pilot.
- Decide whether to implement the pilot across all teams simultaneously or stagger it through different teams and at different times, allowing initial adopters to support subsequent teams in embracing the improvement.

Solution Selection: Too Many Solutions to Pilot?

Start to evaluate the potential impact of the solutions in relation to each other. More than saying that some problems are more important than others to solve, this is about helping to determine where to start and narrow the team's focus on a few solutions rather than all the solutions, which can be overwhelming, and is in keeping with a key principle: start smart.

Let the team come up with their own categories/elements to rate the solutions. Again, this could be overworked, so perhaps start with this list and see if the team want to make any changes. Each of the solutions could be measured by these five components:

- **Impact:** the level of impact and benefits that the solution will likely have.
- **Speed:** how quickly the solution will be embedded post pilot.
- **Ease:** how easy it will be to embed the solution, taking into account the resources needed.
- **Alignment to strategy:** how relevant is this solution to improve the core work we perform and alignment to priorities, strategy and purpose – or is it peripheral?
- **Risk:** how risky is the likely solution we pilot? Is there a chance of significant consequences if the pilot goes awry, or is the risk insignificant?

Have the team abide by a rating scale for each of the components, where 1 is not good, taxing or poor, and 5 is good, strong or worthwhile.

Rating of 1	Element	Rating of 5
Limited positive impact	**Impact**	Significant positive impact
Will take a long time to embed the solution	**Speed**	Likely rapid solution implementation
Hard and resource heavy solution	**Ease**	Simple and cost-effective solution
Peripheral to strategy	**Alignment to strategy**	Aligned to strategy
Solution would have significant inherent risks	**Risk**	Almost without risk

For quick team feedback on a scale of 1–5, use the Fist-to-five tool (refer to Appendix 1 for more details). If there's a range of numbers as the team feedback their estimations, simply average them out. Precision and consensus on ratings are not crucial; the goal is to gain insights into the relativity between solution options.

In the absence of performance data, the team is providing anecdotal suggestions based on their experience, knowledge, and reflecting on the customer experience. A full and clear understanding of the impact of the solution will come only with the data gathered on a solution during the pilot, but as much as your team can at this stage, emphasise facts and data over subjective opinions or feelings.

Tips for Running This Session

If making fast decisions using these techniques is new to your team, then most of your energy as a facilitator will be spent making sure that the team use the tools when they're asked as opposed to falling into conversation.

To alleviate this, make sure the team understand how the tools are used, and obtain agreement at the start of decision-making sessions that these tools will be used to guide decisions.

Be clear on the primary reason for using these tools – to reach a good decision faster, saving everyone time. Remind the team of what time the session is planned to finish, and convey that if they apply the tools properly, then they will finish ahead of time. The facilitator's role is to make sure that happens. Have the team convey their permission to the facilitator to keep the session on track, which enables and emboldens the facilitator to keep the conversation on point.

CHAPTER 12

Embedding Proven Solutions

The sustainability of continuous improvement hinges on maintaining new performance levels without regression. Establishing a stable foundation of consistently good performance based on a previously embedded improvement provides the crucial platform for future improvements. All improvements need to be robustly embedded for the next improvement to be built on, and the full realisation of benefits.

A critical aspect of ensuring this success is having effective measures. Good measures provide insights into performance, enabling teams to act and sustain improved levels in various process areas. While the ultimate goal is continuous improvement, maintaining and enhancing current performance relies on these foundational measures.

PROCESS IMPROVEMENTS ARE BUILT INTUITIVELY INTO THE PROCESS

When designing and communicating a new process, it's crucial to go beyond the initial implementation. The new process needs to be embedded so that it is seamlessly integrated into the daily workflow, with subsequent steps being intuitive or built into the process itself to prevent team members from getting stuck or reverting to old processes. This includes mistake proofing the process, making it simple and safe so that errors don't occur and the resulting disapproval of the new process is significantly reduced. The ultimate goal is to create a process that team members can follow without frequent reference to documentation.

To enhance your approach in embedding solutions, focus on incorporating the process directly into the workflow. Instead of relying on external process documents, aim to integrate essential instructions into the process itself. For example, if there's a new document that the team needs to fill out in the process and a new step that they need to perform after that document is filled out, you have the clear explanation of what that next step is on the document itself, so the team clearly knows what they need to do next.

That might sound somewhat manual, and it is, but in an automated context, workflows can be configured to automate these steps, streamlining the entire process. Either way, what we're looking to do is build the process in such a way that it becomes a mistake-proofed and intuitive version of the documented process. The less dependency on process documents, the more effective and streamlined the overall workflow becomes.

PERFORMANCE REPORTING OF EMBEDDED SOLUTIONS

To help embed good and proven solutions, and the right behaviours to support those solutions, we'll focus on better reporting of performance.

To successfully integrate the solutions and foster a culture of continuous improvement, enhanced reporting mechanisms are essential for highlighting and documenting the continuous benefits:

- **Start validating benefits early:** begin verifying the advantages of the solution as soon as it's implemented, ensuring its impact aligns with expectations.

- **Enhanced monitoring for informed decisions:** utilise new reporting tools to monitor performance, facilitating better decision-making based on real-time (lead) data.
- **Continuous evaluation:** establish the new practices, keeping a close eye on the emerging metrics. This continuous scrutiny helps identify further improvement opportunities.
- **Assign ownership:** appoint a dedicated individual or team responsible for tracking, capturing and substantiating the long-term benefits realised.
- **Communicate benefits:** visually share the benefits, making the outcomes and improvements clear and understandable to all stakeholders.
- **Ongoing improvement:** seek out any levels of performance that may require additional refinement, keeping the cycle of improvement perpetual.

Implementing these steps ensures not only the successful adoption of solutions and a continuous improvement mindset but also the establishment of a systematic approach for capturing and communicating the value generated over time.

INITIATIVE ROLL-OUT AND POST IMPLEMENTATION REVIEW

Improved reporting on the performance of a process or system is likely to complement the implemented solution. To drive the right behaviours within the team, it's essential to measure performance effectively. The true realisation of benefits often occurs post-implementation, and it's crucial to capture and share these benefits.

This not only benefits the teams directly involved in the improvement, but also serves as valuable case studies for other teams. These success stories become compelling reasons for other teams to embrace a continuous improvement mindset in their own operations.

CONSTANT REVIEW OF PERFORMANCE

We've already talked about reviewing performance with better measures displayed on visual boards and discussed with the team in daily stand-ups. Now, let's explore other vehicles for sharing performance across the organisation.

Dashboards

With good solutions embedded, we can focus on producing better ways to visually represent current performance for leaders and their teams to monitor and continue to improve.

As a recap, we've analysed and improved our processes, there's a good chance we recognised that we didn't properly measure our processes. Since then, we've developed some good measures of our processes and the right behaviours that underpin the right performance in our processes. We're going to want to stay on top of these measures and understand what they are telling us about the health of our process. Now let's capture and compile these measures in a dashboard.

Your team has likely already determined the measures that should be on the dashboard (likely during the pilot stage), but other questions that need to be answered are:

- Who is responsible for updating each of the metrics and when/ how frequently will they be doing this?
- Who will be sent a copy of the dashboard or notified when the dashboard has been updated?
- Will there be a commentary (as an overview of the performance) that will accompany the dashboard, and if so, who will put that together?
- Do we need to put alerts on the dashboard when certain metrics fall below certain values to alert us that we need to take action?

The test of the effectiveness of a dashboard, especially in terms of the ease of it being understood, is exactly the same as that of a process map. Give it to someone who's unfamiliar with it and ask them to explain what they see. Simply, if they can understand it and explain it back accurately, then you've got a correctly configured dashboard.

Your dashboard will likely expand over time as you refine and improve more processes, developing new metrics for each one and incorporating them into the dashboard.

It is important to note the distinction between a dashboard and a visual board. A visual board primarily caters to the team, showcasing ongoing work, team-related information and items under focus. Complementary to a visual board, a dashboard serves leaders and stakeholders of the process, offering comprehensive performance data and insights into the overall efficiency of the process. While a visual board is centred around the team's activities and improvements, a dashboard can provide a broader perspective of performance across teams and processes.

SUSTAINING THE MOMENTUM: KEEPING THE IDEAS FLOWING

Once you have gone through one full cycle of determining problems, capturing data on the problems, and then developing and sustaining good solutions, the focus turns to the continuity of this – ongoing (continuous) improvement.

Decide on and design how your organisation is going to continue to capture all future ideas for improvements from the team. Underpinning this will be the team's ability to get data on, and evaluate current performance.

Rewarding the thinking which produces potential improvement ideas is essential for nurturing continuous improvement. Care for those ideas, as undermining the ideas kills the thinking and generation of future ideas. The thinking behind the idea which conveys the right mindset and a heighten engagement in the work, is exactly what we want as leaders and what the team deserves to feel. Too often, we forget that any improvement idea is based on the foundation and level of understanding of our purpose.

> ## Improvement ideas are to an organisation what currency is to an economy.

The vibrancy, velocity and freedom to share ideas is determined by the culture. Ideas, especially those to better the customer experience, are crucial elements of the continual improvement of performance for every organisation. To really dig into an idea, you can lean on tools like problem statements, which are helpful to properly frame problems, offering a fuller picture when the team presents an issue that needs fixing, and the Improvement Initiative Plan for mapping out and initiating those improvement efforts.

SUSTAINING THE MOMENTUM: TRANSITIONING FROM CONTINUOUS IMPROVEMENT CAPABILITY TO NEW WAYS OF WORKING

Moving to new ways of working makes sense. Similar to gemba, it's about getting people out from behind their desks, which can contribute to siloed work, and having teams work more collectively together. The cornerstone of this transition is the daily stand-up, centred around a visual board that showcases crucial and comprehensive metrics of performance, and the good conversations that instigates.

Identifying these metrics is a process refined through the pilots undertaken during continuous improvement initiatives. While monitoring these metrics is essential, the goal is not to make daily stand-ups repetitive or stale, where we are looking at the same metrics day in and day out.

Instead, the focus is on leveraging continuous improvement principles to influence, improve and evolve the metrics we are using for performance insights. The dual elements of daily stand-ups involve looking at the key performance metrics to understand how we're performing, and discussing improvement initiatives in flight and other novel approaches we are adopting to improve the performance of those key metrics and the processes that we own as a team.

The daily stand-up should never become the feel of just a mandatory meeting but needs to remain a forum where the team is eager to participate because it offers vital insights for the day and boosts team energy levels.

Continuous improvement principles, such as data-driven decision making, understanding root causes, customer focus, the right behaviour-driving metrics, problem-solving capabilities and cross-team collaboration play a crucial role in shaping the culture for the new ways of working. These principles, ingrained during continuous improvement initiatives, become integral to the team's approach in the evolving work environment. Here's an overview of how all those components experienced in adopting an improvement mindset contribute to a transition to new ways of working.

Binding/phasing **continuous improvement** into **new ways of working**

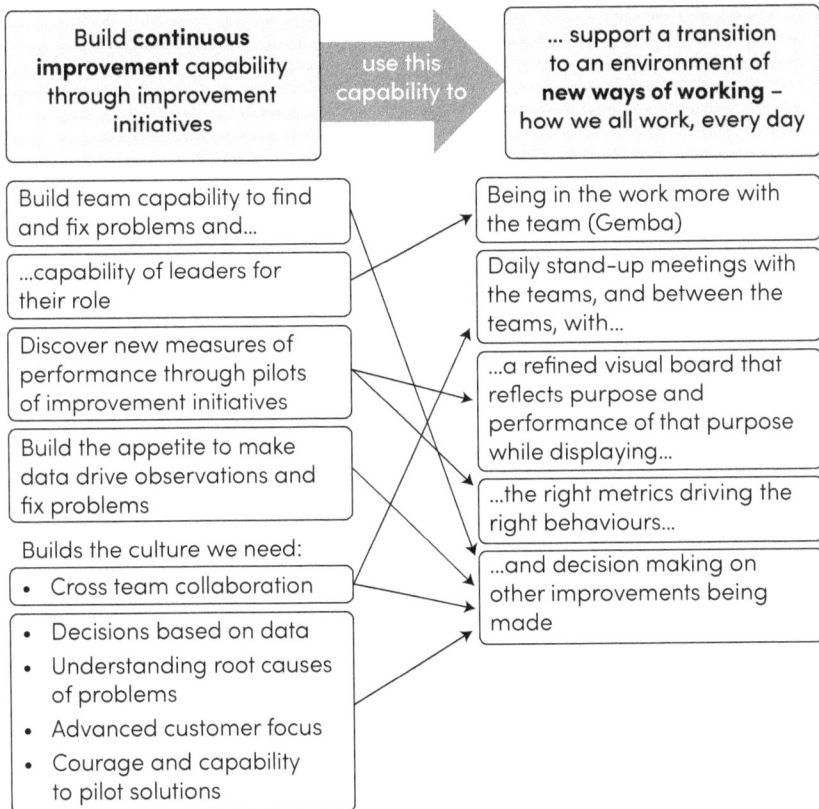

Build **continuous improvement** capability through improvement initiatives

use this capability to

... support a transition to an environment of **new ways of working** – how we all work, every day

Build team capability to find and fix problems and...

...capability of leaders for their role

Discover new measures of performance through pilots of improvement initiatives

Build the appetite to make data drive observations and fix problems

Builds the culture we need:
- Cross team collaboration
- Decisions based on data
- Understanding root causes of problems
- Advanced customer focus
- Courage and capability to pilot solutions

Being in the work more with the team (Gemba)

Daily stand-up meetings with the teams, and between the teams, with...

...a refined visual board that reflects purpose and performance of that purpose while displaying...

...the right metrics driving the right behaviours...

...and decision making on other improvements being made

TIPS FOR LEADERS

Take any nuggets of gold from this section.

> The best leaders consistently demonstrate the courage to believe in and invest in their teams and are prepared to let their teams unleash their capability to challenge and improve the system.

Two Questions to Ask Your Team to Help Establish Good Measures

Whenever I lead or support a team to adopt continuous improvement, there are two questions I ask that provide incredibly insightful answers:

1. What do you need from me to do your best work?
2. What will your best work look like – we'll know you're doing great work when *what* occurs?

Asking these two questions together is crucial because they form an *if/then* statement. *If* this is provided, *then* this is what can be expected. Measures of performance become very clear and easy to monitor.

These questions provide the team with the platform to unleash their potential and measure performance without any surprises about what those measures are, and an understanding of what they need from the leader to contribute to high levels of performance. If the measures articulated aren't aligned to the *purpose* of the team, which is a problem, then this is also exposed through the asking of these questions.

Yes, the answers to these questions will change over time – as they should in a dynamic environment, so ask them regularly. These two simple questions have served me well to get crucial insight on what the team needs to effectively lead themselves, and have an agreed understanding, right at the outset, of expectations of support and performance. These questions are not about forming a contract (anyone going down that path does so at their own peril), but about working together to support and better a team's performance. I hope that by sharing them they help you also.

The Role of Consultants

Consultants can be expensive, so, to get great value, make sure that they leave behind capabilities rather than just solutions for problems. The consultant's role should be to build the continuous improvement capability in the team. Select consultants who can set up the dynamic in the team and the environment to build and unleash the capability of your team to make life easier for themselves and your customers, and to get the team moving with improvement initiatives swiftly.

He kai nā tangata, he kai tītongitongi; he kai nā tōna ringa, tino kai, tino mākona noa

You can only nibble at another's food, but with food that you have cultivated yourself, you can satisfy your appetite. Māori proverb – Whakataukī

Engaging Support

The best continuous improvement practitioners know that:

- they don't know best, so they don't come up with the solutions themselves. Instead, their role is to facilitate how to garner the best solutions from the team with the crucial insights from the customers and their experience
- their role is to act as a translator between the improvement initiative team, senior leadership, the organisation and the customer. They convert the voice and messages from one team to resonate with another team. They understand what the customers want, make sure that the team understands clearly what is being asked for, and that the leaders understand the value of what the customer wants and the work that the

improvement initiative team is performing. The same thing is translated in different ways.

Look for a practitioner/consultant who has the mindset that they are there to help discover problems that others are too busy to recognise – that their role is to help you and your team discover problems (through good facilitation) that you've been too busy to recognise (and again, to build that capability in the team).

Graceful Leadership for Performance Improvement

How leaders react to news of poor performance will drive related behaviours in their teams. If there's a lack of grace, fortitude and resilience displayed when receiving poor news about performance, the behaviours that drive the team will be equally poor: Hiding or doctoring performance results, justifying, minimising, rationalising, or making excuses for performance. None of those behaviours are good. They are traits of denial (de Becker 2000).

Here's the fix: teams who look to adopt continuous improvement must start with building and supporting healthy team dynamics. Only with healthy team dynamics can you have honest conversations about the performance being experienced, and more crucially, why you are experiencing the levels of performance that you are.

The support of the chief executive and senior leaders is critical for the adoption of continuous improvement throughout the organisation. The leaders must be absolutely committed to the team, building their capability to not only perform their work well, but to study the work to continue to improve it to make life easier for themselves and their customers. Commitment needs to be given to keep continuous improvement on their agenda so there is consistent and frequent messaging about how important continuous improvement is to the organisation.

Leaders and process owners might need some high-level training to provide the following:

- defining continuous improvement and its essential principles
- the core four stages of continuous improvement initiatives

- the leadership behaviours that support the adoption of continuous improvement by the team
- team dynamics needed to underpin continuous improvement
- the leader's role in continuous improvement
- decision making at crucial points in the improvement initiative
- benefits for leaders and benefit realisation for the organisation
- case studies of results already experienced in your organisation.

Sponsors would receive additional training after being through leadership training to cover:

- the role of the sponsor
- assessing problem statements
- the sponsor's role in each stage and tools available to support
- the sponsor as a stakeholder.

For training others in the wider team, consider a continuous improvement induction with the following options:

1. **Basic continuous improvement induction (approx. one hour):**
   - What is continuous improvement?
   - The core four stages of continuous improvement initiatives.
   - Essential principles of continuous improvement.
   - Case studies of results already experienced in your organisation.

2. **Comprehensive continuous improvement training (approx. 3–4 hours):**
   - Includes what is covered in the basic induction above.
   - Core continuous improvement tools, including:
     - ~ facilitation techniques
     - ~ decision-making tools (e.g. Fist-to-five tool)
     - ~ problem statements (highlighting future opportunities and areas of team awareness and frustration)
     - ~ Improvement Initiative Plans.
   - One hour to, in their teams, develop and build their problem statements for problems in their respective areas.

The problem statements generated could then be worked up into Improvement Initiative Plans where they could be coupled with a sponsor and a team to start the improvement work.

Better Meetings

We commonly have meetings to enrich our problem-solving by incorporating diverse perspectives from different minds tackling the same issue. Additionally, meetings often serve as a platform for team members to share their knowledge and insights with others. Given that the right measures drive the right behaviours, it's essential to ensure your meetings are equipped with appropriate metrics. Surprisingly, many meetings currently lack any measures whatsoever. Here are four fantastic ways to significantly improve your meetings:

1. **Interruptions tally:** count interruptions (where one person has interrupted another) during meetings without noting individuals. Summarise interruption totals at the meeting's end. Although the total may seem inconsequential, regularly sharing the tally encourages the team to consciously reduce interruptions over time, fostering a self-awareness of respectful communication. Keep a record, especially for recurring meetings, to track trends. A decreasing trend means progress towards a better team dynamic and richer and more thoughtful conversations.
2. **Conciseness tally:** track how often team members express overly lengthy points. While somewhat subjective, a simple tally at the meeting's conclusion motivates the team to consciously enhance their ability (or at least focus) to communicate succinctly.

After these two measures are established then you can look at two further measures:

3. **Pause time tally:** record instances of a three-second gap or longer between statements. This measure aims to encourage thinking time before responding, fostering more thoughtful

contributions. What we want to establish here is *thinking time* as opposed to reactionary statements with little thought. Generally, the more thinking that takes place, the better. Give people the opportunity to talk *and* the time to think.

4. **Diversity and inclusion**: capture the frequency of each team member's contributions to assess balance. While perfect balance isn't necessary, the purpose is to identify significant imbalances. Compare the contribution numbers of the three least contributors to the average of others to see if there's significance in the gap. This advanced measure requires a team mature enough to develop its own rules for ensuring diversity of conversation and balanced contribution (being inclusion) in its meetings.

References

de Becker, G. (2000). *The Gift of Fear: Survival Signals That Protect Us from Violence.* London: Bloomsbury.

Lee Sye, G. (2022). *Process Mastery with Lean Six Sigma: A Complete Body of Knowledge for Lean Six Sigma Practitioners.* Soarent Publishing.

Maister, D.H. and Harvard Business School (1984). *The psychology of waiting lines.* Boston, Mass.: Harvard Business School.

Martichenko, Robert. 'What's the Problem with Continuous Improvement?' *Logistics Quarterly Magazine 10.* Issue 5 – Article 1 – LQ Archives.

Robinson, S.K. (2010). *Bring on the learning revolution!* Available at: https://www.ted.com/talks/sir_ken_robinson_bring_on_the_ learning_revolution?language=en.

Seddon, J. (1999). *Systems Thinking in the Public Sector: the Failure of the Reform Regime... and a Manifesto for a Better Way.* Devon: Triarchy Pr.

Appendices

APPENDIX 1: FACILITATION

Good facilitation of sessions and workshops means facilitating the collective ability of the team to solve problems. Too often, in poorly facilitated sessions, great ideas are not allowed to leave the mind to be shared, built on and enacted. Whether it be because a naturally introverted person can't find the right time in their mind to share the idea, or the dynamic of the meeting is such that there isn't thinking time for those who need time to think – and they need to think before they share, as opposed to those that need to share out loud so they can think something through – the good facilitation of any meeting or session is crucial to yield the collective good of the team through enabling a good environment for all.

As a snapshot, this means that the facilitator assists in running a meeting or discussion by conducting the conversation so it stays on topic. This enables a team to quickly determine decisions and remain focused on the outcomes that need to be realised from the meeting or workshop.

Facilitation concerns itself with all the tasks needed to run a productive and impartial meeting. It serves the needs of any group who are meeting with a common purpose, whether it be making a decision, solving a problem, or simply exchanging ideas and information.

You usually do one of three things when you are running a facilitation session: either you're looking to **share knowledge across the team**, so there might be a team collectively mapping a process together and becoming aware of other steps in the process that they didn't have a great understanding of, so there is a common knowledge at the end of the facilitated session shared across those who participated. Or it is a **strategy** session where the team is working together to find a way to do something; it might be something to be improved or working out how to leverage a competitive advantage. And the third reason might be some type of **arbitration or finding middle ground** between two or more teams to get some level of cooperation and collaboration so the teams can work better together.

It's hard to say that there's a perfect number of participants when facilitating a session, but in my experience, any number between four and 12 is usually manageable and it keeps things personal, which is important. As a facilitator, having a number in this range means you can monitor everybody's interaction with each other and even out the contribution across the team.

Preparation

To prepare to be a facilitator, there are some key elements you need to know:

- The purpose of the meeting or workshop. Know the objectives and which are the most crucial to be completed and the tools you might need to use. And, crucially, you have to make sure that the participants also know the purpose of the meeting or workshop – and they know what they need to do ahead of time to prepare to contribute.
- If there is likely to be a lot of writing and note taking involved, have a *scribe* appointed. While the facilitator could also time keep, the roles of facilitator and scribe are usually too involved to be combined. It is important to know the agenda and time limits for each of the agenda items.
- Planning the sections of the meeting or workshop are important. There might be three crucial questions that need to be investigated, if not answered during the meeting, and we need

to plan what time should be spent on each of those questions so that we get to cover them all.

- Of course, be conscious that as much as the facilitator plans the workshop, and all planning is good, the workshop will never go to plan, so there needs to be a degree of contingency planning.

Starting the Meeting

Team discussions are more effective if they have structure. Begin with a brief background about the items to be discussed and what the objective of the meeting is.

Facilitators should make sure that everybody is clear on what that meeting is about and that there are no surprises during the meeting or workshop. Surprises are not good things. Facilitators need to be up front about the reason for the workshop, what will be done during the workshop, why we are doing those things during the workshop, and conversely, what won't be done during the workshop – what is out of scope. The more the participants understand these aspects prior to the workshop the better.

Instructions the facilitator suggests for the team need to be delivered one instruction at a time. That means providing the team an instruction and then letting them perform it before they get their second instruction. Too often, facilitators will provide four or five instructions and then unleash the participants to fulfil them, and most participants won't remember the instructions. Providing instructions one at a time makes it easier for the participants to better comply.

Facilitators need to be conscious of the language that is used during the framing of instructions, so it's precise, clear and simple to understand. The measure of a good instruction is when a participant thinks: 'I can do that' after reflecting on what has been asked of them. One thing at a time.

Establish and convey the rules and the roles for the meeting: Who is the timekeeper (if not the facilitator), who is the scribe and who will manage the parking lot? The parking lot is used when ideas are raised but are not central to the objective of the meeting so are recorded and parked for discussion sometime after the meeting, or are points to be reviewed at the end of the meeting (just not at the time that they were brought up).

The use of parking lots is crucial for the flow of the conversation during the workshop. What parking lots do is quickly capture and enable the team to move on from conversation topics that are unrelated or only partially related to the core purpose topics of the workshop. Parking lots are a tool to simply keep conversation on track.

Facilitating the Meeting

A key role of the facilitator is their use of judgement on when to allow conversations to develop and when to intervene to direct the discussions. It is never easy in making this call. The facilitator should intervene when the team needs help bringing focus back to the objective. It is a judgement call when to intervene if the team is talking about a sideline issue based on whether or not it is felt that they will quickly return to the central topic.

Intervention will also occur when the conversation is being dominated by a few and remaining on the same point. It is the role of the facilitator to make sure that everybody has the opportunity to be involved, whether or not they choose to use that opportunity is up to them. The role of the facilitator is to enable that to happen.

Others who haven't found the opportunity to state their thoughts might have an idea or thought which is fresh and relevant and can help the team find a solution and move on. As the facilitator, you provide the platform for their voice to be heard by conducting the conversation and checking in with the quieter members of the team.

The meeting has to be run in such a way that it is safe for everyone to speak and share their views and the data they have. Of course, don't confuse facilitation as a forum to get leverage for your thoughts; the facilitators' role is to fairly facilitate the thoughts and ideas of the team. The role of the facilitator is to set the platform where all participants of the workshop can equally contribute. That is the core role, so the facilitator should very rarely, if ever, share their opinion.

Solving the issues that the team face is not the role of the facilitator; the role of the facilitator is to produce an environment for the team to work together to solve the issues they face. Facilitate a session so that people have the time to talk equally and are afforded the space to think – this is the perfect team dynamic and conversation.

As an overview, your actions during the meeting will be a combination of:

- being silent, patient and listening to the conversation while evaluating the direction of the conversation, whether it is helpful to the objectives being reached
- posing questions or paraphrasing statements or decisions made to clarify for the team
- guiding the team to suggest actions or choices and helping the team to decide
- checking for the agreement of the team on an issue
- using decision-making tools to see if the team is in relative consensus on the proposed solution or action. If the team can't reach a consensus, you might need to facilitate the team leader to decide on the solution or action for the team to adopt.

Closing the Meeting

In closing the meeting, perform all of the following:

- thank the team for their conduct and participation
- scan through the parking lot for any issues that need to be resolved now before the end of the meeting or workshop
- summarise the main points and any decisions made as well as actions decided on and owners
- summarise any outcomes that still need to be worked through by the team and make sure that all these elements have been captured accurately by the scribe
- articulate what the next actions will be, and who will be involved.

Tips for Facilitation

Try to have the facilitator role allocated to someone who isn't a member of the team – that way you're not losing a team member's input, as being a facilitator is a demanding role. It will also mean that your team has a neutral facilitator who is focused solely on the progress of the meeting or workshop.

Have a facilitator as often as you can as their neutral role can be valuable in maintaining the momentum of the conversations, which will help develop real outcomes quickly.

As a facilitator, take the opportunity at the end of the meeting to evaluate your contribution with the team leader and understand what you can improve on and what you did really well, which is a strength for you to continue to display as a facilitator.

If it's not possible to secure a neutral facilitator, then take on the role as a leader. Avoid proposing solutions yourself, but instead, support the team in generating solutions.

Here's a quick tip: Have your next meeting around the smallest table to fit (relatively comfortably) your team. It's a great way to keep the meeting personal and connected. Too often, when teams have meetings, they sit around a table that is way too large for them. Too large meaning there are big gaps between each of the team members. When we use the term 'I feel close to you' it is really in terms of proximity. People innately feel closer to each other when they are literally physically closer to that person. That physical closeness is a real thing!

A technique that can help the team stay focused on any task at hand is knowing the *cost-of-conversation*. We have all experienced those meetings that totally got off track and nothing got resolved. They were essentially a waste of time. In my experience, this happens because the team aren't kept on point – focused specifically and wholly on the purpose of the meeting. One of the better tools the facilitator can use is sharing the cost of conversation: a short statement about what needs to happen to recover the time we will be spending in this meeting.

For one team I had, we realised that we needed to sell a unit for every 12 minutes that the team was in our meetings to just re-coup the expense of the meetings. So, to us, that meant that the meetings had to be purposeful and deliver coordinated improvements to the organisation.

Facilitating Decision Making

The use of decision-making tools is crucial to make sure that conversation is being converted into decisions been made, and that everybody is involved.

Another great reason to use decision-making tools is to stop what I refer to as *snipers*. Snipers are those people who seemingly agree with the decisions that have been made as a team but don't overtly commit to the team decisions, and as the meeting advances, they raise a point that was made or agreed on, say, 20 minutes previously. This derails the team and the whole conversation reverts back to the point that the wider team thought had concluded. That is why I refer to them as snipers – they sit and wait for their opportunity to cause massive harm to the team dynamic in a passive aggressive manner. The use of team decision-making tools relieves us of the effects of a sniper.

Decision-making tools enable teams to come to a consensus quickly. They can be used in a wide variety of situations, including ranking the relative importance of issues, problems or solutions and checking for understanding.

A great way to facilitate decision making is the *Fist-to-five* technique. This gives everyone the opportunity to quickly articulate their feelings towards something proposed.

Benefits of Using Decision-making Tools

The use of decision-making tools builds commitment to the team's choice through equal participation in the process. This is because it allows all team members to rank issues whilst limiting pressure by others and putting quiet team members on an equal footing with more vocal members. It also makes a team's consensus, or lack of, visible, allowing disagreement to be highlighted, discussed and resolved. Using numbers to express how the team feels about an issue or solution speeds up the conversation and highlights specific areas that do need discussion.

Below is the overview of the Fist-to-five tool. There is also the multi-voting tool, for which there is an overview on page 98.

Fist-to-five

This is a decision-making tool that allows people to show support, agreement or understanding by showing a fist or a number of fingers corresponding to their opinion.

- **Fist:** A no vote – dead set against the proposal.
- **1 finger:** Need to discuss certain significant issues or suggest critical changes.
- **2 fingers:** Relatively comfortable with the proposal but feels some minor issues need to be discussed now before accepting it.
- **3 fingers:** Reasoned idea, comfortable enough to let this decision or proposal pass without further discussion.
- **4 fingers:** Considers this a good idea or proposal. Happy to work with it.
- **5 fingers:** Great idea.

The leader states or restates a decision the group may make and asks everyone to show their level of support by showing the number of fingers corresponding to their opinion.

Make sure that you state what a fist and five digits means in plain language. For example: 'Team, please let me know how you feel about the proposed solution being the one we trial first – fist means I'm completely against that solution being used and five means I completely agree, let's go with it.'

If anyone raises two or less fingers, they need to state their objections and the team should address their concerns. Those who show two fingers or fewer are up next to share. The facilitator will ask them: 'What's needed for you to progress with the team?' or 'What do you need to move forward with the team?'

The responsibility is on them to be specific about what it is they need, which is often a point they want to express for the team to be aware of.

Continue the Fist-to-five process until your team achieve consensus (being everyone is three or more fingers) or decide they must move on to the next issue.

This tool might feel a bit awkward to use at first but continue with it and it will be used often and will quickly feel natural.

APPENDIX 2: VISUAL BOARDS

It is a widely accepted principle that you can only improve the things that can be observed; that you can only manage what you measure. Visual boards are based on this principle and provide information about the activities the team are working on so that others in the team and visitors to an area can easily understand and interpret. Anybody should be able to walk up to your visual board and quickly know what is being worked on by your team and the status of that work.

Crucially though, any visual board has to contain information that helps the team do their work. Focus the elements on the visual board to be elements and insights to help the team perform their work, rather than the results of their work. I'm guessing that the results are already captured in reporting that's done – from the team leader through to senior management, so there's no need to replicate this on the visual board with data that doesn't primarily help the team perform as well as they can.

Visual boards also provide a basis for the daily stand-up meeting for the team, where everyone is kept up to date and can have performance-driven conversations.

Benefits of Using Visual Boards

- A visual board shows the 'big picture' – they provide the ability to identify, at a glance, what tasks the team is performing and how those tasks are tracking.
- The board can visually aid the team's activities by highlighting any issues needing attention.
- The board is a quick way for the team to understand the work being done by others in the team.
- Boards can be used to inform anyone of the current status of the team. They stimulate greater and more regular team involvement and motivation.

Generally, your visual board will likely display two types of work – work that is part of a rhythm (business as usual work; for example, on the 8th of every month you've asked all contractors to have submitted their invoices), or project work like continuous improvement initiatives.

Work that is part of an ongoing rhythm and work that is a stand-alone improvement initiative will be displayed differently. Likely, work that is part of an ongoing rhythm will be a list of what events need to have occurred by when, and improvement initiatives will have short descriptors to denote the work being done – sometimes being a single sticky note. Either way, the overview of each type of work will have a descriptor of what it is, when it is to be done by, and the owner.

Capturing Improvement Initiatives on Visual Boards

Visual boards are used by the entire team to convey the activities they own, what they are currently working on, when they are projected to be finished, and any roadblocks they have encountered. It is a visual display of what is going on in an area and how the work is going.

There will be places available on the board for the visual representation of the work a team is doing, what stage each of the work is at and where people can make comments, add information, or highlight issues that may be occurring.

Designing a Visual Board

Designing a visual board is a team event. It is a relatively simple process:

1. Discuss key principles and concepts of visual management and show examples of other visual boards.
2. Now unleash the team to brainstorm focus areas and what needs to be conveyed on the visual board, for example:
    a. What elements of work will be displayed and the various stages that work can be at?
    b. What key measures of performance and critical success factors that apply to the team, including team attendance for the week (who's on annual leave and when)? What key

information should be visual, such as first aiders on site, and visitors expected today?

c. What should be on it from the customers' perspective?

A quick note: what likely won't be on the visual board is information that doesn't support the team to perform and understand their performance. For example, if the elements are in managerial reports (and therefore already covered), do they really need to be on the visual board?

3. Sketch designs for visualising the focus areas. As a tip, use Fist-to-five to quickly work through design options – which items are to be placed where. As a tip, you don't need team consensus about whether an element is to be included or not on the visual board – who knows until you try it to see if it is worthwhile. That said, it might be best for the team to not overwhelm the board with elements right at the start.

4. Check back to ensure all crucial focus areas are included in the sketch design.

5. Decide which focus areas of the sketch are the priorities and how this might influence the design.

6. Develop a mock-up of the design that encompasses those priorities but make sure there's something on the board that means something to each member of the team and the work that they contribute, and that it includes customer insights or something that affects the customer that the team needs to monitor.

7. Build the board but hold off on beautification and digitisation of the visual board – focus on it being functional only.

8. Find a location for the visual board. Place it in the vicinity of the most frequent users, approximately at eye level and with adequate space for conducting stand-up meetings. Also, make sure the visual board is complemented with resources that are close to hand, such as sticky notes and markers.

9. If your team will have daily stand-up meetings, decide on the
    time of the meetings and the key daily agenda items, and have
    this overview on the visual board.

The team will have produced a good design if board elements can
be easily understood without the need for verbal explanation. The
board should also be easily read from a distance – up to about two
metres – which will suit the team for the stand-up meetings.

Don't strive for the perfect visual board straight away, that
objective will soak up a lot of the teams' time and it's an impossible
objective. Just start and the board will naturally evolve as the team
finds new ways to make it suit and better convey information about
what activities the team is working on. Know that the first version
of your visual board won't last long before your team updates
it, so don't invest much time overthinking the layout and the
presentation of it.

Things to keep in mind when using a visual board:

- keep it simple: avoid too much information – people do not
  have time to read it all
- keep it clean and up to date
- use colours, photos, graphs and drawings – anything that is
  helpful
- make it big enough so it can be read from a short distance
  and put it where people can see it. Boards can be made out of
  Corflute, which is cheap. It is also easy to hang as it is light,
  and the boards can be marked up into sections with coloured
  masking tape.

Adding Activities on the Visual Board

An activity on a visual board is represented by a sticky note or
similar. For the sticky notes to properly represent an activity, make
sure it has these three elements of information:

Each activity description should start with a verb ——● Capture baseline data of current performance

Each is allocated to a person to lead. This could be by an avatar used on the sticky note or a specific colour, or simply a name

Each activity sticky note has an end date stated ——● 14 Feb

Using Visual Boards in a Stand-up Meeting

A visual board should be the central piece of the daily stand-up meeting. The daily stand-ups are usually conducted in the morning, lasting about 10–15 minutes, during which, each team member states in about a minute, three elements:

- what they accomplished since the last stand-up
- what they're working on today
- what roadblocks, barriers or issues are preventing them from achieving what they have planned to work on today or soon.

Roadblocks are not bought up during the stand-up to have solutions produced for them but are raised to find those who can help with resolving the roadblock outside of the stand-up meeting.

Team members can take turns facilitating and timekeeping during the stand-up meetings.

Someone (usually the team leader) is assigned to update the board on a regular basis, though this can be done during the daily stand-up meetings.

A visual board smooths out and speeds up the flow of work in the team as it enables decisions on resource management based on what we see, who we know, who is working on what, how important that activity is to the team and when it needs to be done.

Make visual boards (and stand-up meetings) part of your engagement with stakeholders. Make the visual boards available to them (and indeed the wider team) and invite them to attend your stand-up meetings.

APPENDIX 3: IMPROVEMENT INITIATIVE PLAN TEMPLATE

An *Improvement Initiative Plan* usually includes these sections – and of course adjust the plan (and its name) to suit.

Improvement initiative name: Plain language name

Date and version of this plan: e.g. 17 November 2026, version 1.0

Process description
Name of the process (or part of the process) and a short overview of the process – what the process is for (its purpose), where it starts and finishes (the first and last process steps), and the metrics that process performance are measured by.

Process problem statement
A problem statement will likely be 2–4 paragraphs and will answer these questions:

- Where is the problem occurring in our organisation?
- How frequently is the problem occurring?
- When the problem occurs, how severe is the problem? What is the measurable impact on our organisation and our customers?
- When did the problem start, or when did we first notice the problem, and over what time period do we have data on this problem?
- What will be the measurable effects on our organisation and our customers if we don't address this problem?

Is there any graphical representation of the data you want to include?

Expected outcomes
Include a summary/a bullet point or two on how improving this process will contribute to the performance of our organisation and what the expected outcomes are.

Aligning with values
In what ways does this improvement initiative contribute to our values?

O	Insert a value here	How this improvement work aligns to or supports that value
O		
O		
O		

The Wider Improvement Initiative Team

- *Initiative champion/sponsor:* The name of who is funding/ allocating budget to this initiative.
- *Service or process owner:* The name of the person who is responsible for/owns the process. Ownership means that they can sanction changes to the process. If there are multiple owners, define their boundaries within the process.
- *Initiative team leader:* Include their name and the time they will dedicate to this improvement initiative per week.
- *Initiative Team:* List the roles in the team, the team members' names and the time they will dedicate to this improvement initiative per week. For example:
  - ~ Process officer, Andrew Han, ~32 hours per week
  - ~ Clinical lead, Alan Wikler, ~20 hours per week
  - ~ Business analyst lead, Grant Robinson, ~20 hours per week
  - ~ Performance and culture lead, Navlene Singh, ~1 day per week
  - ~ Change specialist, Jeremy Markham, ~1 day per week
  - ~ Improvement specialist, Melissa Ludlow, ~20 hours per week

In Scope

Bullet-point the related aspects that will be improved through this stage of the improvement initiative.

Out of Scope

Bullet-point the related aspects, though potentially important, that will *not* be fixed or improved in this stage of the improvement initiative.

APPENDIX 4: PILOT PLAN TEMPLATE

Improvement initiative name: Plain language name – Pilot stage plan

Date and version of this plan: e.g. 17 November 2026, version 1.0

Pilot overview
Talk to the scope of the pilot, including:

- an overview of the purpose of the pilot and the solution being tested and the root cause of a problem we are looking to solve.
- how long we are going to run the pilot for and the start date of the pilot
- all the types of benefits that we are testing the solution for in the pilot.

Pilot team
List the team to be involved in the pilot and what their roles will be – including which customers (all or a sub-group) will be involved.

Pre-pilot set up and prep needing to be performed
Bullet-point/list all the actions that need to be done to set up for the pilot, and the owners of those actions, and include:

- documents that need to be built
- training that needs to be conducted to prepare the team involved in the pilot
- comms that need to be sent out prior, and customers that need to be contacted prior of the pilot.

Potential issues we've planned for in the pilot
Bullet-point/list a summary of issues and risks and ask:

- What are the contingency and roll-back plans if significant issues occur during the pilot?
- What specifically would cause a roll-back out of the pilot back to business as usual?

Validating the pilot and solution performance

What data we are collecting

Convey the metrics we are measuring, including:

- how frequently will we capture the performance metrics during the pilot
- who is responsible for capturing what data
- who (stakeholders) it will be delivered to and when.

The pilot success criteria

State what metric or performance level reached will determine the success of the pilot – how we determine whether the solution is effective. For example, the success criteria might be simply reducing the number of occurrences of customer queries by 20%.

Confirm and list the baseline performance data we need to understand the improvements through the likely benefits listed above in the pilot overview section.

Comms and stakeholders

List who needs to be kept informed through the pilot and what information and performance metrics need to be sent to them, how frequently, and via what method (personal catch ups, email, short video summary updates, etc.).

Post pilot plan

Describe what will happen to the pilot in the time between the scheduled end of the pilot and the embed stage.

APPENDIX 5: EMBED STAGE PLANNING TEMPLATE

Improvement initiative name: Plain language name – Embed stage plan

Date and version of this plan: e.g. 17 November 2026, version 1.0

Overarching plan

- What are the high-level elements and tasks of the embed plan that need to be performed, the timing for each of the elements, and the resource requirements?
- What are the risks that might occur during the embed stage?
- List what all other teams affected by the solution, directly or indirectly, need from us.

Training plan

Who will be trained and when, and what are the resource requirements of that training? How will we know if the training has been effective?

New performance tracking and visual representation/dashboards

Who's collecting which data and how? Who is building the visual representation of the performance?

Stakeholder updates of this performance data

Which stakeholders will be updated with what information and how frequently through the embedding of the solution?

Continual tracking of the benefits

How will future benefits of the solution and the impact of new levels of performance be captured?

Continual tracking of core elements of performance data to ensure continuous improvement of solution

Who is responsible for continual improvements to this process, and will they have all the tools and insights they need?

Ongoing ownership and handover

What else needs to be done to hand over the new process to the team in the process and the process owner and when is that planned for?

APPENDIX 6: TEAM DYNAMIC EXAMPLE

Our *Kaupapa*˙ are the impactful principles and disciplines that support the start of the adoption of continuous improvement culture and new ways of working. Adopting these principles and disciplines supports the whole team, with a better culture of inclusivity to equally contribute to the improvement of performance.

How we will connect

We connect personally as a preference over connecting digitally when in the same building – we use Teams to organise catch ups rather than to communicate.

When we connect, how we will communicate

- Always using simple and plain language – not using words a customer won't understand (whether we are talking to a customer or not).
- Being specific and not taking shortcuts as we converse – using names of people, teams and elements, (not 'it', 'she', 'they', 'them') and not using acronyms – especially around others, for example, not using 'CI' but 'continuous improvement'.
- Be accurate in our conversations – talk to data and what we know.
- Making sure what we share and say is purposeful – as when we talk, it can be at the consequence of another.

How we will work collectively

- Stop talking when people are making notes – provide our teammates time to capture their thoughts.
- Give people the opportunity to talk, **and** the time to think.

---

* *Kaupapa* is a te reo Māori term meaning principles, policy and ideas that act as a base or foundation for action. Change the name or reference to the team dynamics to something meaningful for your team.

APPENDIX 7: SAMPLE SIZE CALCULATIONS

Calculating the needed sample size for discrete and continuous data involves different approaches. Let's break down the methods for each type. It's worth noting that various factors, such as the type of analysis or study design, may require adjustments to these basic formulas. Additionally, specialised software or online calculators can provide more precise sample size calculations based on specific study parameters and statistical techniques.

Sample Size Calculation for Continuous Data

When dealing with continuous data, such as measurements on a scale or numerical values, the sample size calculation typically revolves around estimating means or averages. The key parameters to consider are the desired level of confidence, the standard deviation or variability of the data, and the acceptable margin of error.

For calculating the sample size to estimate means, the most common formula is based on the standard deviation (σ), the desired level of confidence, and the margin of error. The formula is as follows:

$$n = \left(\frac{Zs}{\Delta}\right)^2$$

where:

- n is the required sample size
- Z is the critical value corresponding to the desired level of confidence (e.g. for 95% confidence level, $Z \approx 1.96$)
- s is the standard deviation of the sample
- Δ is the desired margin of error.

By plugging in the appropriate values for Z, s and Δ, you can calculate the sample size needed to estimate the mean accurately. Here's an example:

We've collected thirty samples of data on how long in hours (and the additional minutes) it is taking us to process each application for our customers, and from that data, the standard deviation is 7.16 hours. So, we're wanting to know how much data we need to collect to be 95% confident, that the mean of this newly (about to be) captured sample data would reflect the population (all data) within what we've chosen to be ± 2 hours (being the margin of error). With that, we know that we need to capture 50 data points of how long applications take to process, with us being 95% confident that the calculated mean is no further than 2 hours from the actual mean.

$$n = \left(\frac{1.96s}{\Delta}\right)^2 = \left(\frac{1.96*7.16}{2}\right)^2 = \left(\frac{14.03}{2}\right)^2 = 49.24 \approx 50$$

Sample Size Calculation for Discrete Data

When working with discrete data, where observations fall into distinct categories or groups, the sample size calculation often revolves around estimating proportions or percentages. To determine the necessary sample size, you can use formulas based on the desired level of confidence and the acceptable margin of error.

The most commonly used formula for calculating sample size for discrete data is the formula for estimating proportions. It takes into account the expected proportion (or prevalence) of the characteristic being studied, the desired level of confidence, and the margin of error. The formula is as follows:

$$n = \left(\frac{Z}{\Delta}\right)^2 P(1-P)$$

where:

- n is the required sample size
- Z is the critical value corresponding to the desired level of confidence (e.g. for 95% confidence level, $Z \approx 1.96$)
- P is the estimated proportion or prevalence of the characteristic
- Δ is the desired margin of error (expressed as a decimal to represent a percentage).

By plugging in the appropriate values for Z, P and Δ, you can calculate the sample size needed to estimate the proportion accurately. Here's an example:

We've collected thirty samples of data on how often (as a percentage) we have to send incomplete applications back to our customers, and from that data, that's occurring 30% of the time. So, we're wanting to know how much data we need to collect to be 95% confident that the actual percentage of incomplete applications in this newly (about to be) captured sample data would reflect the population (all data) within what we've chosen to be ± 5% (being the margin of error). With that, we know that we need to capture 323 data points of applications to understand the percentage, knowing that we are 95% confident that the real percentage is within 5% of our sample percentage.

$$n = \left[\frac{1.96s}{\Delta}\right]^2 P(1-P) = \left[\frac{1.96}{0.05}\right]^2 0.30(0.70) = (39.2)^2 * 0.21 = 322.69 \approx 323$$

APPENDIX 8: GEMBA QUESTIONS FOR LEADERS

When you are out with the team in their work environment, or meeting a team for the first time and want to understand the performance, here's some questions to ask as a starter:

- Know and articulate that you are there to gain knowledge and awareness of the work – ask: What is the purpose of their work?

- Ask any questions for you to be clear about the levels of performance the team are expressing – so it is clear to you how the team think performance of their work is measured, and which elements of performance might be viewed as more important than others.

- Find out how this performance is measured, the full range of current measures, and how the team know how they are performing, both individually and at a team level. Compare those measures to the purpose of the work as they defined it – is there congruence? Are there any vital measures or insights that are missing that would better help the team perform or better understand their performance?

- How often are the measures of performance available and are they visual?

- In terms of the levels of performance – and why we have the level of performance that we do:
  - ~ some elements will be related to customers – find out what they *know* about the customer experience and engagement
  - ~ some elements will be related to problems. Once you understand the nature of the problem that is being shared, understand it fully by trying to find out how often the problem happens (as a number, whether it be the number of times it happens in a week or month, or the percentage of time that it occurs) and when it does occur, what the impact is on the customer and the team (usually that's in terms of time lost fixing the error).

- If they have expressed problems in their work that affect their performance, I like to finish with this final question: ask if they are keen, *and have the time*, to be part of a team to fix the issues they shared. If they are super keen, I make a note in case that problem does become ear-marked to be fixed, so I know who is keen to be part of the team to resolve it (again, the principle of starting where the love is).

- And of course, manners and appreciation – thank the team for their time. Showing you and bringing you up to speed slows down their work. They (most likely) are not measured on how they inform leaders, but only on the work that they get done – something you might look to rebalance through, for example, capturing of ideas of potential improvements from the team by the leaders.

APPENDIX 9: KEY TERMS OF A BENEFIT REALISATION FRAMEWORK

Below are key terms that are part of the benefit realisation lexicon.

Benefits are a measurable improvement, attributable to a specific change or improvement. Benefits will advantage one or more stakeholder and should contribute to the organisation's strategy.
Benefits can be:

- **Quantifiable benefits**, which can be:
    - ~ any trackable movement via data of performance, such as capacity freed up, or
    - ~ a monetary benefit measurable in financial terms. This can be revenue creating or cost reduction through error reduction.

    Just as a word of warning: Any changes in monetary benefits is usually subsequent to other changes that happen in the process and those initial changes are the predetermining factors for the improvement in management benefits, and what we want to measure. Often if we're just measuring monetary benefits by themselves, we're missing predetermining variables or root causes that we should be measuring first, which provides better insight of improvements in our process.

- **Non-quantifiable benefits**, which are benefits that are realised but are tricky or excessively time consuming to measure the exact benefit, such as improved reporting, improved staff morale and reduced staff turnover rates.

Benefits Management is the identification, quantification, analysis, planning, tracking, realisation and optimisation of benefits.

Disbenefit is a negative impact that might occur as a direct consequence of implementing a particular solution. Disbenefits must always be acknowledged and communicated as they are discovered.

Baseline is the data of the current level of performance, which is taken before any pilots are run or improvements occur. The value of the benefits is literally the difference between the new level of performance and the performance data captured as part of the baseline.

Initiative/project/engagement are terms often used interchangeably. They are overarching terms for a specific and focused change and may be part of a program, other projects, business-as-usual activities and plans to achieve any improvements. A benefit realisation framework informs us of the benefits of any initiative, project or engagement.

APPENDIX 10: CONTROL CHARTS

Once good measures (as defined in our *Good Measures* section on page 264) are established, a control chart can be used to measure and graphically represent the performance of a process – especially showing the level of variation that occurs in the process. Control charts provide a graphical representation of the process performance over time and are easy to interpret. This allows the team to quickly determine when any action is required to support process performance. Control charts may be referred to as statistical process control charts.

Benefits of Using Control Charts

Control charts help us monitor variation in the performance of a process. By having visibility of the variation of our performance, we can determine whether or not action needs to be taken – the control chart can serve as a warning indicator for when intervention is needed.

Control charts are also an excellent visual tool to easily compare past and current performance to determine how process performance has changed.

Variation Explained

There are two types of variation we need to be aware of, which will occur in every process:

Common Cause Variation

Common causes are chance or random events that always happen – no two things or performances are ever the same. If you were to write your signature five times, there would be differences between all – this variation is common cause variation. Reducing common cause variation is technical and will likely require management support to make process changes.

Special Cause Variation

This is variation that can be attributed to a distinct event, such as when writing your signature with your non-dominant hand, the variation between your left and right hand is significant. The difference here is special cause variation. This type of variation is usually addressed by the team through mistake proofing or the like to stop or limit special cause events from occurring.

Usually, common cause variation offers little cause for concern whilst special cause variation, such as significant events or trends, likely means that our process performance has been significantly affected. The power of the control chart is that it has been designed to alert us to when special cause variation has potentially occurred.

Special cause variation is not necessarily bad. If we have put in place a solution in a process, our efforts would be justified by special cause variation occurring, reflecting a considerable (sometimes termed a *statistically significant*) improvement. Conversely, if there's only common cause variation after a change, it would mean that the change itself has made no significant impact.

Reading a Control Chart

We use control charts to help us:

- understand common cause variation so we do not overreact to this variation
- detect special cause variation so we can be aware of problems
- ensure process stability by detecting changes in the process over time – such as performance trending in a certain direction
- pinpoint key sources of variation within the basic process as there might be seasonal factors occurring.

A control chart takes data and displays it in chronological order. It is similar to a run or line chart but offers the added advantage that it will show when process variation becomes statistically significant – these are our special cause events.

The control chart usually has these rules built in to highlight when special cause occurs. When these rules are broken, it is time to take action. Although there might not actually be anything wrong, special cause is not statistically likely, so it merits investigation.

Control charts can be built in Excel or through statistical software such as Minitab, and via AI tools. To use an AI tool like ChatGPT, use this prompt for control charts:

> *I have a dataset representing a process over time and I'd like to create a* [specify if you need a specific type of control chart such as I-MR, X-bar, R-chart, for example. Leave blank if unsure] *control chart to monitor the process stability and detect any out-of-control conditions. Here is the data:* [insert data or upload an Excel spreadsheet – and state which columns the data is in]. *Could you please analyse the data and generate a control chart? Additionally, please provide a brief explanation of the control chart and what it reveals about the process stability, including any points that are out of control according to the Western Electric rules.*

Here is an example of a control chart highlighting special cause variation – the points marked with numbers by the points. The numbers respond to the special cause variation occurring. The numbered special cause points marked with a '1' denote that these are data points which are over three times the average distance of all the points from the mean – this distance from the mean (also known as the average) are the control lines – which are three standard deviations away from the mean. These control lines are sometimes indicated with red lines (UCL stands for Upper Control Limit and LCL stands for Lower Control Limit), and the mean by the green line on a control chart. All numbered points of data are where special cause has been detected, and we will investigate to determine if there is the root cause for these events occurring that we need to be aware of and sort improvements for.

Finding a solution to stop these events from occurring is continuous improvement. Other forms of special cause variation also occur in this chart – the numbers next to the special cause points relate to the specific special cause variation rule broken – all meriting investigation.

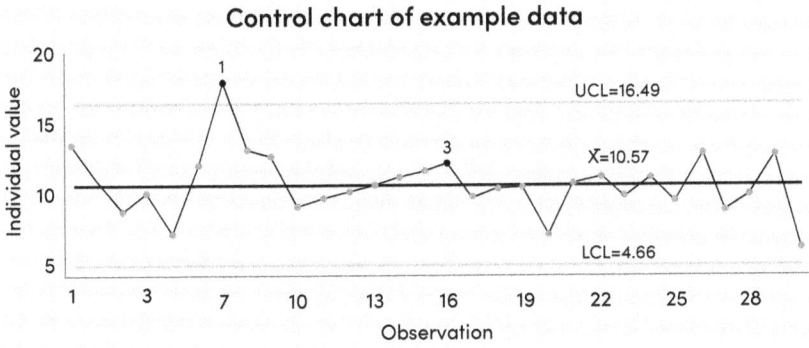

Control chart of example data

APPENDIX 11: PARETO CHARTS

The Pareto principle, commonly referred to as the '80/20 rule', is an effective way to separate the few fundamental issues from the many minor issues.

The principle was named after the observation of Italian economist Vilfredo Pareto, who discovered that 80% of the land in Italy was owned by 20% of the population. This 80/20 rule will also apply in numerous business situations, where often around 80% of the effects can be explained by 20% of the causes.

Benefits of Using a Pareto Chart

A Pareto chart is a powerful graphical representation of a problem and will visually communicate the core issues that stand out above the minor issues. This is where we will want to focus the design of our solutions – being the vital few factors that cause a disproportionately high number of problems experienced by frequency. The chart makes this easy to interpret for teams and stakeholders who might be unfamiliar with the process.

Pareto Charts Explained

To demonstrate if the 80/20 rule applies, a Pareto chart can be constructed. This is a bar chart with categories represented along the horizontal axis. These categories are analysed by the number of occurrences and their percentage contribution to the total number of issues experienced.

Analysis is likely to reveal that a few categories will be the source of most issues. These are conveyed on the Pareto chart by the categories being sorted by occurrence in descending order, from left to right. Once main issues of a problem have been identified, improvement efforts can be focused to find specific causes rather than having the team's efforts diluted across all the issues.
Below is a Pareto chart constructed to understand the occurrences of rework. With the Pareto chart, it is easy to determine that over 50% of occurrences of rework relate to just one category – NZPC.

This clearly demonstrates that if we are to make considerable gains in reducing the occurrences of rework, we should look specifically at NZPC issues first. Only four categories make up nearly 80% (78.7%) of all occurrences of rework.

If the Pareto principle doesn't hold, the bars will be of similar height. In this instance you will need to find another way to analyse the data to find the significant reasons for the problems experienced.

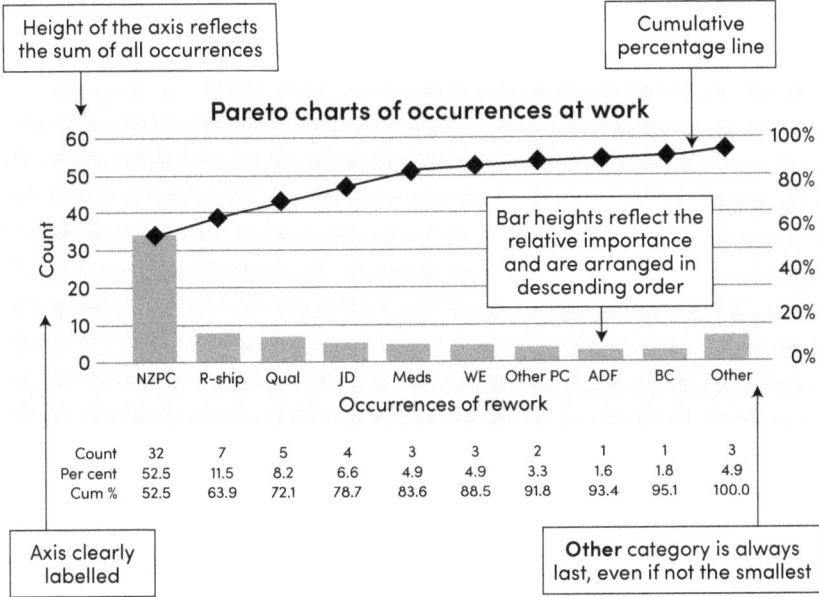

	NZPC	R-ship	Qual	JD	Meds	WE	Other PC	ADF	BC	Other
Count	32	7	5	4	3	3	2	1	1	3
Per cent	52.5	11.5	8.2	6.6	4.9	4.9	3.3	1.6	1.8	4.9
Cum %	52.5	63.9	72.1	78.7	83.6	88.5	91.8	93.4	95.1	100.0

Use Pareto charts to demonstrate to your stakeholders why your team is focusing on only some issues and not others.

Pareto charts can be produced in Excel or through statistical software such as Minitab, and via AI tools. To use an AI tool like ChatGPT, use this prompt for Pareto charts:

I have attached an Excel spreadsheet containing my dataset, and I would like to create a Pareto chart to identify the most significant factors in the data. The data is located in [specify sheet name and columns, e.g., "Sheet1, Column A for categories and Column B for values"]. *Could you please analyse the data and generate a Pareto chart? The Pareto chart should display both the individual values in descending order and the cumulative percentage. Additionally, please provide a brief explanation of the Pareto chart and what it reveals about the most significant factors.*

APPENDIX 12: BOX PLOTS AND HISTOGRAMS

Once good measures (as defined in our *Good Measures* section on page 264) are established, box plots (sometimes referred to as box and whisker plots) and histograms can be used to measure and graphically represent the performance of a process. These tools can offer different analytical views of the same data.

Histograms summarise the frequency of each of the measured values that occur and show the distribution of those values. Box plots also show the distribution of the values to a less granular level and in doing so offer an easy ability to compare the performance of processes against each other.

Box plots and histograms are excellent visual tools to display process data. They display data in an easy way so anyone who needs to understand elements of the process performance can do so without having to view all the data.

Box plots and histograms can be run in Excel or through statistical software such as Minitab, and via AI tools. To use an AI tool like ChatGPT, use this prompt for histograms:

> *I have a dataset and I'd like to create a histogram to visualise the frequency distribution of the data. Here is the data:* [insert data, upload an Excel spreadsheet – and state which columns the data is in]. *Could you please analyse the data and generate a histogram?* [Mention if you have specific bin sizes or ranges in mind.] *Additionally, please provide a brief explanation of the histogram and what it reveals about the data distribution.*

And use this prompt for box plots:

> *I have a dataset and I'd like to create a box-and-whisker plot (also known as a box plot) to visualize the distribution and identify any potential outliers. Here is the data:* [insert data, upload an Excel spreadsheet – and state which columns the data is in]. *Could you please analyse the data and generate a box plot?* [Indicate if you want to compare multiple groups.] *Additionally, please provide a brief explanation of the box plot and what it reveals about the data distribution, including any outliers.*

Reading Histograms

To be able to see the distribution of the values in our process better, we can take all the data and group them into similar values – commonly referred to as a 'bin'. A histogram shows us the occurrence of the different values and can also be used to compare process performance against Voice of the Customer (VoC) – what the customer wants. If a customer is happy to queue for anything up to three minutes, this could be illustrated on a histogram so that you can quickly see how you are performing against the customer's expectations. Comparing Voice of the Customer to process performance is *Capability Analysis*.

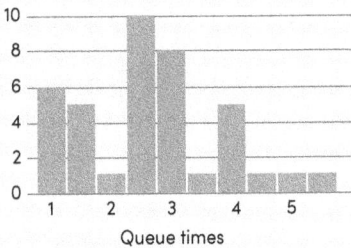

Histogram of queue times

Queue times

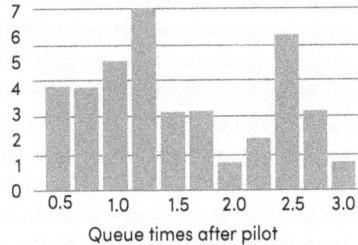

Histogram of queue times after pilot

Queue times after pilot

Here our histogram shows we have too much variation to meet customer needs – our queue times vary from 1 minute to over 5 minutes and often customers are queuing for 3 minutes or longer. With the current process performance, we are not capable of meeting our customers' needs.

Here we can see our histogram shows that we have made an improvement and are now performing well to meet customer needs.

Reading Box Plots

A box plot takes all the data and puts it in order by value, and then equally splits the prevalence of all the data into four quadrants: the top, upper middle, lower middle and bottom 25% of values. The middle value, or the median, is the line in the middle of the box plot. The 50% of data closest to this value is split into a box above and below this line. The whiskers (the thin lines above and below the boxes) are the remaining 50% of the data split up, so each whisker is 25% of all the data. Simply, the box plot is a display of the range and concentration of values.

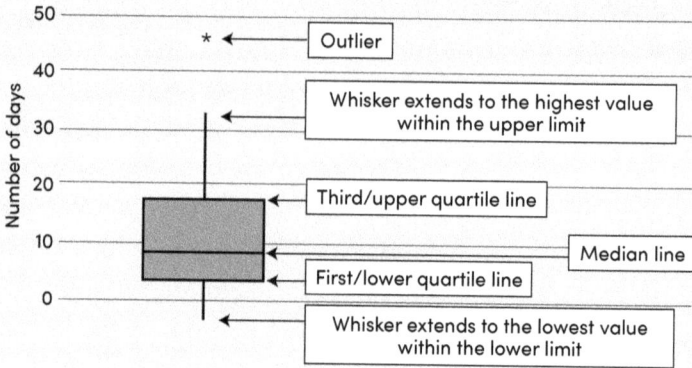

Below, our box plots are used to compare the before and pilot data of the team's improvement initiative to improve the queue times. It's easy to see that there has been a significant improvement. This is the same data from the before and after pilot histograms above, but because the box plots are on the same chart with the same scale, they are very effective in visualising the differences between two different sets of data – in this case, a before and after of queuing times. What you see in this example is that prior to the change, the longest 25% of queuing times, which were about 3.3 minutes or longer, were surpassed during the pilot phase. Even the longest queuing time experienced during the pilot was faster (being less than three minutes) than 25% of the experiences previously. We also see that the median queuing time was cut in half, from about 2.2 minutes pre-pilot to 1.1 minutes experienced in the pilot.

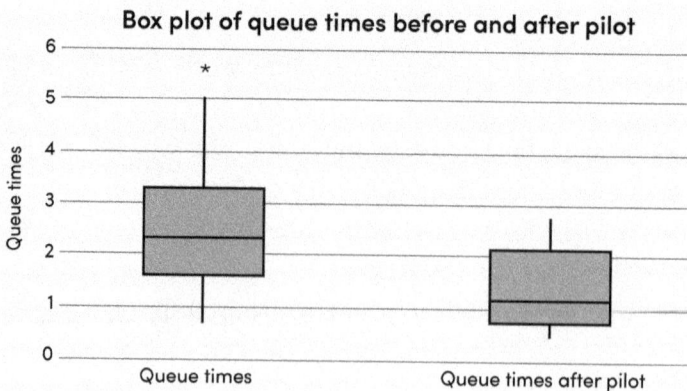

Box plot of queue times before and after pilot

APPENDIX 13: EVERYTHING ON ONE PAGE, THE CHEAT SHEET

Build the team dynamic
    Decision made on what is worked on, and by who (teams formed) – Loop 1

Build a high-level process map
    Brainstorm and add all problems/pain points where they occur in the process

        For pain points, add:
            Frequency
            Severity, refer to:
                Waiting (customer)
                Working (team capacity)   (Important as capacity freed up is the goal)

        Analyse and determine pain point inter-relationships

        Choose which problems to fix now, and for those...

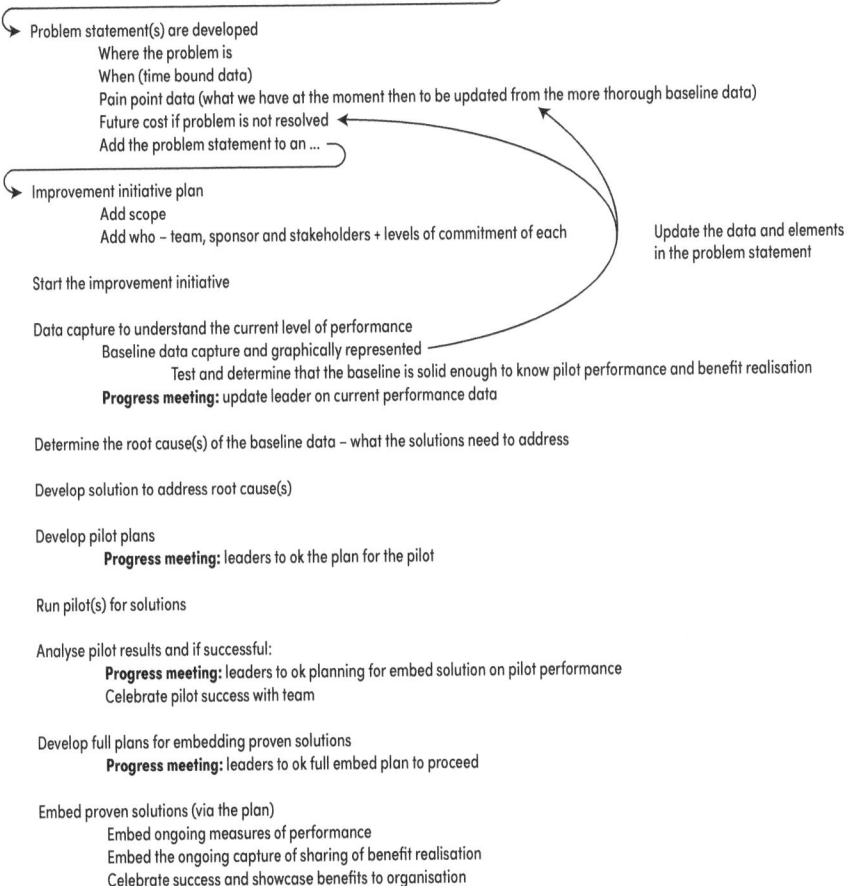

Problem statement(s) are developed
    Where the problem is
    When (time bound data)
    Pain point data (what we have at the moment then to be updated from the more thorough baseline data)
    Future cost if problem is not resolved
    Add the problem statement to an ...

Improvement initiative plan
    Add scope
    Add who – team, sponsor and stakeholders + levels of commitment of each   Update the data and elements
                                                               in the problem statement

Start the improvement initiative

Data capture to understand the current level of performance
    Baseline data capture and graphically represented
        Test and determine that the baseline is solid enough to know pilot performance and benefit realisation
    Progress meeting: update leader on current performance data

Determine the root cause(s) of the baseline data – what the solutions need to address

Develop solution to address root cause(s)

Develop pilot plans
    Progress meeting: leaders to ok the plan for the pilot

Run pilot(s) for solutions

Analyse pilot results and if successful:
    Progress meeting: leaders to ok planning for embed solution on pilot performance
    Celebrate pilot success with team

Develop full plans for embedding proven solutions
    Progress meeting: leaders to ok full embed plan to proceed

Embed proven solutions (via the plan)
    Embed ongoing measures of performance
    Embed the ongoing capture of sharing of benefit realisation
    Celebrate success and showcase benefits to organisation

APPENDIX 14: HOMEWORK

Watch the first 30 minutes of the movie *Moneyball*, about the (then) Oakland Athletics (at the time of writing, it looks like the team will be moving to Las Vegas) for an entertaining and real-life application of a continuous improvement mindset.

About the Author

Darcy Mellsop brings two decades of direct, hands-on experience in facilitating organisations to enhance their continuous improvement capabilities and effectively implement change within their teams. This wealth of experience serves as the foundation for this insightful book. With a persistent drive towards excellence and a natural inclination for improving processes, he was initially drawn to the field through Lean Six Sigma. Darcy's journey has been marked by an extensive exploration of various methodologies identifying the core principles that form the backbone of all effective improvement strategies. This deep dive into the essence of continuous improvement methodologies has sharpened Darcy's ability to connect teams with these fundamental concepts, fostering a culture of growth and efficiency.

Darcy customises a holistic approach to improvement, blending strategy with empathy and insight with action to catalyse enduring change. This comprehensive, bespoke methodology has positioned Darcy not just as a consultant but as a transformative force in the realm of continuous improvement, committed to achieving excellence in a sustainable, inclusive manner.

Over the years, Darcy has meticulously sculpted a distinctive approach, emphasising the importance of grassroots solution development and ensuring that innovations are born from those directly involved in the work. This philosophy not only fosters ownership and engagement but also ensures that improvements are practical, sustainable, and closely aligned with the unique dynamics of each organisation.

Darcy's journey has been one of simplification, optimisation, and empowerment, leaving an indelible mark on every organisation touched by his work and unwavering commitment. At the heart of his mission is a profound dedication to nurturing and unleashing the potential within teams, thereby driving substantial leaps in performance, culture, and customer satisfaction.

Darcy's enthusiasm for continuous improvement transcends professional boundaries, seamlessly integrating into personal endeavours. From minimising environmental impact and waste in daily life to applying iterative enhancement methodologies to his passion for running, Darcy embodies the very essence of continuous improvement in all facets of life. Perhaps a bit too much so – much to the chagrin of his wife and kids. Darcy simply can't help being a customer and sharing how things can be improved. The family, being the audience more regularly held hostage to this analysis, finds it especially painful (apparently) when waiting in a queue with Darcy.

www.ingramcontent.com/pod-product-compliance
Lightning Source LLC
Chambersburg PA
CBHW040752220326
41597CB00029BA/4735